CH

Uncommon Prayer

D1617081

MICHAEL PLEKON

Uncommon Prayer

PRAYER IN EVERYDAY EXPERIENCE

University of Notre Dame Press

Notre Dame, Indiana

University of Notre Dame Press
Notre Dame, Indiana 46556
www.undpress.nd.edu

Names: Plekon, Michael, 1948- author.
Title: Uncommon prayer : prayer in everyday experience / Michael Plekon.
Description: Notre Dame : University of Notre Dame Press, 2016. | Includes
bibliographical references and index.
Identifiers: LCCN 2016023749 (print) | LCCN 2016024400 (ebook) | ISBN
9780268100001 (hardcover : alk. paper) | ISBN 0268100004 (hardcover : alk.
paper) | ISBN 9780268100018 (pbk. : alk. paper) | ISBN 0268100012 (pbk. :
alk. paper) | ISBN 9780268100025 (pdf) | ISBN 9780268100032 (epub)
Subjects: LCSH: Prayer—Christianity.
Classification: LCC BV210.3 .P55 2016 (print) | LCC BV210.3 (ebook) | DDC
248.3/2—dc23

LC record available at https://lccn.loc.gov/2016023749

CONTENTS

IMAGES

ACKNOWLEDGMENTS

I want to thank the many friends and colleagues who helped with this book and made possible its publication. First of all, as in the past, I am grateful to Matt Dowd, editor at the University of Notre Dame Press. He believed in it and worked hard to see it through the publication process. I also want to thank the reviewers who assessed the book and offered suggestions for revision, as well as the board and director of the press. Several friends were kind enough to read through and offer comments on early drafts—Jonathan Montaldo, Robert Thompson, John Bostwick, John Hotrovich, and Jennifer Zamansky. Others, too many to be named, were patient enough to listen to me talk about what I was trying to do here. But among them I want to mention colleagues in ministry H. Henry Maertens, Alexis Vinogradov, John Frazier, Nicholas Denysenko, William Mills, and Seraphim Sigrist, along with my spouse, Jeanne Berggreen Plekon. Regula Noetzli of the Charlotte Reedy Literary Agency and Keelan Pacot of Grove Atlantic enabled permission for the use of poems by Mary Oliver. The photographs, which enable you to encounter the faces of the writers we listen to here, were made possible by many of the writers themselves. Sarah Coakley, Heather Havrilesky, Barbara Brown Taylor, Christian Wiman, Richard Rohr, Rowan Williams, and Sara Miles were kind enough to respond to my inquires, allowed use of images and text, and encouraged me. Thanks go to Paul Pearson of the Thomas Merton Center and Phil Runkel of Marquette University Library and the Dorothy Day archive for use of images of Merton and Day.

There are many others who participated in some way to this book's appearance. I am grateful to my colleagues in the Department of Sociology/Anthropology and former students at Baruch College of the City University of New York, who figure in one of the chapters. I also want to acknowledge the members of the community of the parish of St. Gregory, my church home, who are prominent in one chapter here, as well as the members still living and departed of Trinity Lutheran Church, Brewster, New York, who figure in another chapter. If I started to recall all those from other parishes, from the Carmelite order, from my life who taught me to pray and prayed with me and for me, this brief acknowledgment would become a map of my life. So I will conclude with my departed father and mother, who prayed with me at church and before bed every night and especially in their very lives. They somehow knew that there is no part of life that is not a place and time of prayer.

CHAPTER ONE

Introduction

Prayer in Many Places

Religion and Reality

Religions and religious people often disagree with each other, sometimes even violently. In recent years we might be led to believe that
there is nothing but dispute and divergence among religions and their
members. Stephen Prothero wrote an entire book emphasizing this.[1]
There is a tendency to accept, respect, tolerate other traditions in our
time, and perhaps this leads some to claims that all religions are the
same, that we all have the same God. Anyone teaching or studying
world religious traditions in a comparative way cannot help but recognize really striking convergences, as well as equally powerful differences. Some are not surprising at all, for example, that religious
traditions concern themselves *not* just with doctrine or teachings,
statements about God, gods, or the origin and end of the world and
personal lives. They also have a great deal to say about just how we
live those lives, that is, about ethics — what we should and should
not do.

Religions generally consider what is taught and believed to be real,
for example, how the world came to be or how our own lives will end.
Perhaps the metaphors and symbols used are not always to be taken
literally, in every detail. Yet behind them, through them, something
real and important is being communicated. Alexander Schmemann,

the well-known Orthodox priest and theologian, once told a friend that God was as real and as near as the blades of grass upon which they were sitting in a field. And if God were not that real and that close, he said further, then God was of no use. The mystic from the middle ages, Julian of Norwich, saw something similar. Jesus showed her to be holding in the palm of her hand something small, small as a hazelnut. When she asked what it was, the answer the Lord gave was, "It is all that is made." In this tiny round object Julian understood three things: God made it, God loves it, God keeps it—everything, all of creation. This little hazelnut-like sphere signified for Julian the immense love God had for each of us and everything in the world.[2] Julian would also say, "There is no wrath in God," only forgiveness and love. This vision so permeated her outlook that she could famously say, "All will be well, and all manner of things shall be and all will be well."[3] In our own time, writer and monk Thomas Merton had God say: "Mercy within mercy within mercy. I have forgiven the universe without end because I have never known sin."[4] With his consistent stress on compassion, forgiveness, and tolerance, Pope Francis has become known as the "pope of mercy."[5]

Beyond such examples, hearkening back to an often heard line, "We all have the same God," at least in the three great monotheistic traditions of Judaism, Christianity, and Islam, such a statement, at root, is true, given what these traditions say and believe about God. And in all three, God, for all the commandments, punishments, and wrath, nevertheless is at heart a loving God, one who creates and forgives endlessly. The first and greatest of God's names is that of mercy—*al Rahman al Rahim*, the gracious, the merciful. Not a few religious writers and visionaries have likewise only been able to experience a loving, forgiving God. This they are not speculating about. It is for real.

Anthropologist Tanya Luhrmann's well-received study directed attention to how belief intersects with people's lives in very powerful ways.[6] She examined evangelicals' and Pentecostals' intense experiences of the presence and action of God in the world around them and in their own lives. As an anthropologist, she takes seriously the psychological, political, social, and cultural consequences of faith in peoples' lives. As with the thinking and acting of any people or tribe, she affirms the powerful reality of what these evangelical and

Pentecostal Christians believe and experience in many different ways, from explicit prayer to other events and encounters in their day-to-day lives.

This book takes for granted Luhrmann's ethnography of faith and prayer, and also uses the work of sociologist Nancy Ammerman and her associates, as well as Diana Butler Bass in charting religion in everyday life.[7] You will read about how people experience communion, encounter with God, and more that is usually considered prayer in less than traditional or typically "religious" ways. Following Ammerman's lead, there will be "stories" from people who pray, this being one of her major means of getting at the everyday experience of faith.

Prayer Everywhere

In earlier books, I looked at the search for God, identity, and meaning, a life of holiness and wholeness. I examined the spiritual journeys of a number of writers, theologians, pastors, activists, and others, focusing on a range of examples of the search for holiness.[8] In some cases, the figures and their experiences were very much within classical lines, while in others, they were less than typical, sometimes rather unusual. Over the course of these studies, I wanted to make the point that the call to holiness is for all, that holiness does not require perfection and does not exclude one's humanity, and that failure, doubt, questions, and the like are not impediments. I also felt it important to examine the destructive, toxic aspects of religion, as a number of individuals experience these.

Not only can religion sometimes be destructive and toxic, religion is often captivating, consoling, creative, and transformative. Unlike the way in which we regard religion in our time, as a private matter, a personal choice and pursuit, clearly in much of history it was by definition communal. The Hebrew Bible, particularly in its historical books, narrates the struggle of Israel over against its polytheistic and very local religious neighbors. The God of Israel, but for that matter, all the other gods of surrounding nations, was anything but private and personal. All of life and every person in society, from ruler on down, was subject to divine power, required to follow divine commands, worship, and obey in all aspects of life. There was no separation of church and state, no compartment into which religion fit over against the rest of "secular" society. Religion permeated everything.

We clearly do not think or behave like this today. The oldest texts we have, the scriptures, the most ancient of liturgical services, are not only thoroughly communal, assuming all are involved, they are also cosmic, stretching beyond the local community, city, town, country, nation, or empire. On the one hand encompassing and universal, the tradition nevertheless permeates all of life, not just the temple and its celebrations, but every corner of the everyday. The striking contrast, almost paradoxical, we should keep in mind as we proceed here, on prayer. We tend to restrict religion in general and prayer in particular to the house of worship, the temple, synagogue, or church, and to the scriptures, the prescribed services, the feasts, that is, the prayer of the whole community.

One of the best-known prayer books in English is the *Book of Common Prayer*, largely the editorial and creative work of the archbishop of Canterbury, Thomas Cranmer. It was authorized for use by the Church of England by the Crown in the sixteenth century.[9] Its elegance and cadence have become almost the standard of prayer language throughout the English-speaking world. Yet in all of religious history, prayer has never been restricted to the scriptures or liturgical texts, even though these are fundamental in shaping faith and piety. There are numerous, excellent studies of prayer, such as Friedrich Heiler's classic study.[10] A more recent one that has been of particular value is an almost encyclopedic one by Philip and Carol Zaleski.[11]

Prayer in Life

Here, though, we shall focus on the experiences and activities that individuals searching for God understand as prayer. I want to take these as seriously as Luhrmann does in listening to what believers hear God saying to them. I do not mean here primarily prayers compiled in books or those employed in liturgical services, so I speak of "uncommon" prayer. This does not in any way diminish the value or place of formal, liturgical prayer—far from it. It is prayer in ordinary, everyday life that I will consider here, not prayer in theory or just conceptually, but in the actual experience of people. In a documentary, a Benedictine monk said that there is no such thing as faith or prayer or love, only people who believe, who pray, who love.

This approach is neither primarily an historical investigation nor a technical, how-to-pray approach. Neither is it an academic theological reflection on prayer in the ordinary sense, though clearly many questions arise, and, in what is contained in these chapters, there are many answers. This book is distinctive in searching out the lived experience of prayer.

On the grassroots level, prayer remains a major ingredient in everyday life. A recent survey on prayer conducted by LifeWay Research, a Nashville, Tennessee, based Christian organization, gives something of a snapshot of what people in America pray for or about.[12] Such a high percentage pray for family and friends, 82 percent, which, when added to other targets like people in disasters (38 percent), government leaders (12 percent), those of other or no faith (20 percent), and others in the public eye (5 percent), make it clear that prayer is highly relational or interactional, social. Chapters here about a prayer list and parish events as prayer will give this real support. Yet, the same survey also underscores the personal dimension of prayer: 74 percent pray for their own problems and difficulties, another 54 percent for good things that have happened in one's life, and 42 percent and 36 percent for, respectively, one's sin and future prosperity.

This study found that 48 percent of those queried said they prayed daily. The more detailed list of things they prayed about is at times hilarious, ranging from asking that their favorite team win to finding a parking place, as well as success in things that one had not really worked hard for and for vengeance against one's enemies. Over a third also prayed for their enemies, too!

Various surveys on religious behavior in the United States consistently show slippage in such activity, particularly among younger people, the millennials in particular—more than 20 percent are "religious nones," indicating no membership in churches or participation in communal activities.[13] Yet even among these, religious belief and activity on a personal level like prayer has not disappeared.[14]

Prayer is many things. For some, likely even some readers of this book, prayer is, or rather, must be talking to God, our talking to God. I can also imagine that for some, prayer has to follow those classic modalities mentioned: praise, thanksgiving, and the rest. For still others, prayer surely requires that God be somehow addressed, thought about, aimed at.[15]

Ruth Burrows, known in religious life as the Carmelite Sister Rachel, makes what is a classic, very traditional point in her study.

> Prayer. We take the word for granted but ought we to do so? . . . Almost always when we talk about prayer we are thinking of something *we* do and, from that standpoint, questions, problems, confusion, discouragement, illusions multiply. For me, it is of fundamental importance to correct this view. Our Christian knowledge assures us that prayer is essentially what *God* does, how God addresses us, looks at us. It is not primarily something we are doing to God, something we are giving to God, but what God is doing for us. And what God is doing for us is giving us the divine Self in love. . . . True prayer means wanting GOD not ego. . . . The great thing is to lay down this ego-drive. This is the "life" we must lose, this is the "self" we must abandon if we are to have true life and become that self God wants us to be, which only God can know and ultimately only God can bring into being.[16]

Prayer and Ourselves

A number of the poets and other writers we will listen to in this book affirm that there is a true self as well as a "false" or "shadow" self. Thomas Merton is the best known of them, Richard Rohr another. They also argue that the spiritual life, at least in part, involves discerning between these. One should seek to move away from the false in favor of the true self, the self that God has in mind, that God created.

The larger question is about the self and, by extension, others around us and prayer. Is ego involved in prayer? How could it not be? Is prayer only top-down, one-sided, directed to God, in whom we are to lose ourselves but who will be silent? It is possible to say yes to all of these, but I would also say it is much more complicated. Burrows is struggling to remind us that prayer is not just about the words or the liturgical forms, not just about methods. She knows, as does any wise spiritual director, that it is easy—really the natural inclination—to make prayer into a symphony of ourselves. All the best approaches to prayer likewise tell us that prayer cannot be just the sound of our own consciousness, the stream of our insecurities, hurts, joys, and plans. Prayer is of necessity about ourselves and about the important other people in our lives. But prayer is more. Whether one comes at prayer from God's perspective or that of the individual, there is the tendency to objectivize it, to make it into something. Prayer is far more expansive, diverse, and elusive. Again, consider the monk in the documentary who said that there are no such things as faith, love, or prayer, only *women and men who believe, love, and pray.*

While it is crucial to keep sight of the presence of God in prayer, what about the experience of those who pray? Is it not the case, as we shall hear from Barbara Brown Taylor, that an inescapable reality is the experience of God's absence, God's silence? She invokes Ruth Burrows's fellow Carmelite, John of the Cross, with his famous description of *la noche oscura*, each person's "dark night."[17] Jesus quotes the Psalms on the cross: "My God, my God, why have you abandoned me?" Not only is the absence of God part of prayer—as are doubts and inabilities to use traditional theological language—but so too many other of our feelings, thoughts, experiences, and lives.

Prayer Where You Least Expect It

This book will be radical but also traditional at the same time. Sometimes prayer is not respectfully asking things of God or, for that matter, desperately demanding that God fix things for us. Neither is it always praising God or begging forgiveness. Or expressing gratitude or even exulting in the beauty and presence in the world around us. We will see that for some great souls, it is simply being there in silence, before God, not even trying to imagine God or communicate with God. The point is that in so doing we are much more likely to eventually listen and hear what God has to say to us.

I will suggest that prayer may be the joy of being together with friends and neighbors to eat, to celebrate, and also to work, to make things. Being with others, caring for them, teaching and learning with them, is prayer. So is confronting the dark, what we do not know, what we fear, whether failure, sickness, aging, the bad things we and others do, or death. This too is prayer, as is ragging about the pain and the difficulty in facing the darkness.

Some of those to whom we will listen here, particularly poets, will tell us prayer, more than anything else, is paying very close attention—to the woods, the beach, to the animals both wild and tame—and, by extension, paying attention to the natural world will lead to paying attention to others, and at last to ourselves.[18] Going inside, following what many call the prayer of the heart, is how to find our true selves.

In classes that I teach at Baruch College of the City University of New York, I always encounter a rich, diverse student community. Over a hundred languages are spoken by faculty and students at the college. It is the business school of the CUNY system but also is home to a large arts and sciences school, which services both the schools of business and public administration. We do not have a department of religious studies or theology but a program, that is, a regular offering of courses in religion by trained and interested faculty from several different disciplines—anthropology, history, modern languages and literature, philosophy, sociology, and political science, among others. There are overview courses in the Jewish, Christian, Muslim, Buddhist, and Hindu traditions, as well as a very popular comparative religions course and other more specialized ones that focus on the scriptures of various traditions, specific historical periods, as well as important figures in the traditions. There are seminar-shaped courses in which we read both the lives and the writings of singular persons of faith in the Christian traditions, from Dorothy Day and Thomas Merton to Bonhoeffer, Martin Luther King Jr., and Maria Skobtsova. Gradually additional, still-living writers, poets, and activists were added, such as Sara Miles, Barbara Brown Taylor, Darcey Steinke, Mary Karr, Mary Oliver, as well as a number of others. In another course we read primary sources—memoirs, poetry, and fiction in which authors share their experiences and describe their spiritual journeys.

The three books on holiness, mentioned earlier, were written during and increasingly drew from these courses. This book on prayer in everyday experience continues the mining of others' encounters with God in all kinds of life situations and events. The chapters here listen to and reflect upon what some remarkable individuals offer by way of spiritual experience, by way of their living out of prayer. Those who have read the earlier books will recognize some authors—Thomas Merton, Rowan Williams, Sara Miles, Barbara Brown Taylor, Dorothy Day, Maria Skobtsova, Paul Evdokimov, and Seraphim of Sarov. Others have been read and discussed in class but were not included in prior books—Sarah Coakley, Heather Havrilesky, Mary Oliver, Christian Wiman, Mary Karr, Richard Rohr. In some cases, I have grouped together writers whose thinking collide and merge in a most fascinating manner—this is the case with the theologians and others in chapter 2 and the poets in chapter 4. In other cases, I brought together individuals who did not know each other or even live at the same time but nevertheless complement each other in fascinating ways—Dorothy Day and Maria Skobtsova in chapter 7, Paul Evdokimov and Seraphim of Sarov in chapter 10. And in still other chapters—3, 6, and 11, I focus on one writer only: Merton, Taylor, and Rohr, respectively. These are neither randomly selected individuals nor an attempt to represent an exhaustive range of Christian traditions, though there are Anglicans/Episcopalians, Eastern Orthodox, and Roman Catholic figures, as well as several of no-claimed church affiliation. I hope the gathering and conversation among them will be as fascinating to you as it has been to my students. I also have three chapters that arose out of my own life and experience. A bit more on them shortly.

Listening to Experience

First, we will go to the prayer of theologians. The theologians speaking here are not offering the dense, often challenging material for which they are best known. Rather they offer very personal and accessible witness about prayer. A number of times in this book we will hear that prayer, even that of simple silence and presence before God and the world, is profoundly disturbing, disruptive, and transforming of who and what we are. We will hear of this from theologian and priest *Sarah Coakley*. Along with her, fellow theologian and former archbishop of Canterbury *Rowan Williams* will give us clear and forceful perspectives on what we do in prayer—these coming not from scholarly lectures but from teaching in his cathedral church.

To these important academic theological voices, I want to add those of two women from quite different locations and backgrounds. *Heather Havrilesky* bears no theological credentials whatsoever and, like many younger adults, has moved away from the Catholic tradition in which she was raised. A parent of small children, spouse too, her writing both in print and in the blog world catapulted her to the position of advice columnist for *New York* magazine. Now, why would a serious book on prayer consult a sometimes snarky, always discerning columnist? Even a small sampling of her thoughtful and compassionate response to troubled souls will prove to be an unexpected gift.

And lastly, in the same chapter, to the rich commentary of the three just mentioned I include the colorful, vibrant voice of *Sara Miles*, a chef, former foreign correspondent, radical activist, and now deacon and head of the Food Pantry at St. Gregory of Nyssa Episcopal parish in San Francisco. Her earlier books, *Take this Bread* and *Jesus Freak*, tell the story of her conversion experience to Christ as an adult, with no religious background whatsoever, and describe her work in the ministry of outreach to the people of the Mission district. Here, we will follow her on Ash Wednesday, when with parish colleagues, she distributes ashes and prays with street folk in her neighborhood and tells their and her own story of transformation in the swirl of city life. While we may think that prayer is very much about shutting out the noise and confusion, the all-too-many others and their demands, some voices will say that it is not about escape to peace and quiet at all. Quite the opposite, the crush of the city is where we are fashioned into real souls. And rather than only quiet contemplation, we will hear about prayer as engagement with the world of need and pain around us—feeding the hungry, providing shelter for the homeless and medical care for the ill, and advocating for the powerless. In short, prayer is action.

Next, we will listen to an acknowledged master spiritual teacher, *Thomas Merton*. For all the books on contemplative prayer he produced, what we will hear is very radical and simple yet powerful. Prayer can be as simple as breathing, as going through all the demands of the day with mindfulness, finding not just monotony but also great contentment and joy. We will listen, in particular, to observations he made, first in the journals and then in an essay on what he learned in and from his hermitage. In the last years of his life he was allowed to live in a simple small cinderblock cottage, not far from the rest of the monastery. There, in many ways, he simplified his spiritual life and got down to the basics, thereby following directions that monastic renewal and Vatican Council II were promoting.

Prayer is many things. Yet it is not everything. Prayer is the search for God, doubting God, conversing, even arguing with God, challenging God to be what God really is. The Hebrew Bible, in particular, includes all of these modalities. There, prayer is truly human, and both great mothers and fathers and prophets of the people of God exult, praise, and entreat God, as well as castigate, accuse, and rail against the same Lord. In the classic modalities, prayer has been seen as adoration, praise, thanksgiving, intercession, confession, seeking forgiveness. All of these and more encounters with God in the everyday are what we are looking for here. Encounter is also reciprocal—our encounter with God, God's with us.

After Merton, we move to some poets in the next chapter. "I don't know where prayers go," *Mary Oliver* exclaims in the opening of one of her most beloved poems, "I Happened To Be Standing."[19] Later, after musing over the possible prayer lives of cats, opossums, sunflowers, and oak trees, she also wonders whether prayer is a gift or a petition, or if any of this really matters. For Mary Oliver, who has had no great institutional religious involvement, prayer is identified as simply being present before God—in silence, especially in mindful awareness and in perception of the natural world. But then words come, both to God and from God, to express what has been experienced in the encounter, even if the encounter is deer in a forest, birds on a beach, or wind in the trees around one's house. Or in the face of other people.

Along with Mary Oliver we will read poet *Christian Wiman*. He has taught a course at the Yale Divinity School Institute of Sacred Music entitled "Accidental Theologies," that is, theological reflection and expressions in unexpected, surely non-academic or any other kind of theological locations—in novels, poems, plays, and elsewhere.[20] This is not so different from the goal of this book; actually, it is almost the same. I want to follow individuals beyond prayer books, sacred texts, and liturgies to other places: encounters and experiences in which they see, hear, and communicate with God, the world, and other people. These include the experience of nature, the care of those in need, social and political activism, personal relationships, conversation, creative work, as well as sickness, emotional suffering, doubt, and unbelief.

I believe it is also necessary to look into less joyful, even painful experiences in life to see how prayer figures there. As it turns out, even for her open-eyed wonder at the world, Mary Oliver also writes of grief and loss and coming to grips with them. Wiman, best known for his poetry, reveals another, quite different attitude toward faith and, in practice, prayer. In a collection of journal entries over the course of a year or more, *My Bright Abyss*, he chronicles his struggle with a rare, often terminal cancer, this just after getting married and hoping to start a family.[21] Raised in Texas evangelicalism, Wiman drifted in young adulthood away from the powerful faith of his childhood. Faced with a serious, difficult-to-treat cancer, he returns to faith. But it is not a clinging to the past nor a desperate adherence in the face of pain. It is one of the most riveting accounts of faith that protests disease and suffering. Wiman fights with God and with many important aspects of Christianity through his diagnosis and treatment. Through this journey, one finds a great deal of prayer, yet not in a church building, at a service, or with an open bible.

Mary Karr is also well known as a poet, yet she has been praised for her three volumes of memoirs. In the last of these, the best-selling *Lit*, she confronts her own struggles with depression and alcoholism as well as the breakup of a marriage and the challenges of being a single parent. In all of this, after a life in which faith was absent, she had the powerful discoveries of the community of believers, of the insight of religious writers, and of God. Karr points us to the tangled terrain of one's life as filled with encounters with God, with the experience of prayer.

In the next chapter, we will listen to yet another writer, an Episcopal priest and college professor, esteemed as a preacher too. *Barbara Brown Taylor* has now completed a trilogy of books on spiritual experience and journeying. The first, *Leaving Church*, was a searing account of her experiences in ministry, including her failures. Another book, *An Altar in the World*, looked at the experience of the sacred away from church, out in the ordinary world of everyday life. Finally, the volume to which we will listen here is her encounter with darkness. She challenges us to put our faces and our minds in the darkness of life, in very material as well as emotional and spiritual ways.

In another chapter, the presence of God in serving others and standing for social justice, confronting the political establishment and self-serving policies, is presented as living prayer. Here we encounter the very colorful personalities and the challenging, exciting lives of two women who set up shop in urban locations during roughly the same decades in the last century to aid the neglected and hopeless— *Dorothy Day* and *Maria Skobtsova*.

Skobtsova rightly spoke of "the liturgy outside of the church building," termed by others "the liturgy after the liturgy," that is, when liturgy is continued in our lives.[22] For her, as for Day, this meant seeing the indissoluble link between love of God and of the neighbor. Prayer was of course the liturgy—both the Catholic Worker houses and Mother Maria's hostels had chapels as their spiritual heart. But in addition to receiving communion, prayer for them was the hunt for day-old food in local markets, its preparation and serving—a "second table" after the feast of the holy table of the Eucharist. And for both, doing the works of loving-kindness also entailed speaking out and writing against the war, fascism, racism, and the buildup of nuclear weapons—a witness for the gospel in addition to the works of mercy.

I have included three chapters that are both personal and interpersonal reflections on prayer in remembering, in community, and in teaching. These chapters include some material from my own experience of prayer. Having been a teacher and priest for many years, I think there are some intriguing examples in these callings. In the parish where I serve, there is a great sense of community. Visitors and oldtimers, friends as well as strangers are welcomed, quickly integrated into the community. And this is a community that likes to be together, especially around food. Of course we have the Sunday liturgy of the Eucharist, services for feasts, baptisms, weddings, funerals, and more. These are much loved. But when food appears or when people gather to prepare food, either baking or making that Eastern European delicacy, pirogi, or for that matter, to say goodbye to a fellow member at their funeral or to celebrate the making of a new Christian in baptism or the uniting of a couple in marriage, some very beautiful, powerful webs of interaction emerge, ones I will describe as full of prayer, prayer in ways we do not usually imagine.

I have spent more than forty years of my life in the classroom, mostly teaching undergraduate students and researching and writing articles and books like the one you are reading. I have looked closely at remarkable persons of faith in our time, listened to their words, and followed their lives in order to see what their journeys in faith toward God are like and how these resonate with the rest of us. But in the classroom, I have also observed intense, eloquent, and truly moving moments of confession, of sharing personal triumph, but also great pain from students as their responses to the texts. I have listened to impassioned accounts of racial prejudice and discrimination and what these did to the students who experienced them. In my classes, where students form teams for presentation and discussion of the text we all have read, there is personal discovery, epiphany, outrage, the sharing of these, and more. I will also convey some of the many stories contained in the names that I have written down in the course of the last thirty years or more on a prayer list. I began this list because I did not remember a person in prayer, and it has become a map of my life, my work, and my relationships over decades. It is a powerful image, a living one, of how prayer is remembering, not just cognitively but also in action.

Toward the book's end, we will hear of the lives and thoughts of two persons of faith in the Eastern Church—the greatly loved monk *Seraphim of Sarov*, a kind of Russian Francis of Assisi, and the much admired teacher and writer *Paul Evdokimov*. Both, though a century apart, believed that you had to become what you pray, be prayer incarnate. Last of all we will listen to a contemporary spiritual writer and speaker who echoes the simplicity and force of the founder of his order of friars, the "little poor one," Francis of Assisi: the Franciscan friar and priest *Richard Rohr*, who brings together the best insights of modern psychology and the mystical tradition of spirituality.

Prayer in Many Places

What we will examine in this book—uncommon prayer—manifests the insight of a great tradition, namely, that it is possible to pray always and everywhere, and that the formal frameworks of books, scriptures as well as rites or services, do not restrict us. I intend to show in personal reminiscence precisely how these also come alive in everyday life. Perhaps it is possible to think of how weavers incorporate a pattern into many threads and they move the loom. The pattern is distinct from the threads, but, once woven, it is integral to the fabric, the cloth so produced. Is this not what prayer is really meant to be?

Lastly, elements of the book that should be highlighted are generous quotations, commentary, and rich annotation to further reading. Photographs are included so that the faces of the voices are also accessible. As with my other books, I aim at a carefully researched, thoughtful, but accessible book on the lived experience of prayer that can be read on its own as a contribution to the understanding of contemporary faith in action, twenty-first-century visions of spiritual growth and finding God.

Amy-Jill Levine, a Jewish New Testament scholar, makes the following point—a point this book attempts to drive home—the presence of God and the presence of prayer permeates all aspects of life. She does this very powerfully at the end of analyzing the parable about the kingdom of heaven being like yeast that a woman hid in the dough, actually in three measures, an absolutely huge amount of flour that would produce an enormous amount of bread (Matt. 13:33).

> [F]inally, perhaps the parable tells us that despite all our images of golden slippers and harps and halos, the kingdom is present at the communal oven of a Galilean village when everyone has enough to eat. It is present, inchoate, in everything, and is available to all, from the sourdough starter to the rain and the sunshine. It is something that works its way through our lives, and we realize its import only when we do not have it. To clean out the old leaven allows us to make room for the new, to start, again and again, to feast.[23]

CHAPTER TWO

The Prayer of Theologians and Others

*Sarah Coakley, Rowan Williams, Heather Havrilesky,
and Sara Miles*

The history of Christianity is full of things casually or deliberately forgotten, or left unsaid, in order to shape the future of a
Church or Churches. Institutions religious or secular create their
own silences, by exclusions and by shared assumptions, which
change over time. Such silences are often at the expense of many
of the people who could be thought of as actually constituting
the Church; institutional needs outweigh individual needs. Some
are conscious silences of shame and fear at the institution of the
Church not living up to its own standard of truth and compassion; and there has often been a particular pain meted out to those
who make the silences end. Life is rarely comfortable for the little
boy who says that the emperor has no clothes.[1]

It is worth recalling historian Diarmaid MacCulloch's observations about silence, concealment, and denial in both individuals and
corporately in the church. Theology and theologians are not always
the best friends of the faith.[2] The silences of which MacCulloch speaks
range from the aftermath of the council of Chalcedon and its splitting
up Christians who had been able to negotiate differing interpretations
of Christ to more recent coverups of sexual abuse and the silence of

churches' fear and inaction with respect to the Holocaust, slavery, and the situation of LGBT people.

When clergy and theologians try to break the silence, however, the result is not always happy. How often did now-former Archbishop of Canterbury Rowan Williams find himself attacked—by not just the media and political types but from within the church—when he tried in a talk or essay to deal with the complexities of sharia and other religious codes in a diverse culture or the difficulties of fidelity to tradition when it came to women and LGBT people?[3] Earlier in the last century in Paris, the Russian émigré priest and scholar Sergius Bulgakov was deemed a heretic by some for trying to find ways to talk about God using modern philosophical and literary language. Yet he has been rediscovered as likely the greatest Eastern Church theologian of the modern era.[4] Currently the "pope of mercy," Francis is charged with creating a "mess" and a "confusion" and leaving the Roman Catholic Church "without a rudder" for asking if those marginalized by divorce or their sexual identity cannot be more genuinely welcomed and encountered.[5]

In the face of all this, I think it important to listen to some writers who offer more than silence on living out what they pray. Sarah Coakley and Rowan Williams are clergy in the Church of England and theologians. Sara Miles is a writer and a parish deacon in the Episcopal Church. All are widely published authors. I have also included a rather different voice as well, neither a member of the clergy nor a theologian, not identifiably religious at all—Heather Havrilesky, the writer who responds to readers' letters in the column in *New York* magazine "Ask Polly." She offers a fresh, startling honesty in responding to others' confusion and pain—the prayer of healing and friendship.

Sarah Coakley: Prayer as Transformation

Sarah Coakley's work is profound, dealing with gender, the body, and the Trinity, among other subjects. She conveys a fierce commitment to her vocation as a priest, and more specifically, to prayer within that calling.

Sarah Coakley

The venerable journal the *Christian Century* has, since the 1930s, periodically asked important church leaders and theologians to respond thoughtfully to the question, "How my mind has changed?" In an account for that journal of what has changed in her work, outlook, and life, Coakley chose to focus on the profound transformation of her intellectual, professional, and personal life brought about by prayer! In it, she presents a vision of her scholarship and thinking, her body and gender, her relationship to God, to herself as a woman, spouse, parent—all changed by discovery of silent waiting before God each day: not meditation, biblical reflection, or the liturgical prayer of the church, just silence.[6]

When I first read this reflection I was genuinely struck by how so gifted a scholar could describe, in such blunt, forceful terms, what happened by keeping silent before God. Perhaps this kind of shattering experience might come from the desert mothers and fathers, or from the likes of Thomas Merton, a poet and writer as well as monk. Knowing the kind of rigorous training Coakley had—she even notes this in some detail in the essay—to be so changed by silence and presence was even more striking, and all the more so, the extent to which she described its impact all through her life and work.

There is now a considerable literature on what some call "center-ing prayer," and on silence before God. Major contributors include Thomas Keating along with Basil Pennington, Benedictines John Main and Laurence Freeman, and Franciscan Richard Rohr.[7] It figures importantly in Thomas Merton's corpus of writing over decades, al-though not with that description. Merton quite carefully described, for a Pakistani Muslim correspondent, Abdul Aziz, that he has come to pray in a kind of nothingness before God.

> Strictly speaking, I have a very simple way of prayer. It is centered entirely on attention to the presence of God and to His will and His love. That is to say that it is centered on faith by which alone we can know the presence of God. One might think that this gives my meditation the character described by the Prophet as "being before God as if you saw Him." Yet it does not mean imagining anything or conceiving a precise image of God, for to my mind this would be a kind of idolatry. On the contrary, it is a matter of adoring Him as invisible and infinitely beyond our comprehen-sion, and realizing Him as all. My prayer tends very much to what you call *fana*. There is in my heart this great thirst to recognize totally the nothingness of all that is not God. My prayer is then a kind of praise rising up out of the center of Nothingness and Si-lence. If I am still present "myself" this I recognize as an obstacle. If He wills He can then make the Nothingness into a total clarity. If He does not will, then the Nothingness actually seems itself to be an object and remains an obstacle. Such is my ordinary way of prayer or meditation. It is not "thinking about" anything, but a direct seeking of the Face of the Invisible, which cannot be found unless we become lost in Him who is Invisible.[8]

Compare Merton's description to Sarah Coakley's account of what she experienced and then found to be the consequences of prayer as silence before God.

> After many attempts at daily intercession and scriptural medi-tation which seemed unsatisfying (although I am sure they were exactly what was needed at the time), it was in my mid-twenties that I finally found my way into a simpler form of prayer via an

experiment with Transcendental Meditation. I took this up on the excuse of needing an antidote to stress in my first academic job. The impact was electrifying. I hadn't been going longer than about two months with this simple discipline of 20 minutes of silence in the morning and early evening when what I can only call a seismic shift of seemingly unspeakable proportions began to afflict me. Whatever was going on here was not only "transcendental" but severely *real.* . . . Yet it was strangely impossible to step off the spiritual roller coaster which was now in full swing. I recall finding a letter of Basil the Great in which he describes the adventure of prayer as like getting into a boat with the decks constantly shifting under one; this was some comfort, as was the discovery of Bernard of Clairvaux's many meditations on the "fear of the Lord as the beginning of wisdom," fear marking the necessary cracking open of the heart before God if prayer is to develop and deepen. Since the ground was (literally and fearfully) heaving for me too, I had urgent recourse to whatever patristic, medieval and early modern treatises on prayer I could lay hands on. Little was I to know at the time that this was to lead me to a complete rethinking of doctrinal development in the early church and beyond. For as I rapidly discovered, when one came at that history without the forced modern distinction between "spiritual" and "dogmatic" texts, a whole new world lay before one: spiritual growth and doctrinal truth hung newly together. The history of doctrine became likewise the entangled history of spiritual and political struggle—including intense struggles over questions of gender and authority. But this did not reduce doctrinal questions to (secularized) issues of sex and power, as was becoming a fashionable mode of analysis in the wake of Michel Foucault. On the contrary, the commitment to prayer strung one on the rack of the painful internalization of divine truth. For me, this change of approach heralded no nostalgic or romantic return to a premodern era, as was—at the other end of the spectrum from the Foucauldians—also becoming popular in various forms of neo-conservatism. Here the slogan was: "Down with the Enlightenment and back to the Fathers and medievals!" No, for me it was a retrieval of a classic tradition sweated painfully out of the exigencies of prayer encountered primarily as darkness and disturbance.[9]

"Electrifying," a "seismic shift," a ship deck moving, the ground heaving below her feet, a "spiritual roller coaster," "darkness and disturbance." For such a learned individual and teacher and soon-to-be-priest, how surprisingly powerful, tumultuous! And all this from silence before God. How much is changed by apparently so very little. Coakley goes on to identify three major changes, not just in how she conceived of doing theology, but, far beyond it, of the very character of texts and of the intellectual and spiritual life.

First, she discovered "surrendering of control to God," the vulnerability of creature before Creator that she would later write more about.[10] She mentions that noted feminist theologian Elisabeth Schüssler Fiorenza at Harvard told her to stop speaking and writing about such "vulnerability," and still today, there is criticism of Coakley from feminist perspectives for this. Yet, there was much more to this discovery.

> It also took patience to grasp — through the deeper engagement with scripture and tradition that this practice was also drawing me into — that my whole concept of the bounds of selfhood was undergoing change. The meaning of the "body of Christ" in Paul sprang alive for the first time, and with that a mysterious sense of our deep mutual implication in each other's lives as members of that body. And if this was what Christ meant for the here and now, then surely it must signal that my previous assumptions about a past, extrinsic "life of Jesus" as the only basis for Christology was wildly awry and fatally restricted (sorry, Troeltsch). The resurrection had reappeared — reentering triumphantly by stealth through the back door of my consciousness. Moreover, what had started as a frighteningly lonely journey of prayer now seemed to be the least lonely activity that one could possibly engage in — not only buzzing with communication, but positively crowded with angels and saints, the living and the dead.[11]

Coakley also found that the experience of silent prayer forced her to confront the reality of body, sex, and the mystery of desire, not just conceptually or emotionally but in the whole. Sex, the body, and desire cannot just be where conservatives want rules to dominate nor where liberals would prefer us to do what seems right. If the "personal is political," all the more are these definitional aspects of our identity. And thus she would look to the Trinity to think about these realities.[12]

Finally, Coakley found that contemplative prayer pushed her past many of the ways in which she was trained to regard the claims of traditional religious texts essentially cognitively. But when one wants to be critical of Enlightenment limits of rationality, where does one go without becoming a shrill voice of sectarian expression? There must be some way of integrating and taking seriously the truth of texts as well as criticism.

> My own response to this philosophical and theological crisis is one that seeks to analyze the dark testing of contemplation as precisely an epistemological challenge. In other words, I continue to reject another false modern disjunction—that between spirituality and philosophy. It is not that contemplation affords just another sectarian theological perspective, which one can take or leave as one wills. Rather, its painful and often dark expansion of consciousness, its integration of thought and affect and its ethical sensitizing to what is otherwise neglected (including, of course, the poor "who are always with us") all demand that one give an account of how philosophy, and science and politics too, cannot ultimately afford to ignore the apprehensions that contemplation invites.[13]

What holds, in Coakley's view, for academic work in religious studies and theology has a correlate in the church, where in recent decades there seems to have been one war after another regarding sexuality, gender, and similar issues.[14] Coakley has written and spoken in interviews about how being a priest intersects with her profession as scholar and teacher. She produced a particularly forceful account of the power of prayer, taken from her experience in chaplaincy training in correctional facilities.[15]

She also has written about how seriously she takes the canonical obligation of a priest to pray the daily office, the truly "common prayer" of the church, as well as to celebrate the Eucharist. In a collection of essays with others, she makes clear that this tradition of the daily office is not just a museum-piece of English cathedrals and their choirs but a powerful way of witnessing to one's faith in a visible, public way in the church building.[16] She notes how strong a force daily prayer is in keeping one's priorities clear, in putting the distinctive vision of Christ and the gospel to the many troubles in our everyday life, from poverty and abuse to war and conflict among political parties and perspectives in our own country. She also has noted the ways in which prayer also connects with others, both in her priestly training in prison chaplaincy as well as in interaction with students, both graduate students and those preparing for ordination. She left Harvard after painful conflict with the administration and others about the place of theology in such a university over against a more secular study of religion.

Coakley's account of her own experience with prayer in silence before God, the remarkable vulnerability it engenders in connection to power, also the grounding of it in desire, the body, the erotic, makes for a lot to ponder, much to contest. However there is also something else easily missed.[17] Coakley really is showing what the present volume is all about, namely, the flow of prayer into and, thus, its presence in all of our life, the breaking down of the easy categories of sacred and profane, divine and human, of formal prayer and just living.

Is it possible that there are forms of prayer and things to be discovered that we are simply unaware of, given how we formalize and box in this action? The genius of Coakley's ideas, which we must trace back first to the Hebrew Bible and then the New Testament, is that prayer leaves no aspect of our identities and lives untouched. Coakley makes this clear in her writings, explicitly talking about the connections between her vocations as scholar and priest and the other statuses and roles in her personal life—parent and child, spouse and friend. She also strongly emphasizes the realities of the body, of sexuality and of one's gender identity. The life with God, and then of course prayer, is related to all of these social and personal identities for her. This is surely one of the most important realizations in this book: that prayer touches every aspect of our lives and identities.

Rowan Williams: Prayer as Full Humanity

Growing in prayer is not simply acquiring a set of special spiritual skills that operate in one bit of your life. It is about growing into what St. Paul calls "the measure of the full stature of Christ" (Eph. 4:13). It is growing into the kind of humanity that Christ shows us. Growing in prayer, in other words, is growing in Christian humanity.[18]

Even while he was the archbishop of Canterbury, Rowan Williams, not unlike Sarah Coakley, continued to lecture, write, and also function as a pastor, visiting parishes of his diocese of Canterbury, offering retreats in Lent, presiding at the liturgy both on great feasts and ordinary Sundays. He began his career at major universities, studying at Cambridge, teaching at Oxford, and now, after his time as archbishop of Canterbury, back at Magdalene College, Cambridge, as master.

In a recent collection of talks given as bishop of the Canterbury diocese at the start of holy week, Williams crafts, as only someone who is also a poet can, rich and beautiful reflections on the basics of

Rowan Williams

Christian life that are striking in their simplicity. Drawing on the scriptures and liturgy, he offers what would have also been extended in the early centuries of the church, namely *mystagogia*, lessons on the essentials of baptism, the Bible, the Eucharist, and prayer. In the ancient church these would have been the final "lessons" for those preparing to be received into the church by baptism at the Easter vigil, on the night of Holy Saturday into the New Day of Pascha, the resurrection. They would first receive the Eucharist at the same liturgy in which they became Christians.

It is one thing to learn about the two great sacraments by which one is united to Christ and then to all sisters and brothers in the church by faith and by communion of the Lord's body and blood. It was also necessary to open up for new members the constant teaching both of the "word of God" in the scriptures and of the life of prayer, not just prayer form and formularies to be recited. In this last aspect, prayer as what holds all of life together, Williams makes an obvious yet startling suggestion. One should put oneself in the place of Jesus, just as the Lord's Prayer, the "Our Father," does. Jesus, in fact, gives this prayer in response to his disciples asking him to teach them how to pray, something that surely as faithful Jews they already knew, but now wanted to know more about from their teacher.

Williams consults with possibly the greatest preacher and teacher of the early church, Origen, sadly later cast aside because of accusations of heresy at a church council and only more recently thoroughly rehabilitated by scholarship. Much of what he was accused of was not his perspective.

Origen suggests a few things that will be noted over and over in this book. One is that we can and should pray anywhere. Not just in church or at services or with the Bible in front of us—though all of these are wonderful, and most of Origen's writings are precisely commentaries on the scriptures. Another is that we would do well to put aside our anxieties and obsessions, the things that overwhelm us, not because God cares little for these but so as to make us more attentive to God, more at peace, and then able to hear God and put one's life into sync with God.

Out of all this there begins to emerge a model that became very popular in the early church: a threefold pattern of learning to pray. You start with the "practical" life: learning ordinary self-awareness, the common sense of the Christian life; recognizing when you are being selfish and stupid and acting instead with an increasing degree of generosity. You move on from that to the freedom to see God in the world around you. When you have got your ego and all its fussiness a little bit in its place, then actually you see more; the world is more real and more beautiful. You see order and pattern in it, and your heart and your imagination expand until at last you arrive at the third level, at what Origen rather unpromisingly calls "theology" (by which he does not mean a degree in religious studies).

The intensity and clarity of what you see in the world around you trigger a sort of "leap in the dark"—or rather into the light— and into God. Your vision is clarified; your actions are gradually disciplined; the divine life slowly transforms you; and, to use one of the best expressions that Origen comes up with, we move into a condition where "the whole of our life says, Our Father."[19]

It is crucial to see that for Origen and for Rowan Williams, and, as it will turn out, just about everyone you will hear from in this book, prayer is not an escape, though it takes us elsewhere from where we presently are. Also, Williams reminds us not only of the opinion of early Christian teachers but of the New Testament itself, namely, that prayer is very much about the seemingly nonspiritual, areligious clutter of daily life. After all, a central petition in the Lord's Prayer is "Give us this day our daily bread." Not a new theological perspective, though a new outlook on our living may be precisely the gift we receive from our asking. Possibly, then, Williams suggests, we may come to see God where we did not see God before. We may begin to accept that there are details we cannot change and that may frighten us but that are not in themselves horrible. Lastly, Williams sounds a theme that will be heard here throughout. Prayer, if we really pursue it in life, will necessarily help us become more mindful, more aware of the others around us, of the world in which we dwell. Prayer does this by freeing us from ourselves in order to really be ourselves, to be in communion with others. How strange this sounds, in our twenty-first-century world, in which we are, all of us, so exquisitely aware of ourselves—the hurts, pains, inadequacies, as well as the achievements, accomplishments, skills, education, and experience that have enriched us. And this is not to mention how we look, how much we weigh, or how old or young we appear to be.

Williams consults Gregory of Nyssa and John Cassian, two other important writers in the early centuries of Christianity. From Gregory, a poet before everything else, we learn that prayer is the healing of all that is broken in our connections with God, with others and ourselves. And from Cassian, we hear that prayer is not so much or just what we think, feel, or do, but God doing, thinking, feeling, being in us.

Rowan Williams's essays, while archbishop of Canterbury, routinely were misinterpreted, misread, and even distorted in the media. Occasionally even his supporters complained that his mind was too complex, his vision too comprehensive, his stances too carefully stated. They wanted blunt, provocative positions. Sometimes he provided these, seemingly only to throw more fuel on the flames. Commentators charged that his writing and speech were too nuanced. They most often did not make for sound bites and headlines. But contrary to all this, I heard from a most intimate teacher and friend of his, Canon Donald Allchine, that one could not find a better pastor or confidant, that Rowan Williams was the best parish priest you could ever find, and that he was a loyal and supportive academic mentor.

In these talks on the essentials of the faith he shows himself to be these things as well as a consummate teacher and poet. I wanted to listen to him very early on in the book so as to encourage readers that what they would be getting was accessible and heartening, not just intellectually demanding prose or pious, overly sweet nonsense. To me, it is encouraging that three ancient, sagacious writers like Origen, Gregory of Nyssa, and John Cassian as well as two discerning, eloquent teachers and priests who are our contemporaries, Sarah Coakley and Rowan Williams, are emphatic about prayer being rooted in life—tumultuous, sometimes discouraging, seemingly hopeless life, in which we are so small and vulnerable and unable to make things turn out as we want.

Prayer in "Ask Polly"?

For those looking into a book about prayer, it would not be so surprising to turn to a wise pastor, a theologian, or a poet for advice. But recently, I was struck by the wonderfully sensible and sensitive reply given by writer Heather Havrilesky in the "Ask Polly" column in *New York* magazine: "Aging is scary and life is a struggle: why keep going?" "Polly" or better, Heather, provides a thoughtful if edgy response. Havrilesky has written for numerous venues, starting with Suck.com in the '90s and moving on to Salon.com, Bookforum, and the *New York Times* magazine, among others. She also has published a memoir, *Disaster Preparedness*. As with the other writers we are listening to, I can only invite you to go to her work, much of it accessible online, to really sample not only her sometimes snarky but usually hilarious and always compassionate perspectives.[20]

Havrilesky's writing is startling in its direct response to lives in trouble—troubles with one's close friends and significant others, troubles with one's own family of origin and experiences growing up, troubles in self-image and self-identity. There are sick dogs, a filthy house, writing deadlines passed, children misbehaving, comments on current events. In mentioning a *New York Times* magazine article she's published, the panelists on the TV show *The View* refer to her as "the mom" who wrote the fascinating piece in the Sunday paper. What, she wonders, happened to her name, her identity as a writer, to everything else about her except being "mom"?[21]

Heather Havrilesky

Somehow her life, with her work and her family, with her many readers with whom she interacts—this life is full, something wonderful, for which she is profoundly grateful. Gratitude is a powerful element in her spirituality because it is essential in her attitude toward herself, others, and her life. She urges her readers to become not just mindful and decisive but grateful.

In her memoir we follow her childhood, a tough one, marked by her parents' divorce and her sense of loss of them despite both living in the same location, Durham, North Carolina.[22] Comparing Havrilesky's no-nonsense, self-critical reflections in the memoir, one can quickly see how her life and experience have shaped what she nowadays has to say to those who pose questions about self-esteem, relationships, loneliness, and love.

Her mother, reminiscent of Patricia Hampl's in her memoir, is a survivor, one tough cookie.[23] Actually, both her parents seemed intent, in the 1970s, on making sure their children could face the ambiguities and disappointments of life by, more often, *not* solving problems, not smoothing them over or even consoling their kids.

While still a child at home, in the balcony of Sacred Heart Roman Catholic Church, she mused during mass about whether any of the ritual and creed had anything to do with God. A "test" of God's existence and power to act is set up, an easy trick, but God fails to accomplish it, so God fails. The story is not to be taken at face value. There is discernment in this passing glance at childish religion. Later on, in her replies to personal pain, there is an ocean of grace and wit, and even a little mercy, actually quite a lot of mercy.[24]

I suspect hardly any of her fans or readers would take her to be a leading spiritual voice, even if one rising up from dirty laundry, interrupted work, and the just-below-the-surface terror of someone entering her forties. But what she says is the real thing. In her replies to readers, despite an often caustic, edgy tone, there is a very solid humanity in how she sizes up and responds to the problem they serve at her. In the passage below, she senses the writer is being pulled into depression, not by irrational or cooked-up fears but by the real and inevitable prospects of aging, failing, illness, death, and loss. Her response is beyond mindful. She even shares a visit home to her aging mother and what she learns—a great deal and mostly not to pity the woman—by quietly observing an orderly, good life lived by someone who she's not embarrassed to call "old." Here is how Heather finishes her reply to the reality: "Aging is scary and life is a struggle: why keep going?"

Uncertainty and failure might look like the end of the road to you, but you know what? Uncertainty is a part of life. Facing uncertainty and failure doesn't always make "Two who are Mostly Good" weaker and weaker until they give up. Sometimes it wakes them up, and it's like they can see the beauty around them for the first time. Sometimes losing everything makes you realize how little you actually NEED. Sometimes losing everything sends you out into the world, to breathe in the air, to pick some flowery weeds, to take in a new day.

Because this life is full of promise, always. It's full of beads and dolls and chipped plates; it's full of twinklings and twinges. It IS possible to admit that life is a struggle and also embrace the fact that small things—like sons who call you and beloved dogs in framed pictures and birds that tell you to drink your fucking tea—they matter. They matter a lot.

Stop trying to make sense of things. You can't think your way through this. Open your heart, and drink in this glorious day. You are young, and you will find little things that will make you grateful to be alive. Believe in what you love now, with all of your heart, and you will love more and more until everything around you is love. Love yourself now, exactly as sad and scared and flawed as you are, and you will grow up and live a rich life and show up for other people, and you'll know exactly how big that is.

Let's celebrate this moment together. There are twinklings and twinges, right here, in this moment. It is enough. Let's find the eastern towhee.[25]

Would you recognize this as a spiritual statement, a homily, a prayer? Likely you would not. But Heather Havrilesky speaks with great caring, discernment, and strength to someone distressed. And cannot the lines about belief and love and their contagion echo with so many lines in the letters of John and the Gospels? Do we require specifically religious imagery, symbols, and language to make something spiritual, prayerful? As Alexander Schmemann put it, prayer, particularly that of the liturgy, seeks not to waft us away to another world but rather to enable us to perceive the new world precisely around us, to see the cleansing effect of water, the nourishment from bread and wine.[26] We are what we eat, echoing Feuerbach, Schmemann insists, and thus all our prayer is not about other worlds, others things, but about our being alive in the world, the only world we have, the world created, loved, and given us by God. Rather than rants about secularism and secularization, Schmemann, and along with him Rowan Williams and all the others to whom we will listen, direct us back continually to our world, our lives, and those in them.

In the aptly titled *Disaster Preparedness*, Havrilesky shows us many moments of her frazzled, disordered existence, from childhood on up to her marriage and family life with two young daughters. There is more than a hint of irony in the "disaster" part of the title because, as one winds through her account, there is some heartbreak and chaos, but also deep, strong affection, forgiveness, acceptance of the "otherness" of even so intimate others as one's own mother and father. It is not a bizarre life but rather an ordinary one, with many of the experiences we all encounter in late-twentieth- and early-twenty-first-century America. Good work, in one's profession of training, is not easily found, yet it does exist and is worth struggling to locate. Likewise, a partner with whom to share life is not just hanging on a rack in your size and color and cut. Like many, Heather bumps her way through boyfriends till finding the one who will be her spouse, and she is careful about the details of this precious man and co-parent.

It is not just the searing, surprising replies Havrilesky provides to her blog and column readers that make her stand out as an unexpected, far-from-obvious but important voice. It is even more the way in which she is able to come to terms with her own self and the web of life around her, captured in the conclusion to her memoir.

> I love this fucking clown show of mine. The unruly dogs, the distracted husband, the alternately sweet and enraged two-year-old, the enormous baby who still wakes up at four a.m. even

though she clearly has the fat stores to hibernate through a long winter. I love them all, along with my emotionally overwrought teenage stepson and my little, overheated house and my hairy rugs and my smudged windows and my scrappy, overgrown yard, and all of the imperfect manifestations of this imperfect life. I am flawed, flawed, flawed, and I will rarely feel shiny and complete and utterly calm and prepared. And sure, while I'm at it, I will never be gorgeous and rich. . . . But look how hard we try, you and me, us and them, everyone. Isn't it sort of sweet, to see how determined we are to do better, to be stronger, to make sure our kids and our mothers and our partners and even our dogs know they're loved? . . . We are frazzled and unruly, you and me. We are desperate and wistful and restless and funny and frayed at the edges. We can worry we're doing it all wrong . . . we can be ingrates and role models, we can flinch and be heroic, we can be courageous and also melancholy. . . . Please remember, we were not a disappointment. Not at all, not even close. We were gorgeous and strong, you and me. We were terrible and troubled and utterly divine.[27]

Heather Havrilesky needs no theological degree or frequency at church to be able to recognize the need for hope, the urgency of mercy, the omnipresence of beauty, everything as gift. I heartily recommend reading her columns and memoir. They will give you a shot of joie de vivre as well as comfort in messiness. It is true, she often chooses to answer queries full of self-centered obsession and entitlement and usually unmasks these for what they are without destroying the fragile human being often huddled beneath them. Here, to someone unable yet to come to terms with time and its passage, she covers lots of issues. In short, celebrate now, don't think you can see all the joy and peace that someone else has experienced simply because you judge their situation frightening, discouraging, hopeless. Realize that uncertainty and fear are inescapable. There is much to rejoice over and love, despite what saddens.

There is not the slightest mention of God or anything religious here. But I would challenge anyone who would say this is not prayer. There is concern for another, suffering, an effort to affirm forgiveness, compassion, to see things not as we want them but as they are. For that matter, long stretches of the scriptures leave God and religion behind in the swirl of battle, political intrigue, desire, and more.

Origen, Rowan Williams, and Heather Havrilesky remind us that we cannot separate our faith or the Spirit from the messiness of the world, the hardness of the heart, for right there, as Descartes saw, is the movement of grace. God is not somewhere else. God is with us, in us, closer to ourselves than our own hearts, as Augustine said. God is also concerned with everything, not just the really monumental issues that flood the news—endless war all over, Afghanistan, Iraq, Syria, Gaza, and Ukraine, battles without end in government, poverty, illness, aging, death. When we are able to rediscover God in the midst of all this and more, it is not sorcery or magic, nor will all the bad disappear, whoosh, and the rabbit pop out or the doves fly away.

Sara Miles: Prayer in the Streets

> Inside and outside of church buildings, on Ash Wednesday and every other day, the people of God keep talking with God. We saturate our cities with worship, in eager imitation of God's saturating holiness. We mix up remembered prayers and misremembered rituals, calling on ancestors and accidentally encountered strangers whose own conflicted conversations with God leak into us. We kneel, we cover our heads, we cross ourselves, we invent more ways to kiss, kiss, kiss. We shout hosanna, hallelujah; we say sister, brother, mother, father; we sneeze and say God bless you; we curse and speak in tongues. And because voice and gestures are never enough, we pile on things: rosaries, roses, petals, pennies on a dead man's eyes, amulets, icons, books, bread, wine, water, milk, honey, oil, salt, fire, ashes, more. More. Mix it all up. More.[28]

You catch it only a few lines into anything Sara Miles has written: the exuberance, the passion, but also the freedom from clerical-ecclesiastical restraint and decorum. Sara is yet another writer in the Anglican tradition, not a Cambridge product, like Coakley and

Williams, but a former journalist in war-ravaged Central America, a chef-in-training in New York City, a struggling freelance writer. As she documents in her memoir *Take this Bread,* her grandparents were missionaries, extremely devoted to the church, worship, and Christian life, so much so that her parents held onto the spirit but distanced themselves from institutional religion and thus raised Sara and her brother without conventional religious training or experience of church.[29] In this she has much in common with others here like Dorothy Day, Thomas Merton, Maria Skobtsova, and Mary Karr, who came to faith later in life.

Take this Bread is a hard-edged, gritty memoir of a most adventuresome life and early adulthood. We follow Sara through New York City restaurants, into Mexico and Central America in times of social upheaval there in the 1980s. Sara gets pregnant, has a daughter, finds a partner, has to support herself and contend with the one with whom she is living, as all in relationships must. Sara also recounts the dismal San Francisco Sunday morning when, down in most aspects of her

Sara Miles

existence, at the age of forty-six, she wandered into St. Gregory of Nyssa Episcopal Church during the Sunday celebration of the Eucharist. Not at all clear what was being said, sung, or done, she extended her hands for the bread distributed and took the cup offered, and experienced someone she had never encountered in her life up to then—Christ. Sara's Christian formation and catechesis occurred after her initiation, not all that rare a happening in our time, something that the community and clergy of St. Gregory have thought about, discussed, and published on. After receiving communion, Sara grew into membership in that local church fellowship. As she narrates it, she, having really no religious upbringing, was experiencing the faith, scriptures, sacraments, community, and the works of loving-kindness for the first time. Unlike the customary initiation path of learning followed by baptism and communion, she first took the bread and cup, ate and drank, and then grew into what she at times became very disillusioned with, namely, membership in the church.

Given her training and experience both in the food industry and political action and community organizing, she soon became a lay preacher and minister at her parish. One of her realizations was that the community could be doing a great service in helping feed the hungry just as they were fed at the eucharistic table. After some resistance—"Poor people in our new church building, picking up produce, messing up our new hardwood floors, disrupting our schedules . . ."—she took the advice of a former Jesuit in the congregation and got over her disillusionment and established a food pantry that not only feeds hundreds each week but also has set up a network for food distribution elsewhere in the city.

The history of St. Gregory of Nyssa Church is one of giving a central place to liturgy, with everything else radiating from this core. The very design of the building was intentionally focused on the awareness of the communion of saints both heavenly and earthly surrounding the holy table and the lives of all members. Up in the dome are fresco icons of ninety holy women and men, from all historical periods, from different parts of the world and religious backgrounds, professions, and work. Thomas Merton is included, as well as Mother Maria Skobtsova.[30] These saints follow the Risen Christ in the cosmic dance that is the eternal liturgy of the kingdom of heaven. Down below, in the space of the church building, the congregation also wends its way in sacred dance from the place of the liturgy of the words, the readings and homily, to the eucharistic table. While this is a parish of the Episcopal Church in the USA, with *The Book of Common Prayer* as its foundational liturgical tradition, the walls are adorned with icons and the liturgy employs processional crosses, umbrellas, and liturgical dance steps from the Ethiopian church, and the sacred music traditions of the Russian, Greek, and Black churches, among many others. The center of worship is the great thanksgiving, the Eucharist, the sharing of the bread and cup with all. Carved on the altar are words from the Gospel of Luke 15:2, "This man welcomes sinners and eats with them."

Many other groups and activities emanate from this liturgical core, "liturgies after the liturgy." There are a number of learning groups, as well as the food pantry in which all the produce, bread, and other groceries are laid out around the altar for people to take according to their needs. There are classes in music and iconography. And there are groups of parishioners who do outreach into the community during the week.

As a deacon in her parish, Sara Miles has described in another book visiting the elderly, the sick, the imprisoned, and more, which she and others regularly do.[31] More recently, she has recorded in great detail and color the way in which she and other laity and clergy from St. Gregory Episcopal Church take the rite of imposing ashes out of church and into the Mission district. The reminder of mortality, of the body and humanity on Ash Wednesday, rich as it is as Christian symbol, quite literally collides with grandparents out shopping, street musicians performing, sick people coping, parents getting kids to school. Miles's perceptive eye reveals the neighborhood to be the *City of God*, the title of this most recent account of faith in action. So much of everyday life is full of prayer.

Ash Wednesday begins, and coincidentally ends, for Sara at home but also in church. She allows us to start the day at her home. Then there would be three services at St. Gregory, a Eucharist in the morning, another in the evening toward the end of the day, and an afternoon service out in the streets, actually in the square in the midst of the Mission district. Doing anything liturgically—and St. Gregory is a most elaborately, colorful, and ecumenically liturgical church—takes time, preparation, and a lot of things. She describes lighting candles, getting on vestments—she had to change into these on the rector's insistence—putting out appropriate icons of the Mother of God, John the Baptist, and the prophet Amos for the celebration that would begin the season of Lent. There is the flagon of wine and the baked bread for communion. And the incense—they use lots there—and today, most importantly, the ashes. These have to be made by burning the palms from last year's Palm Sunday.

No sooner is the morning service done, with a borrowing of the circle of individuals begging each other's forgiveness from the Eastern Orthodox Forgiveness Vespers that start Lent, then in cruises a well-known local, "Mr. Claws," his nickname due to overgrown fingernails, who is in bad shape physically. So the "liturgy after the liturgy" involved getting him down the hill to the nearest hospital ER. The hospital evokes memories for Sara of her own arrival in town, going to this county/public facility for food stamps. Now it was the first place in which the non-church liturgy of the day would begin, in trying to follow up on Claws, who already had been seen, treated, and discharged by the time Sara got there. At the hospital, a priest who ran the chaplaincy service would later assist in the street celebration of Ash Wednesday. Sara gives a vision of what the whole day is about.

Some people meet God in a hospital bed. Some meet God in the wilderness, in the majesty of mountains, or under night skies; some feel God in the intimacy of trees shading a garden or in old, small villages. . . . But for me, it's cities that make the presence of God most real. In a way St. Gregory's first taught me this. Certainly the rituals, the candles, the incense, the icons, the teaching and preaching, hymns and prayers I found inside that beautiful building opened my eyes. Certainly the torrents of Scripture I heard there—Psalms and parables, prophecies and Gospel stories—opened my ears. But it was the unedited, often uncomfortable experience of being jammed up bodily next to strangers at church, in liturgies and at the food pantry, that cranked my heart open to the Word made flesh. And that Word becomes even more vivid outside. On crowded urban streets, just as in the waiting room of the General [Hospital], it's harder for me to avoid the knocking-together of lives that the Holy Spirit seems to relish so much. In the haphazard sprawl of a city, only the astronomically rich and walled-off can pretend that human ideas of order—like the geometric grid of county roads laid over the Great Plains, or the forced sameness and cleanliness of suburban shopping centers—are stable. The sheer unpredictability of city encounters makes it impossible to presume, as many churches do, that God's grace is sequential—measured out at regular intervals in baptism, confirmation, communion, marriage, burial—and will happen to everyone at the prescribed time, in the same way. In a city, grace falls all over the place. People march around in front of a supermarket carrying pictures of the saints, and I'm invited to kiss them. Strangers build altars in the courtyard of a housing project or denounce the *migra* on the plaza, and I'm invited to hold hands and pray with them. Jesus keeps dredging up odd fish in his net and dumping us all out, wriggling and shining, to reveal his Church.[32]

After loading up all of what a theologian has called the "cultic apparatus" needed for doing a service and giving out ashes down in the Mission district—censers, incense, vestments, banners, prayer books—Sara takes readers on a tour of not just the larger city but especially this area that is called "Mission" because it surrounds the original Spanish mission compound. The mission church Dolores, of Our Lady of Sorrows, continues the tradition of the Franciscan friars who once gathered indigenous natives and colonists for worship, work, learning, and often protection. The string of these mission communities, part friary, part parish church, part settlement and farm and workshops and even military barracks, stretches up and down the California coast.

Today's San Francisco, of course, and the Mission in particular, are a hodge-podge of ethnic groups, rich and poor, techies and day workers, senior citizens and little children. There are quite a few churches in the Mission too, mainline denominations like the Episcopal, Lutheran, and Roman Catholic, and then the Pentecostal, Evangelical, and storefront and traditional naves. But Sara notes, "It's not just inside church buildings that you can find God: in the holy city, God is the temple and dwells among his people. . . . The city might be far less religious than most if measured by the number of people who attend churches, but in its streets it's the city of God."[33] We're reminded of lots of traditional religious activity out in the streets—the holy week processions in Italy and Spain and across Latin America, in Buddhist and Hindu temples, porous to the streets around them, Muslim prayers done in courtyards and shops, processions in small Greek villages, and more.

Just as in her other accounts of her work, Sara goes on for most of the rest of this book with one person, one character after another encountered on this Ash Wednesday, not just at the outdoor "street liturgy" in the afternoon but also before and after. We already met Mr. Claws. We meet the neighbors on the block where Sara lives, have glancing views of her partner as well as of the larger neighborhood, learn how both the recession and gentrification affected it, and discover the permanent needs of undocumented immigrants, kids, and their families who need medical care, food, education. Upscaling was nibbling away at grand buildings from the past that have gotten worn out but which were ripe for restoration. The clash of inequality, so battled about in the media and political circles, clearly exists there in the blocks around the church and her home.

Even before Sara can get to the square, her car temporarily blocked by a double parker, the sight of her in the black cassock triggers a stream of friends and neighbors: "Oh good, hi! Ashes, can we get some?" says her neighbor Linda, and almost immediately there is another, elderly Don Miguel, with his sick wife, Doña Luz, then Rafael, the playground coordinator and truant officer:

> "*Mujer*," said Rafael, his spooky, pale green eyes boring into me. "How are you? Sorry about the car blocking your driveway. Gimme some ashes too?". . ."Remember you're dust," I said, "and to dust you will return." I could hardly breathe. My hand was shaking.[34]

Later, at the gathering place where a short service and distribution of ashes would take place, we meet a real assortment of church folk assembling for the event: a former woman vicar of another Episcopal parish, the seminarian intern from her parish, a choir member, another parishioner who worked in hospice, a neighboring rector, the hospital chaplain mentioned earlier. The history of the outdoor service is told, then some of the fascinating details of beginning with a silent procession, burning the Aztec incense Copal, which many Mexicans would recognize by smell. Bilingual posters are taped up on the plaza fence: "Life is very, very short"; "More forgiveness." A group of Brazilian drummers join the procession and bang wildly away. That was when the service began several years back. The Ash Wednesday Sara describes was a little less from the prayer book and more like the setting, informal, less than orderly.

In describing the growing trend for many churches to have public "ashes to go" on the day, distribution at commuter rail stations, parks, and plazas, Sara reflects on the ever-present tension between the beautiful order of service within a church or even cathedral building, with choir, organ, all the vestments, and historic ritual. It is telling that despite her completely areligious upbringing and absolutely secular, politically engaged adult life as a cook and reporter, Sara herself cherished the beauty of liturgical worship she encountered first at St. Gregory's. She eventually came to realize that there was a wide variety of styles of such worship and that she has come to prefer the rich but colorful, slightly populist and folkloric mix of traditions that St. Gregory's fostered—a little Greek, a little Russian, some Ethiopian, a bit Anglican, and more in the music, the icons, the vestments, the architecture.

Yet for all this, her own activist personality demanded that there be a vibrant, humane "liturgy after the liturgy," outreach visits to home-bound sick people, the enormous project of organizing, financing, and then each week running the food pantry. Her good friend, St. Gregory's rector Paul Fromberg, had told her that there are "priests of the Church, and there are priests of Jesus," sensing that she was less enthusiastic about rubrics and rituals and more committed to outreach and pastoral care and evangelism, especially as one who came later in life to the church.

Indeed, it was tempting to imagine myself, romantically, as a solitary "priest of Jesus," unencumbered by and superior to the Church that baptized me and gave me communion. It was tempting to think I'd figured out how to be a Christian—a better, smarter, less boring kind of Christian—all by myself. But I had to admit this was impossible. Still, my life at St. Gregory's hadn't endeared me to churchgoing so much as it had allowed me to fall precipitously in love with what God was doing in the world. My experiences in that beautiful building opened my eyes to the holy everywhere: strangers offering each other banana bread in line at the food pantry, Martha bringing a bunch of wet, white calla lilies to our next-door neighbors, a woman giving Mr. Claws a cup of water in the pharmacy waiting room. I'd learned, by paying attention in the ordinary streets of this larger, un-housed Church, that things which were cast down—a strange gardener, a weeping teenage mother, a sick old man—were being raised up. I'd glimpsed that things which had grown old—my prejudices and self-righteousness, for example—were being made new, whether I liked it or not.[35]

These words of Sara connect with the others in this chapter— Sarah Coakley, Origen, Rowan Williams, and Heather Havrilesky's calm way of bringing her reader back into connection with the hard but inevitable realities of aging, sickness, and death. The care and attention they all give is not rooted in ordination but in mercy—God's first of all, and then theirs.

Sara Miles also describes a funeral service performed away from church, for a *salsero*, a street musician named Chucho. There was just a bench in a plain multipurpose room off the housing project's courtyard, the prayers right out of *The Book of Common Prayer* for the burial of a Christian, a few simple but dignified words of eulogy from fellow *salseros*. The last word from one of them: "Jesus—in heaven or wherever, may Jesus love him." To this she adds another brief description of a very short interment service, this time at St. Gregory's, of the ashes of a member. They are interred into the columbarium, the interment spaces, which is close to the outdoor baptismal font at the church. In a driving rainstorm, the images of baptism, tears, death and the same Easter refrain is sung by everyone:

Christ is risen from the dead, trampling down death by death and upon those in the tombs bestowing life.

Sara extends this back and forth between liturgy and life, between ritual and existence, in a reflection on the omnipresence of the Virgin Mary in the Mission district. She is known by so many names: Dolores, Mercedes, Soledad, Consuelo, Milagros, Estrella, Luz, that is, Our Lady of sorrows, mercies, solitude, comfort, miracles, stars, light. Above all comes the Virgin of Guadalupe, the Mary who appears as one of the people, dark-skinned, pregnant, looking almost like the Mother of Corn and Bringer of Life, the goddess Tonantzin, whose ancient temple once was there on the hill of Tepeyac. This woman, Mother of God, now one-of-the-people is everywhere, in tattoos, lampshades, vases, sides of buildings. December 12, her feast day, Sara describes, as she and Katie, her daughter, and two other friends, Kevin and Anibal, stand with the rest for *mañanitas*, the service of songs and prayers the morning of the feast. The *mariachi* bands, the smell of the pastries from the bakery, the singing, the way in which the Virgin transcended all ethnic and class differences, swept up in her hands and cloak, churchgoers and doubters, the healthy and sick. It is a gorgeous vision of street liturgy, popular religion, of the back and forth, of prayer and food and music and community all interpenetrating.

And so Sara ends her account with the afternoon procession and distribution of ashes on the plaza. Moving on down the street, they encounter an old lady licking an ice cream cone. She also stops and presents her forehead: *Recuerda que eres polvo, y al polvo volverás.* Then two teenagers, one dubious, recoiling from this weird, adult group, then being pushed by her friend to receive the ashes with a grudging "Amen." Then into shops, a *taqueria*, a Chinese bakery, a hipster bar, the neighborhood cultural center. Along the way Filipinos, Arabs, Latinos, almost everyone, seeing the black cassocks, the thuribles smoking, the baby food jars of ashes call out: "Hey, over here, can I have some too?" The proprietor of a hair salon tells his clients in their chairs, "Look what I brought you, I brought you the cross." Someone sees the poster about forgiveness and tells them, "I saw your sign that said 'Forgive more.' That's what I need in my life right now. I need to forgive more."[36]

On and on the parade of ashes goes, all through the late afternoon. One man coming off the bus falls to his knees and asks one of the priests for confession right there on the sidewalk. One of the last to receive ashes was a virtual newborn, whose mother unwrapped his blanket and said, "He's one and a half weeks old." He too was told he was dust and to dust he would return.

> Church is small. Church is so much more cowardly and less imaginative than it has to be; it's so mindlessly stubborn about its own correctness, proud of its own power, petty, judgmental, and unkind toward those who disagree. But these failures of the institution, as the experiences of Ash Wednesday reveal, are precisely the same as my own. My nostalgia, my desire to stay indoors, to refuse new experiences, to ignore demanding neighbors, to hide from the Spirit in the habitual—these are the sins that call for repentance. Because though incarnation is at the center of Christian faith, it can be scary to experience it as we say in my neighborhood, *en su propia carne*, in your own meat, here and now. It feels too dangerous to mix up the grungy facts of our bodies—blood, sex, breath, illness, dirt, death—with the Spirit, which most of us would prefer to imagine as elevated and immaterial. Bodies aren't stable: they're vulnerable. And when random bodies slam into each other unplanned, the way they do in the streets of a mestizo city, anything can happen. Sometimes it can feel safer to worship indoors, in a temple of stone, where the company is more predictable. Where the fire will seem smaller and the overshadowing cloud less dark and the holy ground more neatly fenced in. But a spiritual life is a physical life, shared with other people. Those who hunger. Who thirst. Who sing. Who are born to teenage girls on the wrong side of town and die as criminals; who eat with their hands and yell at their friends; who spit and kiss and groan in labor; who bleed and stumble and drink cool water; who breathe on one another and create, out of these crudest physical facts, a mystical body. Church is small. But the good news is that any temple made by human hands must always be too small to hold God. And so the rowdy, heterodox Church of God's whole bickering body is set loose in the creation God made to praise him, set loose in the incarnate meat of Jesus, set loose all over the world.[37]

It is impossible to follow up such power in Sara Miles's contrast of how small church can be yet, at the same time, so huge, even cosmic.

Three of the writers in the chapter come from liturgically rich, elaborate traditions, truly "high church" in worship. Only the Eastern Church, standing in the heritage of the "Great Church" of Constantinople, Hagia Sophia, bests the Anglican Communion, though the Roman tradition is close.

So it might seem to some readers odd indeed that for these writers there is a sense or even a warning about the church being or becoming "too small." How could this possibly be, with gorgeous choirs and chant and candles, processions, vestments and icons, even in the tiniest chapel, all sorts of saints surrounding and praying along with you and the rest of the congregation? Some decry the loss of such mysticism and otherworldly transcendence in the use of ordinary, vernacular language rather than Greek, Slavonic, or the sixteenth-century cadence of *The Book of Common Prayer*. How could all of this become too small?

"Small" here has nothing to do with the sweep of a cathedral nave or the expanse of its windows and vaulting, and surely not the soaring sacred music and the sense of a heavenly court in the liturgical ministers vested and performing the actions of the service. It has to do with the constriction of sensibility, the shrinking of vision, a kind of sectarianism that all too often afflicts believers. Mother Maria Skobtsova profiled precisely this in several of her "types" of religious existence.

The liturgy, in principal, may be ecumenical and catholic—terms connoting vast expanse, even cosmic in extension, given that in the psalms everything from mountains to small rock badgers, everything that breathes, praises the Lord. But at the same time, Sara Miles reminds us this same expanse must be there in the heart, a heart open to all as Christ's.

CHAPTER THREE

The Prayer of a Hermit

Thomas Merton

Life consists in learning to live on one's own, spontaneous, free-wheeling: to do this one must recognize what is one's own—be familiar and at home with oneself. This means basically learning who one is, and learning what one has to offer to the contemporary world, and then learning how to make that offer valid.[1]

A Master or One Struggling?

I never cease being amazed at how Thomas Merton could put things so concisely and accurately, as is the case in the quote above from his essay for a collection by alumni of Columbia University. He wrote it in 1967, though it was not published till after his death, so it is one of many stunningly honest things he expressed as he settled into a period of real peace, not knowing it was the end of his life. Toward the end of this essay is an even more provocative summation of where he went in his life after Columbia.

> I always felt at Columbia that people around me, half amused and perhaps at times half incredulous, were happy to let me be myself

(I add that I seldom felt this way at Cambridge). The thing I always liked best about Columbia was the sense that the university was on the whole glad to turn me loose in its library, its classrooms, and among its distinguished faculty, and let me make what I liked out of it all. I did. And I ended up being turned on like a pinball machine by Blake, Thomas Aquinas, Augustine, Eckhart, Coomaraswamy, Traherne, Hopkins, Maritain, and the sacraments of the Catholic Church. After which I came to the monastery in which (this is public knowledge) I have continued to be the same kind of maverick and have, in fact, ended as a hermit who is fully identified with the peace movement, with Zen, with a group of Latin American hippie poets, etc., etc.[2]

Close to fifty years after his death, Thomas Merton remains one of the most influential spiritual writers in America. His hundredth birthday was in 2015, celebrated by numerous conferences and new publications about his legacy. Yet since he died, decades ago, his face in photographs is frozen in his early 50s. I do not think that his age at death keeps him "forever young." Rather, what keeps his books being read, and numerous articles and books and dissertations published each year, is the honesty as well as the humanity of his effort to live the spiritual life and share his struggles, both his accomplishments and failures. Like others in the literature of the spiritual life, from Augustine on down to Teresa of Avila, Pascal, and Merton's contemporary, Dorothy Day, there is an exuberance that makes him—and them—classics. Still very appealing, provocative even, is his determination to continue to seek God, to come to terms with his own gifts and defects, his commitment to continue to find his "true self," the person, the saint he was made to be.

Many of his books remain in print, surely the sign of a powerful and enduring voice. His letters and journals, now published, are remarkable records of his experiments with ideas, his rants, as well as his coming to terms with crises, disappointments, and difficulties, of which there were many. However, in the journals, as well as in several published volumes of letters from an absolutely enormous correspondence Merton maintained, there is a great deal of joy and beauty both observed and expressed. Here and there in his writings, some things sound off, anachronistic, such as his use most often of "man" and

Thomas Merton.
Photograph by John
Lyons. Used with
permission of the
Merton Legacy Trust
and the Thomas Merton
Center at Bellarmine
University.

"men" for all people. His musing on details of everyday life brings us
back to America in the 1960s. In his journals for those years, Merton
has a lot to say about the civil rights movement, about the anti-war
movement, about the place of the church in the turbulence of those
days. His comments halted abruptly with his accidental death by elec-
trocution on a trip to Southeast Asia. When he speaks of the president
he means LBJ. He is torn apart by the assassinations in the last year of
his life, 1968, of RFK and Martin Luther King Jr.

By the time he finally was allowed to live at his hermitage, in the
last few years of his life, Merton had come a long way from the idealistic author of the best-selling memoir, *The Seven Storey Mountain*.
Released a quarter century after his death, his journals and letters
show the extent to which his faith and spiritual practice evolved. Victor Kramer and, especially, Jonathan Montaldo, have both stressed the
journals' power in documenting not just the changes in Merton's

understanding of prayer and the spiritual life but of the struggles, weaknesses, and work in his own life.[3]

> Scholars of repute call Thomas Merton a "spiritual master," and publishers lace the back covers of his books with avowals that he is one of the most important spiritual writers of our century. Merton's own assessment of his achievement was more modest. He even insured a more complex reception of his spiritual legacy by writing journals that scandalize the reader who seeks in them a spiritual success story to emulate. . . . They reveal instead a disconcerting journey of his descent into an ever-deepening spiritual poverty. . . . They disclose . . . Merton's being mastered by the Spirit as his willfulness is purified in the furnace of failure, and his self-absorption is transfigured into compassion for everyone else. Merton's mature journals are a sustained narrative of redemption from his having to wear the self-fabricated public mask of holy monk. In them his readers have a final accounting of the "lucky wind / That blew away his halo with his cares" and of the "lucky sea that drowned his reputation." His journals elaborate his parable of hard-road enlightenment through a loss of status. Readers of his journals witness their "spiritual master's" deepening foolishness and the manner by which his polished ego arrived at tarnishment: an inveterate exhibitionist's happy fall from public grace.[4]

Montaldo speaks most powerfully to Merton's constant struggle to become what he was created by God to be, what the Iranian psychiatrist A. Reza Arasteh, whom Merton admired, called "final integration." Even at his death one could say Merton's pilgrimage was ended, though not his journey toward selfhood. Is this not one of the reasons his writings remain so compelling, drawing us into his own attempts to see clearly, to recognize failings and limits, to appreciate what is good and beautiful? Michael Mott's biography, the one authorized by the Merton Literary Trust, does justice to this soul never content, restless, constantly becoming.[5] I have heard similar things from a few Gethsemani monks who lived with Merton and knew him well.[6]

The Writer-Monk Becomes a Hermit and More

Merton had wanted more solitude for years. Earlier in his monastic career, he believed he had the vocation to live as a hermit or in a much smaller community. His hermitage, about a mile from the main monastery buildings at Gethsemani, was anything but an isolated retreat as it turned out. He complains in his journals of fans as well as stalkers who surprise and occasionally terrify him and who generally became a nuisance. This same hermitage was in part the site for an important gathering of peacemakers. It was November 1964 before he actually started living there, and these few days, now chronicled by Gordon Oyer, included the Berrigan brothers, Jim Forest, John Howard Yoder, A. J. Muste, and W. H. "Ping" Ferry, among others.[7] It was only in August of 1965 that Merton was allowed to actually live at the hermitage. He could sleep and work there as long as he continued to come to the monastery for talks and for some services.

A hermitage, for solitude? Jonathan Montaldo reminded me that the psychiatrist Gregory Zillborg said that Merton wanted a neon sign in Times Square, reading "I, Thomas Merton am a hermit. Keep out!" Later, Merton's old friend and classmate Ed Rice did a photo spread on Merton in the hermitage for *Jubilee* magazine. So much for solitude and isolation! So the hermitage, like much else in Merton's life, was a paradox of paradoxes. The guest list grew over the years, all noted in the journals. Joan Baez would visit, as would Jean Leclerq, Will Campbell, Sister Therese Lentfoehr, Jacques Maritain, John Howard Griffin, Wendell Berry, Denise Levertov, Ralph Eugene Meatyard, Guy Davenport, longtime friends Tommie O'Callaghan and Dan Walsh, and many more. Meatyard captured some of the visits in his photos.[8] In the hermitage and nearby monastery woods, Merton was able to eat and drink—he loved his beer, as much as he could get hold of, he said. The hermit conversed with friends and had a life unlike that of silence at the monastery enclosure.

Merton wondered if his life was sliding into disarray without more scrutiny and structure as at the monastery proper. The facts suggest there was a slide or, if not, at least big changes from the ascetical existence he formerly had. There were numerous rides into

Louisville, visits with his therapist and friends, dinners out, drinks, and then there were stops at taverns on the ride home and the beer and other drinks brought out to the woods for picnics. Some over-indulgence was duly noted in his journals. There was also the intense, impassioned relationship with the nurse, a number of times together, poems written for her as well as phone calls and letters and pages of reflection, almost obsession, in the journals on himself and his love for her.

Out of control? Reversion to the supposedly dissolute life of wine, women, and song he lived before he entered, both at Cambridge and Columbia? A clergy colleague of mine put down Merton's writing in disgust after he read about all of this in the journals. For him, Merton was a failed monk and priest, not a spiritual writer to be trusted any longer. He had desires, strong feelings, got angry, impassioned, broke rules, followed his heart, not always his head. He was beautifully, imperfectly human. Another colleague, one with a truly radical commitment to both Christian faith and religious life, similarly cannot stomach Merton, who for him is more celebrity and slob than anything else. Again, too many faults, flaws, character defects, weaknesses. Neither can he take seriously anything such a spiritual dilettante would offer by way of reflection on faith and the search for God.

But one can take all these inadequacies, weaknesses, and failings along with strengths and gifts as signs of Merton being a "living icon." This is Mother Maria Skobtsova's brilliant way of describing the people of God, assembled for liturgy, struggling in all their radiant and not so admirable humanity, to seek God and resemble God in their lives.[9] To be sure, Merton is no plaster saint to be placed on a pedestal and admired, surely not the sanctity that Dorothy Day feared being registered into and then dismissed as more virtuous than the rest of us. Rather, his life is more a mirror that reflects back to us our own tangled existence, our own struggles to find holiness, and peace, and joy.

Michael Mott takes all this narrative as just a part of an entire life and vision in his Merton biography, and his still strong assessment is one shared by those scholars who spent years with Merton's journals, letters, and other writings—Lawrence Cunningham, Christine

Bochen, Jonathan Montaldo, William Shannon, Victor Kramer, and Brother Patrick Hart, who was Merton's secretary in his last years. Also others who knew him well, fellow monks Matthew Kelty, John Eudes Bamberger, Jean Leclerq, Paul Quenon, James Fox, Flavian Burns, David Steindl-Rast, James Conner, and Basil Pennington, have been honest and admiring in what they have written or said.[10] Restless, gifted, sensitive, and easily hurt, always inquiring, Merton was no perfect monk, no model of guileless action. As Montaldo observed, his journals show him less the "spiritual master" and much more one searching and struggling with his identity, with faith, with his life, with mystery—with God. Merton was most human, in some ways absolutely given to his vocation, in other ways, a complainer, a critic, always capable of strategy to achieve his hoped-for ends, wounded by the realization of what he was not.

How Did the Hermit Pray?

We shall listen carefully to what Merton has to say about life, prayer, God, and his identity as he moved to a new phase of his time as a monk, that of living at the hermitage. There are several things Merton says and does and thus passes on to us about looking for God, living in the spirit in our twenty-first century, one he could not himself enter. I think they can be described as returning to simplicity, mindfulness, attention to the world and oneself, doing away with much dualism, all the while celebrating the ordinary and the everyday, and passing on what one has received, what the Dominicans called *contemplata aliis tradere*. While most of these are to be found all over Merton's writings, they are in a special display in his hermitage years, in the journals, but also in other places, such as retreats he gave to contemplative nuns and talks he gave in Alaska and at various Asian stops at the end.

"Sometime in May, 1965," as Merton's journal entry has it, comes the short, feisty piece, "Day of a Stranger."[11] Having recently moved into the concrete block construction hermitage built for him not far from the main complex of Gethsemani monastery, Merton wrote a description of his daily routine as at least a part-time hermit. He described time and his activities in the hermitage in a piece for *Holiday* magazine entitled "Rain and the Rhinoceros."[12] He was toward the end of his time as novice master and thus he still went down to the monastery for the daily Eucharist, lectures, and supplies. To begin with, he was allowed to spend part of the day at the hermitage, the rest at the monastery. Later on, more improvements would be made to the hermitage including plumbing, electricity, and a small addition for a chapel where eventually he would celebrate his own liturgy. On August 20, 1965, he would be done as novice master, and by vote of the monastery council was allowed to take up full-time residence, working and sleeping at the hermitage.

Merton wrote "Day of a Stranger," one of his most creative, self-critical, but also witty and beautiful essays, in response to a request from the Argentinian poet and editor Miguel Grinberg, Merton's friend, for some journal passages describing a day in the life of a hermit.[13] The first, short version is edgy, confrontational at points.[14] There was to be a second and then later, a third, longer version.[15] The final version retains the edge of the first, a kind of coiled intensity. But Merton adds reflection, even a short question and answer exchange, as well as detailed descriptions of everyday chores, "rituals," he calls them: washing the coffee pot, approaching the outhouse carefully because of the snakes who like to lodge inside, spraying for insects, closing and opening windows for either a cooling breeze or to shut out heat. No great cook, he even described the simple meals he made for himself, as well as the coffee or tea he prepared for rising very early in the morning for prayer and reading.

We ought to be grateful to Montaldo for pointing out Merton's very important letter to Ludovico Silva. In it he previews but also enlarges on what he would say in "Day of a Stranger."

> The religion of our time, to be authentic, needs to be the kind that escapes practically all religious definition. Because there has been endless definition, endless verbalizing, and words have become gods. There are so many words that one cannot get to God. . . . When [God] is placed firmly beyond the other side of words, the words multiply like flies and there is a great buzzing religion, very profitable, very holy, very spurious. One tries to escape by

[words] of truth that fail. One's whole being must be an act for which there is no word. . . . My whole being must be a yes, an Amen and an exclamation that is not heard. Only after that is there any point in exclamations. . . . That is where the silence of the woods comes in. Not that there is something new to be thought or discovered in the woods, but only that the trees are all sufficient exclamations of silence, and one works there, cutting wood, clearing ground, cutting grass, cooking soup, drinking fruit juice, sweating, washing, making fire, smelling smoke, sweeping, etc. This is religion. The further one gets away from this, the more one sinks in the mud of words and gestures. The flies gather.[16]

These lines bring to mind "religionless Christianity," Bonhoeffer's phrase. This is Merton at his most discerning, recognizing the excessive and overly specialized verbiage passing for theological language. Merton is aware of the entrapment of faith in the culture and sentimentality of the past.[17] Most of all, the account in this letter, like that in "Day of a Stranger," is a clear recognition of God alive and present in all things, in every activity, even the most basic and ordinary in the little house there in the woods. In the sweeping and soup making, in the reading and sleeping, writing and reflection—real religion was being experienced. In a defiant turn of phrase, Merton claims that the faith he is experiencing there in the simplicity of the hermitage is that of the New Testament, an almost outrageous claim, but one about which Merton is quite serious. This is no beat sarcasm. As the rule of Benedict said, if one wants to pray, he should go pray. Merton's entire daily life, he came to see, could be, in fact, was . . . prayer.

In all of the versions of "Day of a Stranger," Merton lists writers who speak to him in the solitude, from the ancient Syrian mystic Philoxenus to contemporary poet Nicanor Parra. The list is greatly enhanced in the last, longer version. He adds Asian authors, more contemporaries like Ungaretti and Zukovsky, as well as almost half a dozen women writers, including Julian of Norwich and Flannery O'Connor.

In his introduction to the first American publication of a longer version of the piece, Robert Daggy makes much of the self-characterization by Merton as "stranger."[18] The South American destination of the piece, the journal *Papeles*, would render the word as *extraño,* and there are layers of meaning here in the very title and self-image of one who is an alien.

Merton is "stranger" to his own North American society and culture—this is stressed throughout—even though America would claim him as a citizen, consumer, and supporter of government policy. As in the rest of his journals and other essays in the last decade of his life, Merton was anything but a booster of American values, politics, lifestyle, or anything else. "Wealth is poison," he shouts in the text, also decrying the pollution of water and soil. There is affluence but also hunger and poverty in the United States and the "full bellies" have produced "dementia" rather than peace and satisfaction.[19] In a passage that does not appear either in the first or the third drafts, this is put rather forcefully.

> I do not intend to belong to the world of squares that is constituted by the abdication of choice, or by the fraudulent choice (the mass-roar in the public square, or the assent to the televised grimace).
>
> I do not intend to be citizen number 152037. I do not consent to be poet number 2291. I do not recognize myself as the classified antisocial and subversive element that I probably am in the file of a department in a department. Perhaps I have been ingested by an IBM machine in Washington, but they cannot digest me. I am indigestible: a priest who cannot be swallowed, a monk notoriously discussed as one of the problems of the contemporary Church by earnest seminarists, wearing bright spectacles in Rome.
>
> I have not chosen to be acceptable. I have not chosen to be unacceptable. I have nothing personal to do with the present indigestion of officials, of critics, of clerics, of housewives, of amateur sociologists. It is their indigestion. I offer them no advice.[20]

Yet as we know, Merton, while in important positions such as novice master and teacher of student monks, was also in many and fairly complicated ways a stranger to the Gethsemani monastery and to aspects of monasticism and the church more generally. His years of conflict with his abbot, James Fox, are well known, documented in excruciating detail in the journals.[21] But also there, one can read a great deal of Merton's own transformation, as noted, from the idealistic, romantic monk who wrote *The Seven Storey Mountain* to one who looked at the "cheese empire" at Gethsemani, along with the infantilism/paternalism of the abbot's authority and style. Further, he questioned whether the "business" of food production and marketing was at all constructive for the monks. He was convinced it was not. There were numerous other aspects of monastic life as well as the Catholic Church, not to mention the United States government and its policies, that profoundly troubled him. Merton followed closely the paths of Catholics who spoke out for more freedom both in the church and the country. He sadly recognized the institutional power that saw such protest as great threats and so ostracized and removed such voices of prophetic protest, both from the ranks of the clergy and from civil society.

The journals document a great deal of personal struggle: failure but also growth of the stranger in the years to follow, the hermitage years. I have mentioned all the visitors, celebrities and lesser known, the exchanges with other writers and critics, both in letters and in person, and the falling in love with "M," and so much soul searching and anguish that surrounded it. There was also movement toward integration. Whatever can be said about his relationship with "M," Margie, the student nurse he met in the hospital in Louisville, this was a precious, life-changing encounter. It is true that we only know of it from his point of view. Nevertheless, Merton learned that he could be loved and that he could love. And imperfect as it was—isn't all love imperfect—he did love her.

Out in the Woods Yet Still in the World

Merton refused to be part of the American dream and the crowd that runs to work in the morning, works frantically all day, only to run home to "leisure" time and activities. Merton has already been turned inside out in the epiphany described in a well-known journal entry, "In Louisville, at the corner of Fourth and Walnut. . . ." He is no longer the one who had run away to the paradise of the monastery, to fast and sing psalms, and be ever in love with God. Such was the infatuation of his early monastic years. By May 1965, much had changed, not just in the larger world of which he is part but within Merton himself.

Even out in the woods, with the birds, foxes, and snakes, in silence, the world is with him, in him. And so, he carries the world and the many people with whom he corresponds, whom he knows both at Gethsemani and beyond, with him in the early hours as he chants psalms and reads from the scriptures and other writers. This is a huge realization for him, especially poignant in the start of this new life out in the hermitage. There is no longer separation of either the world or God from this poet-hermit. And this will become a central theme as he talks about prayer in one's life.

As distant as the hermitage is on Mt. Olivet, a good twenty-minute walk from the monastery (he describes his hike to and from it), Merton's "day" is punctuated by the world and in often threatening appearances. He watches the jetliners full of passengers en route from Miami to Chicago. There had been no 9/11, but with the Cold War and Vietnam alive and well, he imagines the atomic weapons in the bomb bays of the military planes flying overhead.

He lists words that penetrate the silence of his rising at 2:15 am for praying the psalms and the rest of the scriptures. *Magna misericordia*—great mercy, also "wash me," "destroy iniquity," "I know my iniquity," "I have sinned." "Concepts," he says cynically, "without interest in the world of business, war, politics, culture, etc. Concepts also often without interest to ecclesiastics."[22] Merton begins to sound as though he is writing in our time, the twenty-first century, not over fifty years ago but now, when we are tired of hate passing for politics, abusive clergy and their ecclesiastical protectors. Onward the chain of vocabulary winds:

> Blood. Guile. Anger. The way that is not good. . . . Out there the hills in the dark lie southward. The way over the hills is blood, guile, dark, anger, death: Selma, Birmingham, Mississippi.[23]

We are back in the civil rights conflicts of the 1960s, and even closer is Fort Knox, with gold reserves and material for nuclear weapons.

Quite a "day," especially for a monk, a hermit, poet, mystic!

Then the short, sharp sentences that are the best known from this narrative, in mock beat style:

> This is not a hermitage—it is a house. ("Who was that hermitage I seen you with last night? . . .") What I wear is pants. What I do is live. How I pray is breathe. Who said Zen? Wash out your mouth if you said Zen. If you see a meditation going by, shoot it. Who said "Love?" Love is in the movies. The spiritual life is something that people worry about when they are so busy with something else they think they ought to be spiritual. Spiritual life is guilt. Up here in the woods is seen the New Testament: that is to say, the wind comes through the trees and you breathe it. Is it supposed to be clear? I am not inviting anybody to try it. Or suggesting that one day the message will come saying NOW. That is none of my business.[24]

Such language, for a monk who says his hermitage is "full of ikons of the Holy Virgin"! This has to be the Merton that Montaldo was talking about, not a "spiritual master" but one very much struggling with himself, with others, with God. He announces that

> In an age where there is much talk about "being yourself" I reserve to myself the right to forget about being myself, since in any case there is very little chance of my being someone else. Rather it seems to me that when one is too intent on "being himself" he runs the risk of impersonating a shadow.[25]

Irreverent. Smugly sarcastic. Playing the proverbial wise guy, as in his letters to his friend, Robert Lax. But also quite serious. One hears in "Day of a Stranger" an account of authentic growth and conversion. Maybe he would soon be in inner disarray, cut loose from the monastery and watchful eyes. Later in the journal, as mentioned, he wondered if he'd returned to the wildness of his youth, drinking too much, talking too much, too many friends visiting. In the next year he would meet the nurse in the Louisville hospital, fall in love, write and write and write to her, about her, about finally having a relationship with a woman. Merton did struggle—with his abbot and the limits imposed on him, with the visitors, his celebrating with them, with his concern about the future of the monastery and monastic life.

Of course, he could not know that in the last three years of his life he would be allowed a hermitage and solitude. He would never have thought he would fall in love. As for the world beyond the monastery and so much going on in it—the Cold War's aggressive nuclear arms race, then the Vietnam war and the civil rights movement, the growing cultural upheaval of the 1960s. Merton had long before returned to the world through reading, through his huge correspondence with writers, activists, and like-minded critics of church and society. A year earlier, almost a dozen peacemakers descended on both the hermitage and monastery for a memorable retreat on peace in troubled times.

In his narrative of his "day" at the hermitage, Merton shows himself to have returned to the world far more deeply and in an extraordinary way as a writer, a monk and priest, as a Christian and as a citizen. Of course he still wears the Trappist habit to the monastery, vestments at the liturgy. But beneath it all, not just literally, what he wears is pants, like everyone else.

What he does is the usual for him—unbelievably large correspondence and a volcano of writing: articles, reviews, essays, books, translations. He reads all the time, even while walking outside. But he also makes coffee in the predawn darkness, does rudimentary cooking to feed himself. Cleans house, does dishes. Cuts brush, stacks wood, and feeds the fireplace. All that anyone living alone in the woods would do. He doesn't just recite prayers as he does all this, he discovers, rather, that all of it is prayer!

Mindful of the Everyday, the Little Things

One of the ways of living Merton shows us, without much commentary, in "Day of a Stranger" is *mindfulness*. One could also call it contemplative attention. But whatever description, it is the product of the kind of living prayer he also describes as his existence. This contemplative way of being includes cleaning away a lot of the baggage of institutionalized, stereotypical religion. Getting back to basics means the psalms, the rest of the scripture—"Up here in the woods is seen the New Testament." We don't need even the kind of elaboration Merton employed in earlier writing, like *Seeds/New Seeds of Contemplation, No Man Is an Island*, and similar books. His South American correspondent, a secular poet, would be able to understand the kind of "slow living" as more humane, basic, attuned to the most important things in one's faith and existence.

This is expressed through what Merton saw and chose to capture with his camera. In the many photographs he takes, as Robert Daggy notes, one does not find any specifically religious images or objects. The monastery published plenty of devotional books with monks out in the woods, their backs to the camera, their hoods up, or shots of the monastery church, stained glass, various pieces of sacred art around the buildings. Merton is not interested in writing about such details of church or monastic life and observance, or in stock photography of monastic piety. He may wear the Trappist habit, attend the services in the monastery church, and lecture, but he is no conventionally pious monk. Rather, it is the simple, worn, everyday things inside the hermitage and around it and in the countryside that Merton most frames in his camera lenses and captures—barns, a woodpile, the chair on the hermitage porch, his desk covered with books, magazines, and manuscripts. All these are the sacramental elements of his life.[26] This I take to be another facet of the living, breathing prayer he engages in and tells us about. His prayer is as ordinary as the stool, the little hermitage kitchen, the water can, typewriter, and other objects that are the markers of his space, the tools of his "day."

What he does is live. How he prays is breathe, and it is the wind, the spirit who blows where she wills, that he breathes, the New Testament that he sees. The spiritual life, Zen, love—all this does not get close to the life he experiences in the cinder block walls and out in the woods. In the quiet, the words of the psalms, especially Psalm 51, are clear. Over against iniquity, sin, blood, anger, guile, and death there is mercy—the mercy of God, mercy for us, mercy that becomes ours to give and be. It is the theme that winds its way through all of Merton's pages and life.

> Have you had sight of me, Jonas my child? Mercy within mercy within mercy. I have forgiven the universe because I have never known sin.[27]

[S]eeing the multitude of stars above the bare branches of the wood, I was suddenly hit, as it were, with the whole package of meaning of everything: that the immense mercy of God was upon me, that the Lord in infinite kindness had looked down on me and given me this vocation out of love, and that he had always intended this, and how foolish and trivial had been all my fears and twistings and desperation.[28]

In these few pages describing a typical course of the day in his hermitage, Merton says more than in many of his more focused pieces, ones on contemplation, what it is and is not. Without even using the language of "final integration," or that of the "true" and the "false" self, Merton enacts both integration and contemplation. In these pithy, extremely perceptive lines of "Day of a Stranger," we find not so much a formula or program, but rather an example of prayer lived out and of the attitude or vision that such an everyday prayer creates.

Simplicity

Another important aspect of life Merton shares with us in "Day of a Stranger" is the return to basics, a radical *simplifying* of everything, from prayer to work, food, and schedule. Entwined with this is a serious awareness of not just one's own thoughts, feelings, and actions but of the immediate surroundings, others, and then, the world beyond.

From the start—"The hills are blue and hot"—there is attention to the world of creation, to the need to protect the environment, where Merton knows all the birds that are his neighbors, the snake in the outhouse as well.[29] "The woods and the foxes," the natural world, make for the "cool" that is his immediate existence, over against the "hot medium," in McLuhan terms, of the monastery. This "hot" world is one of "ought" and "must" and "should," despite St. Benedict, who saw the best thing to do was to "cool it." Merton says his life is one in which he does not have to "bundle up packages and deliver them to myself."[30] Cryptic terms? Not really. The "packages" are the trends, the perspectives, the selves with which we are obsessed and obsess over with others.

The air is clean up on the hermitage hill. The Holy Spirit is the wind that comes through the trees. Merton sensed that it had been blowing through his life for years, clearing away a lot of debris. Before his days' end, three years ahead, even more will be cleaned out, revealed, made simple. But there, in that small hermitage, in the simplicity of keeping a house, everything that is necessary is there.

Throughout his journals and published writings, Merton frequently uses the natural world to express his views on contemplative prayer, that is, the utterly simple silence before and with God. A God "out there," or for that matter "up there" or anywhere else but in and with oneself too, became impossible for him. In *Thoughts in Solitude*, he says, "the sky . . . birds . . . wind in the trees is my prayer."[31] All through *New Seeds of Contemplation*, the original of which came out very early, in 1949, we hear much the same.

> A tree gives glory to God by being a tree. For in being what God means it to be it is obeying Him. It "consents," so to speak, to His creative love. It is expressing an idea which is in God and which is not distinct from the essence of God, and therefore a tree imitates God by being a tree. . . . The forms and individual characters of living and growing things, of inanimate beings, of animals and lowers and all nature, constitute their holiness in the sight of God. Their inscape is their sanctity. It is the imprint of His wisdom and His reality in them. The special clumsy beauty of this particular colt on this April day in this field under these clouds is a holiness consecrated to God by His own creative wisdom and it declares the glory of God. The pale flowers of the dogwood outside this window . . . the little yellow flowers that nobody notices on the edge of the road are saints looking up into the face of God. . . . For me to be a saint means to be myself. Therefore the problem of sanctity and salvation is in fact the problem of finding out who I am and of discovering my true self.[32]

By 1965, in "Day of a Stranger," the more pious and theoretical tone is gone, yet the substance is perhaps even more formidable. Don't waste my time with "spirituality" or "love" or Zen. "I am working on knowing myself, becoming myself, my true self," Merton seems to say, encouraging us to do the same. The "false and private self" that tries to exist outside God, reality, and life is an illusion.[33] It is in the "love and mercy of God" that the secret of identity is hidden and where it is to be found.[34] Even in his early work, Merton already disclosed the real heart of what we are shown in "Day of a Stranger." We have to empty ourselves, radically simplify—our daily existence, activities, possessions, even thoughts and prayer so that we can be in and with God. As Merton would describe his prayer to another correspondent in Pakistan, Abdul Aziz: "Strictly speaking I have a very simple way of prayer. It is centered entirely on attention to the presence of God and to His will and to His love."[35]

I think this simplicity of prayer is one of the most important gifts of Merton to us today. Prayer is never just a formal, obligatory activity. Here he knows from hard experience, for when he entered the monastery, not only did the Trappists sing the canonical office, all the hours in Latin every day, they also performed the office of the Blessed Virgin Mary and, often, the office of the dead. On some days the hours in choir for this formal prayer could have been six or seven if one also included the mass. Merton had the prayer of the church, the hours or the divine office, integrated deeply. Even on his final trip, to Asia, he was praying the psalms and readings from his breviary.

So too did these formal "hours" define his "day" at the hermitage. From the middle of the night—he rises at 2:15 am for night vigils—the day is framed by prayer. He quotes from just one psalm, but there are a hundred and forty-nine others he sings, along with Alleluia in the Gregorian second mode.[36] At the time he writes this account of his daily activities, he is still trudging down to the monastery to finish his teaching of the novices, to take part in the daily community liturgy. This pattern of formal prayer will continue, even when he spends most of his time at the hermitage.

He returns, water bottle filled (this is before his plumbing and power have been hooked up). He notices a bumblebee humming in the eaves, the larks singing as they rise from the tall grass. There will be quiet for reading and reflection in the afternoon. He says he's married "the silence of the forest."

> The sweet dark warmth of the whole world will have to be my wife. Out of the heart of that dark warmth comes the secret that

is heard only in silence, but it is the root of all the secrets that are whispered by all the loves in their beds all over the world. So perhaps I have an obligation to preserve the stillness, the silence, the poverty, the virginal point of pure nothingness which is at the center of all other loves. I attempt to cultivate this plant without comment in the middle of the night and water it with psalms and prophecies in silence.[37]

For all the quiet of the woods, the companionship of the animals, and the release from the demands of monastic community life, Merton was no slacker in his "day." He continues to produce text—reviews, articles, essays, and letters, hundreds of them. He is hard at work, even in the calm of his hermitage.

I won't list them all, but I counted over thirty authors in the various drafts of "Day of a Stranger," a wide variety as mentioned already, from Isaiah and Jeremiah to W. H. Auden, Camus, and Sartre. There are great voices of the sacred tradition as well as doubters and critics of the same, visionaries and hard realists. Good reading, continual nourishment of inner life, and while he does not mention it, he was writing like crazy, Merton was. And he was talking to the novices not just about the desert mothers and fathers but T. S. Elliot's *Little Gidding*. Merton connected first the novices, later the student monks and anyone else who attended his talks, to a really vast array of writers and themes, always retaining scripture, the tradition, and monastic sources but constantly introducing authors and issues that made his listeners part of the larger world. At the Thomas Merton Center at Bellarmine University, in Louisville, Kentucky, the collection of recordings of these talks over many years reveals the sheer breadth of Merton's learning, all of which he carefully shared with his community. There are the classical monastic and spiritual writers like Cassian, Pachomius, Ephrem the Syrian, Philoxenus, Jerome, Anselm, Bernard, and less known Cistercians like Guerric of Igny and Isaac of Stella. Merton led many sessions on monastic history but also the contemporary need for renewal. He also introduced Sufism and Buddhism to his fellow monastics. He spoke on classic literary figures such as Blake, on whom he wrote his master's thesis, John Donne, and Nietzsche, but there are all the modern authors: Beckett, Camus,

Joyce, Rilke, Auden, Kafka, Weil, and Foucault, among others. The
death of JFK is discussed but also contemporary Russian writers like
Pasternak, Bulgakov, Berdyaev, various approaches in Marxism, racism in the South and throughout the country, Dr. King. This is just
the audio portion. Readers know well the enormous correspondence,
all the reviews, essays, and articles and then the many volumes of
notes and comments in his journals. Merton was a walking university.
The hermitage may have been rural peacefulness, solitude, and silence,
but the world of ideas blazed there too.

*"Paradise is all around us and we do not understand . . . the gate of
heaven is everywhere"*[38]

At the First Spiritual Summit Conference in Calcutta, on his Asian
journey, Merton introduced his prayer thus:

> I will ask you to stand and all join hands in a little while. But first,
> we realize that we are going to have to create a new language of
> prayer. And this new language of prayer has to come out of some-
> thing which transcends all our traditions, and comes out of the
> immediacy of love. We have to part now, aware of the love that
> unites us, the love that unites us in spite of real differences, real
> emotional friction. . . . The things that are on the surface are noth-
> ing, what is deep is the Real. We are creatures of love.[39]

The beautiful prayer that immediately follows shows the mindfulness,
the contemplative attention and simplifying, the clarification of vision, and the love for the world and for the other that the hermitage
helped Merton achieve.

> Oh God, we are one with You. You have made us one with You.
> You have taught us that if we are open to one another, You dwell
> in us. Help us to preserve this openness and to fight for it with all
> our hearts. Help us to realize that there can be no understanding
> when there is mutual rejection. Oh God, in accepting one another
> wholeheartedly, fully, completely, we accept You, and we thank
> You, and we adore You, and we love You with our whole being,

because our being is in Your being, our spirit is rooted in Your spirit. Fill us then with love, and let us be bound together with love as we go on our diverse ways, united in one spirit which makes You present in the world, and which makes You witness to the ultimate reality that is love. Love has overcome. Love is victorious. Amen.[40]

Simplicity is a crucial gift Merton has been given and gives, along with mindfulness and then commitment to love and service of others—contemplative attention to the world. In Calcutta we hear the results of the reading and prayer, the conversations and reflection of the "stranger" in the hermitage.

In "Day of a Stranger," there is no valuing of one action over another. All have their place—the psalms, scriptures, liturgy, the reading from all the writers mentioned and many more, the talks for the novices and Gethsemani community, and then the work of writing about trying to find God and God's way, in the civil rights and antiwar movements, in the Vatican II renewal in the church, and much more. Oh yes, and the laundry, making coffee, a supper at day's end, sweeping, stacking wood, cutting grass and weeds and the rest.

If God is everywhere and fills all things, as a prayer of the Eastern Church puts it, then prayer, like God, finds a way into, around, and through concern for ecology and peace, as well as for the constant struggles of one's own person—feelings, disappointments, hope. Merton did not know that he had only three more years, but full, productive, and turbulent years they were. Describing his day as a stranger, one marginal but yet still present in his community and world, he unwittingly echoes an ancient, scriptural perspective, namely, that we are always strangers and pilgrims, that our real home is heaven.

Understanding heaven not to be "up there" or "after" this life, but here and now, Merton's own search for home, orphan that he was as a child, was not just for a street address and a building. Much as he longed for and fought for his hermitage, he makes it clear not long before and even on his last Asian trip that he needed greater solitude at least part of the time. I think that had he lived, he would certainly have remained a monk of Gethsemani and the stranger in the hermitage on Mt. Olivet, though likely there would have to be better security of the location, maybe a more remote one as the present hermitage is easily accessible through the woods, from Monks Road, if you know where it is.

But, "home," for this "stranger," also was his "true self." I believe he prayed his way to his true self. But this was because he prayed, as Paul said, everywhere and all the time. I close this chapter with Jonathan Montaldo's discerning and beautiful words.

> Merton gradually abandoned hope for a suddenly perfect life in some perfect place always elsewhere than where he actually was. He surrendered himself instead to the slow heart-work of seeking God one day and one night at a time in the place where his eyes opened and shut every morning and every evening. He got up and fell down, he got up and fell down, and he got up all over again. Merton's journals are a confession of the necessity for us all to move insistently forward through our daily experiences of both absence and presence to that Voice of Love calling each of us to Love's Self. As he acknowledged his road to Joy was as curved as everyone else's, and that, in the face of his life's contradictions, all he might really have left was prayer and hope in God's mercy. . . . Thomas Merton might have stumbled home, but he has made it home. No longer an orphan or an exile, no longer solitary or a prodigal, Merton now waits in joyful hope for the complete and final epiphany of his Lord. . . . As each of us stumbles falteringly forward toward the one, true Voice of Love, calling us each by our names, may the Holy Spirit who is searching our hearts for us, hurrying like a mother toward the sound of all our cries, find us quickly.[41]

CHAPTER FOUR

The Prayer of Poets

Mary Oliver, Christian Wiman, and Mary Karr

Mary Oliver's Praying in Looking

> My work is loving the world. . . . Loving the world means giving
> it attention, which draws me to devotion, which means one is
> concerned with its condition, how it is being treated.[1]

> I like to think of myself as a praise poet . . . . I acknowledge my
> feeling and gratitude for life by praising the world and whoever
> made all these things.[2]

An Unlikely Poet of Prayer?

I suspect few would think of poets as sources for the experience of
prayer. For giving voice to beauty, to love, yes—but prayer? But then,
there is Gerard Manley Hopkins and, long before him, John Donne.
Actually, the closer one looks, the more one sees poets in pursuit of
the sacred, capable of exquisitely expressing their experience of the life
of the Spirit—from Joseph Brodsky to E. E. Cummings, Wallace Stevens to Emily Dickinson. So it is almost comedic to be surprised by
the spiritual in poets!

That said, perhaps there could be no writer less likely to be connected to prayer than Mary Oliver, at least at first glance. As beloved as she has become to lovers of poetry in our time, most readers do not celebrate her for spiritual vision or for a prayerful attitude toward creation and human existence. She has never really been a part of organized religion or a member of a church body, though after the death of her partner she did connect with the local Episcopal parish. One will look in vain for much explicit religious, let alone theological language in her direct, lovely poems. Yet, this is to miss the point, both of her writing and her person, and that is why she is here in this book, so that we can listen to her.[3]

Poets have a gift for clarity: not just the ability to express themselves with beauty and lucidity but to convey, in their own "purity of heart," their powerful encounter with the world and others around them. Here Mary Oliver, for all the simplicity both of her life and her writing, excels.

Virtually every available biographical account says the same thing. Born in 1935 in Maple Heights, Ohio, she leaves for good upon

Mary Oliver.
Photo ©
Don J. Usner.

high school graduation. Only just recently, in an interview, she admitted to being sexually abused as a child, having a thoroughly dysfunctional family life, and having been deprived of the intimacy and care only parents can give.

As a young woman, still in high school, she visited Steepletop, in upstate Austerlitz, New York, the former home of poet Edna St. Vincent Millay. An admirer of Millay, the first woman to win a Pulitzer Prize for poetry, a feminist way ahead of her time, Mary Oliver was able to find a home and worked there for a number of years, living with the poet's sister Norma and her husband, cataloguing papers and assisting in what became a center for poets. While there, with support from a benefactor, Oliver attended Vassar and Ohio State but never earned a degree.

It was at Steepletop that Mary met photographer Molly Malone Cook, and as she says, "I took one look and fell, hook and tumble." They were partners for over forty years till Cook's death in 2006 from cancer. Oliver cared for her in her illness. Cook ran a gallery and later a bookstore while Oliver walked the woods and shore and wrote and wrote.

Oliver taught at a number of schools, including Bucknell, Sweet Briar, Case Western Reserve, and Bennington. Like Millay, Mary Oliver won the Pulitzer in 1984 for her volume *American Primitive*, and before that a Guggenheim in 1980 and the National Book Award for *New and Selected Poems* in 1992. She is also the recipient of many other awards and honorary doctorates.

While there are critics of her focus on the details of the natural world and of everyday life, not the least of which being the many dogs she has had over the years, and her lack of explicit attention to lesbianism, there are more who laud her awareness of the body and the physical and at the same time her ability to capture what is transcendent, spiritual, and other in the everyday.

A Worldly Spirituality

> I definitely believe that [it's possible to contain the spiritual world and also be of the "real world"]. . . . And I think if you skimp on the one or the other, you're not getting the whole show. You have

to be in the world to understand what the spiritual is about, and you have to be spiritual in order to truly be able to accept what the world is about.[4]

Oliver's unassuming poems are nevertheless very powerful visions of the world around her on sea and shore near Provincetown, Massachusetts, where she lived for almost fifty years till moving to Florida. She looks and then writes of the world, of her relationships with others, including her beloved pets, of the world of her own life and experience. Her poetry, I say, is, among other things, the prayer of awe before beauty in nature. Sometimes her encounter results in the explicit question: is what I am seeing, feeling, thinking prayer? More often than not the depth of the encounter simply gushes forth in a psalm of joy, wonder, and even pain. However, it is not just the prayer of discovery, of presence, that Oliver's poetry expresses. Despite her reticent and very private personality, there is the prayer of connection evident in her work—the connection with a partner and of loss and grief at her death, and with others in the course of her life.

The very spare yet direct language of Oliver's poems is full of spiritual intensity. Only rarely are there explicitly religious symbols or language. Yet there is an abundant and consistent sense for the presence of something transcendent—in a grove of trees, in the face and excitement of her dog, in an unexpected encounter with a deer. Whereas in her early years there seemed to be no other human beings present in the poems and very little of the poet herself, in time this ascetic austerity diminished.

Mary Oliver fans argue and disagree wildly about which are her best poems. Perhaps it is better to leave this in the realm of preference and agree that each will have favorites. I want to look at some of what are for me the ones that best express her vision of things that are ordinary yet extraordinary at the same time, prayers that have no "Amen" or even specifically religious language or tone.

The Summer Day

Who made the world?
Who made the swan, and the black bear?
Who made the grasshopper?

This grasshopper, I mean—
the one who has flung herself out of the grass,
the one who is eating sugar out of my hand,
who is moving her jaws back and forth instead of up and down—
who is gazing around with her enormous and complicated eyes.
Now she lifts her pale forearms and thoroughly washes her face.
Now she snaps her wings open, and floats away.
I don't know exactly what a prayer is.
I do know how to pay attention, how to fall down
into the grass, how to kneel down in the grass,
how to be idle and blessed, how to stroll through the fields,
which is what I have been doing all day.
Tell me, what else should I have done?
Doesn't everything die at last, and too soon?
Tell me, what is it you plan to do
with your one wild and precious life?[5]

Probably the last lines are among those most quoted of Mary
Oliver's poems, the subject of at least one screamingly bright poster.
Yes, the line about not knowing what a prayer is drew me to the poem,
but really, that is hardly the best, most striking line. Even if you do
not enjoy the great outdoors as she does. Even if you find it hard to
allow yourself to just stroll the fields, the woods, the beach, plop
down somewhere, on the grass, in the sand or leaves, even if you haven't the slightest bit of curiosity about the origins of fish or fowl, this
poem comes up and caresses you.

If for Oliver paying attention to the world is crucial to her writing, it is just as crucial to her own existence, to her spiritual life, even
if she rarely uses that description. No matter which period of her
writing one looks at, she consistently lets you in on a discovery she
has made, a connection she sees very gently, subtly. You don't see it
coming: it's as if a bird or a squirrel were over there in the woods,
minding its own business, part of the scene, and only after attending
to the creature you notice something you had not before. Hanging
out, walking around with her pad, looking, and seeing—these are
her work ethics, her habits. And there is always a find, a sight, a
realization.

Wild Geese

You do not have to be good.
You do not have to walk on your knees
for a hundred miles through the desert, repenting.
You only have to let the soft animal of your body
    love what it loves.
Tell me about despair, yours, and I will tell you mine.
Meanwhile the world goes on.
Meanwhile the sun and the clear pebbles of the rain
are moving across the landscapes,
over the prairies and the deep trees,
the mountains and the rivers.
Meanwhile the wild geese, high in the clean blue air,
are heading home again.
Whoever you are, no matter how lonely,
the world offers itself to your imagination,
calls to you like the wild geese, harsh and exciting—
over and over announcing your place
in the family of things.[6]

In "Wild Geese," the title signals us to look for these migratory fowl, but here the deeper thought comes first, at the start. It's not virtue nor is it the asceticism we associate with pilgrims and pilgrimages that makes for an inner life. Rather it is affirming your own self, your body importantly, that is mentioned before mind or soul. You love what you love and your love, I think she is saying, defines you. Relationship to another is so basic, so important.

And for so seemingly solitary an individual and poet, connection with another seems important, necessary. Your despair first, then I'll tell you mine. The sky of the wild geese, the prairies, woods, the world over which they head home—we exist in terms of these, we have a place in relation to them.

I hear voices of what could be called master-teachers of prayer echoing in these and many other Mary Oliver lines. I hear desert monastics with their homespun sayings and little stories, since they were not urban intellectuals but small-town farmers and craftsmen. Also I hear, much closer to our own time, Thomas Merton, almost from the start of his monastic and writing career being taught by trees and by seeds floating from plants in the wind in the Kentucky knobs and woodlands around his monastery and later, just outside his hermitage door.

Loss and Connection

The volume *Thirst*, dedicated to Molly Malone Cook, who had died a year earlier, contains probably the most extensive collection of Oliver's poems that have specifically religious imagery and narrative. Its epigram is the famous passage from *The Sayings of the Desert Fathers*, in which Abba Lot visits Abba Joseph, seeking further counsel on what he can do in his spiritual life, in addition to what he already is doing by way of prayer, fasting, and keeping at peace. The elder, Joseph, does not tell him anything specific but raises his hands to heaven. His fingers become like ten lamps lit, and he tells Lot, "If you will, you can become all flame."[7] You can become your prayer, or, your prayer becomes who you are. Well chosen, Mary Oliver!

After Cook's death, Oliver seems to have been befriended by the local Episcopal parish, St. Mary of the Harbor, in Provincetown. In "After Her Death," Oliver describes trying to find the reading for the day in "the book which the strange, difficult, beautiful church has given me," to be sure, the *Book of Common Prayer*.[8] In the very next poem, "Percy (Four)," Oliver says, matter of factly, that among a lot of other things done, she made her way to church.[9]

It is impossible, even in the terse recital of ordinary activities on a Sunday, not to feel the grief, the emptiness, the effort to find solace in the everyday routines. Bills are paid, the dog walked and played with, the laundry completed, flowers watered, and a name, "her name," spoken "a hundred times." Several poems back-to-back are explicit and reveal Mary Oliver's presence at St. Mary's. "Coming to God: First Days" is a conversation with God, this by a poet who asked what prayer was earlier on.[10] She acknowledges being a beginner of sorts, one just entering upon the language of prayer and transformation, just discovering stillness, and seeing there on the altar the bread and cup of the Eucharist.

She asks when her eyes of rejoicing will turn peaceful, her joyful feet grow still, her heart stop prancing over the summer grass. She'd climb a tree if that would bring her closer. She will learn to kneel down "into the world of the invisible, the inscrutable and the everlasting," and "move no more than the leaves of a tree on a day of no wind, bathed in light," a wanderer "come home at last . . . in peace, done with unnecessary things; every motion; even words."

Really, why would the poet need to calm her rejoicing, slow down her feet or their walking across the beaches and grass and woods? For years she had looked into the world and witnessed to what is invisible, inscrutable, and everlasting! She recognized all this in the dogs who accompanied her, in the ocean, in the partner she loved. In an aside to an interviewer, she said that learning to love and to be loved was one of the greatest things she had done in her life.

Even in the coming to God in church there is that perennial awareness both that prayer is more than words from a book, recited or sung, and that faith is more than doctrine. It is striking that, for a deep soul hardly part of institutional religion and liturgical worship, the simple bread and cup of the Eucharist stands out so powerfully. It does here and in the very next poem. Once again she brings together the Eucharist, the presence of Christ, and Molly.[11]

As poignant as the *Thirst* poems are, a record of grieving time, of connection to a new community within the town, it would be a mistake to settle on just these as indications of her careful attention to the world and the presence within it. In all the volumes published earlier, which constitutes the majority of her work, explicit religious symbols and language are rare and really not necessary.

The trappings or the specific language of religion is not necessary to be experiencing the Spirit, the divine everywhere. This presence despite absence is evident in a poem specifically entitled "Praying":

> It doesn't have to be
> the blue iris, it could be
> weeds in a vacant lot, or a few
> small stones; just
> pay attention, then patch
>
> a few words together and don't try
> to make them elaborate, this isn't
> a contest but a doorway

into thanks, and a silence in which
another voice may speak.[12]

In a longer poem, "More Beautiful than the Honey Locust Tree
Are the Words of the Lord," Oliver alternates between participation
at services inside of church and the familiar world of the outdoors.[13]
She mentions not following along in prayers recited aloud so well, but
also the importance of communion, and suddenly, she is back in a
field, thinking about the deer she's observing and the deer's awareness
of the Creator. And there in nature she remains for several more stanzas, telling us somewhat suddenly how much she wanted to be close
to Christ, even thinking she would like to be a reader or altar server . . .
but "back to the woods" she says she went. There no social distance
is possible, and she, like everything else, rose bushes, trees, birds, is
insignificant and yet loved, a "wild child" like the rest of nature.

Many of the *Thirst* poems contain small bursts of longing, loneliness for the loved one gone.[14] Here and there is the slightest hint that
the divine is everywhere present. God's body, she says, is "everywhere
and everything."[15] But since this must have been a period in which
there was a lot of church going, there are also imaginative reflections—
about the Palm Sunday donkey on which Jesus rode into Jerusalem
and about Jesus and the slumbering disciples.[16]

In Church, Out of Church, Paying Attention Nonetheless

It is all too easy to get excited and enthusiastic about someone previously unchurched getting "churched." If my focus on the *Thirst*
poems makes you think this is my reaction, you could not be more
wrong. For even in these poems, written in a time of loss and sadness,
there are the imagery and vocabulary of sacraments, God/Christ,
formal prayer, and, even though not explicitly named, the *Book of
Common Prayer*. The poet had been looking at the wild world and her
wild life with attention, with love, for decades, as her very first work
beautifully shows.

For most of her life, Mary Oliver belonged to no particular religious tradition and, as far as I know, attended no specific church.
Only rarely, and then obliquely, did she reference religious literature.

And yet, for all this distance and indifference, as I have tried to show here in a small way, her vision is spiritually discerning, so remarkably capable of capturing the reality of the human heart and spirit as well as the reality beyond this that yet dwells in every person. As plain and straightforward as her poems are, they fulfill the theological saying *finitum capax infiniti*: the finite is capable of containing, communicating, the infinite. Emily Dickinson immediately comes to mind, as does, in his own most distinctive way, E. E. Cummings. But as is the aim here, this spiritual sensitivity in the most ordinary of outdoor and everyday contexts is uncommon prayer or prayerfulness at its best.

"My God my bright abyss": Christian Wiman's Prayer of Desperation, Doubt, and Faith

I'm a Christian not because of the resurrection (I wrestle with this) and not because I think Christianity contains more truth than other religions (I think God reveals himself or herself, in many forms, some not religious), and not simply because it was the religion in which I was raised (this has been a high barrier). I am a Christian because of that moment on the cross when Jesus, drinking the very dregs of human bitterness, cries out, *My God, my God, why hast thou forsaken me?* (I know, I know: he was quoting the Psalms and who quotes a poem when being tortured? The words aren't the point. The point is that he felt human destitution to its absolute degree; the point is that God is *with* us, not beyond us, in suffering.) I am a Christian because I understand that moment of Christ's passion to have meaning in my own life, and what it means is that the absolutely solitary and singular nature of extreme human pain is an illusion. I'm not suggesting that ministering angels are going to come down and comfort you as you die. I'm suggesting that Christ's suffering shatters the iron walls around individual human suffering, that Christ's compassion makes extreme human compassion—to the point of death, even—possible. Human love *can* reach right into death, then, but not if it is *merely* human love.[17]

The Making of a Poet

We have looked into a lot of corners in life, to see what prayer looks like there. It surely has not been all light and joy and peace, whether you think of Sara Miles's gritty world in the Mission district of San Francisco or Mary Oliver's serene walks and observation of beaches and woods. Neither Miles nor Oliver were raised with much religious exposure. Hardly millennials, they are particularly articulate voices, forceful examples of what religious "nones" sound like, perhaps, in their particular cases and experiences, with a vengeance! Even a usually acknowledged "spiritual master," Thomas Merton, we found to be quite less than masterful and one struggling like the rest of us. Now we move to a very different poet, Christian Wiman.

In church, especially in the services, in the words of the scriptures, the other liturgical texts of prayers, in the preaching and the hymns—most of the time it is tame, if not rosy. We do not hear readings of violence, fratricide, rape, destruction of everything living, mayhem of all imaginable kinds, from the books of Kings and other literature in

Christian Wiman

the Hebrew Bible. Maybe we actually should hear more of this! Here we shall think about what prayer might mean and look like in the kinds of situations in which we would rather not find ourselves, those of sickness, intense pain, terror, and the facing of death.

Now take a poet, raised in a Baptist church in West Texas. Later in life, he abandons the entire religious project and struggles with the challenges of being a productive writer. The tenacious, intense, almost, as he says, violent nature of the "charismatic evangelical" Christianity of his family just disappeared as he went to Washington and Lee University, hardly a bastion of radical secularism or liberalism! Wiman travels, wins several fellowships, including a Guggenheim. He teaches at Stanford, Northwestern, Lynchburg College, and the Prague School of Economics. Looking back, he considered himself a lousy poet in his first collection.[18] Another volume followed, as well as a collection of essays.[19] An essay on his cancer diagnosis and treatment appeared, attracting a lot of attention.[20] Then came numerous interviews and profiles and appearances—with Bill Moyers and Krista Tippett, in journals from *Bookslut* to the *New Yorker*. *Every Riven Thing* earned the Commonwealth Prize from the English-Speaking Union. It is born of the horrendous experience of his illness and return to faith.[21]

In the first year of marriage, Wiman was diagnosed with a rare, difficult to treat, and almost impossible to survive blood cancer— Waldenström's macroglobulinemia. It is usually terminal, but he received experimental treatment including a bone marrow transplant. In an essay reflecting on both the connections and disconnections of poetry with experience, he included one of the most startling descriptions of his own emotional reaction to the news of the diagnosis, in a voice-mail message, on the morning of his thirty-ninth birthday.[22] Rather than everything being intensified, there was a strange attenuation, a distancing or muffling of the objects, people, and space around him. Two poems—one named "From a Window," the other untitled— are further records.[23] In them he documented extreme bodily degradation and pain. Also, twin daughters have come into their lives. Thus Wiman is plunged into the abyss of despair and death, but also the "bright abyss" in which he confronts both his unbelief and belief.

God's Humanity

> My God my bright abyss
> into which all my longing will not go
> once more I come to the edge of all I know
> and believing nothing believe in this:[24]

That's the first stanza and it opens the essays of *My Bright Abyss*. Wiman says he has been trying to feel his way toward the poem's ending. The collection concludes 178 pages later with this very same stanza, the only change being a period rather than a colon at the end. "To experience grace is one thing; to integrate it into your life is quite another."[25] It is challenging to read him.

What follows this first stanza is not quite a journal with daily entries and certainly not a sustained, focused study. His poems are intense, spare. His essays pop as shorter paragraphs, almost epigrams strung together, firing off. He is well read, and the writers he mentions are quoted, including a collection of spiritual notables: Augustine, Merton, Bonhoeffer, Simone Weil, Meister Eckhart, Marguerite Porete, as well as Seamus Heaney, Philip Larkin, Richard Wilbur, and many other poets. Wiman's essays could well be classroom lectures, powerful, eloquent, always written with the poet's sense for the right word.

At first, the medical situation with its harrowing aspects was just overwhelming—a very rare cancer, limited possibilities of treatment, grim prognosis, a new marriage, new children, unspeakable fear and loss. But Wiman's narrative was not obsessed with his illness, though it is the backdrop. Rather we have here an extended meditation on belief but necessarily unbelief as well.

Wiman started off in a strong, expressive religious culture. And like so many, whatever he experienced in that West Texas church, it eventually left him. Although he returned to some kind of faith, his first experience or naivete was irretrievable. God as a "salve" for psychic wounds, or for that matter for any other wounds, questions, fears—such a God no longer worked for Wiman. He sees in the vanishing of Christ from the disciples at Emmaus something important.

Absence makes the perception of presence possible. All the literature and buildings and prayers could disappear, and Christ could reappear, so relative are the structures, so powerfully real is Christ.

This is reflection on that dusty Baptist childhood now gone forever, but it is more, for in our time, there are reasons galore not to believe, some preposterous yet others very challenging. The quote above, at the beginning of this section, is from "Mortify Our Wolves," Wiman's striking chronicle of faith during the terrible cancer treatments. In it he affirms, paradoxically, that even so central a doctrine as the resurrection must be allowed to be doubted. More Christologically basic is the compelling force of Incarnation. In Christ, God now breathes, eats, defecates, feels, suffers, and dies with us, as one of us.

Only consciousness, he writes, enables an approach to God. But God is no object. So one can only "seem" to see God in so many places. Wiman describes how mourners beside a grave become like a black flower planted there, the "shining hive" of embers in a fireplace, the "bare abundance" of a winter tree whose "every limb is lit and fraught with snow."[26] Inside every one of these instances of "seem," the abyss is bright.

Communion

Since all of life is uncertain, seeing God as contingency, with the lack of the absolute, is no longer heretical or offensive.

> If Christianity is going to mean anything at all for us now, then the humanity of God cannot be a half measure. He can't float over the chaos of pain and particles in which we're mired, and we can't think of him gliding among our ancestors as some shiny, sinless superhero. . . . [W]hat is most moving and durable about Jesus are the moments of pure—at times, even helpless: My God, my God—humanity. No, God is given over to matter, the ultimate Uncertainty Principle. There's no release from reality, no "outside" or "beyond" from which some transforming touch might come. But what a relief it can be to befriend contingency, to meet God right here in the havoc of chance, to feel enduring love like a stroke of pure luck.[27]

These lines come from an essay of Wiman's called "Sorrow's Flower." Joy is sorrow's flower. Loneliness, grief, pain are the taken-for-granted realities of his every day, after diagnosis, when in treatment. But then, the cancer is "dormant," as the specialists say, though they are unable to predict when or if it will return. You live with uncertainty of disease and the certainty of death, but also the certainty of the life you have, the communion you have with others. If the humanity of God, *God's entering and remaining in space and time*, is one essential feature of faith, then *Christ as communion*, God and the love of others, is another.

> I can't speak for other people. I only know that I did not know what love was until I encountered one that kept opening and opening and opening. And until I acknowledged that what that love was opening onto, and into, was God.[28]

Wiman flashes to falling in love with the woman who became his wife, also to an older neighbor from his town who still holds onto the love of the man who once was her husband.[29] Wiman and his wife Danielle spontaneously began to pray again when they found each other, though neither had believed or practiced anything for years. Love does not guarantee there will be no loss. A spouse leaves, dies, as does a parent, friend, or even child. We look to strengthen our weaknesses by connecting with others, and often this is what makes love fail. Yet human weakness can encounter God's weakness. Christ's wounds and human wounds connect, and this makes for healing, strength, love.[30]

Wiman recalls how he would sit and argue through Christian teachings, scripture, and practice with the pastor of a church just around the corner from his home.[31] This was during the course of treatment. His medical condition did not improve, neither did his pain, and there was rarely any closure on the conversations. The pastor became a friend. He was able to truly converse, not just teach or correct. These conversations are remembered as very beautiful and dear by Wiman, a form of communion, another love. Toward the essay's conclusion, in the midst of several other memories of that difficult time of treatment, he recalls the isolation that both the treatment and especially the pain created, but also the constancy and love of his wife. Great sorrow, but a small flower of joy—this was all that he could endure then.

The conversations are paralleled by so many other recognitions scattered in Wiman's essays. Doubt, indifference, and unbelief, at least in his experience, are almost necessary stages or paths to faith. Thinking of the Gospels, he reflects on the enormous doubt people had, especially after the resurrection. Would it be easier to believe if somehow we were back there with the disciples, and the world quaked around us, and we were shown the scars in Christ's hands? I remember Kierkegaard arguing that Jesus's contemporaries did not have an advantage over us, centuries later. As for us, Wiman writes,

> in fact the world is erupting around us, Christ is very often offering us the scars in his side. What we call doubt is often simply dullness of mind and spirit, not the absence of faith at all, but faith latent in the lives we are not quite living, God dormant in the world to which we are not quite giving our best selves.[32]

Death takes on a larger role in Wiman's post-diagnosis life than it ever had. We can imagine, we even experience, the death of others, but not our own. The diagnosis, the rare form of cancer, the tiny chance of halting or removing it, brought not only death into view but "suicide ideation" as well.[33] But having fallen in love, having loved and been loved, at only thirty-seven, changed everything for him. So many times does Wiman juxtapose God with his love for Danielle, then their daughters, and her love for him, that I think the connection is so strong that it escapes neat and precise analysis. This love permeates everything for him. He quotes Elizabeth Bowen's gorgeous line: "To turn from everything to one face is to find oneself face to face with everything."[34]

Communion with Danielle is paramount for Wiman. But he does a good bit of communing with the likes of Dietrich Bonhoeffer, Simone Weil, Gerard Manley Hopkins, and a parade of poets, such as Emily Dickinson, Patrick Kavanagh, and Rainer Maria Rilke.[35] Weil's typically cranky claim that "we must believe in the real God in every way" intrigues but also disturbs him. He has trouble even praying except in the most rudimentary way, a "litany of stations," such as thank you, help me, be with, forgive.[36] Not only are we in a data-saturated, media-packed environment, there is little peace inside, where anxiety reigns.

> How does one remember God, reach for God, realize God in the midst of one's life if one is constantly being overwhelmed by that life? It is one thing to encourage contemplation, prayer, quiet spaces in which God, or at least a galvanizing consciousness of his absence ("Be present with your Want of a Deity, and you shall be present with the Deity," as the seventeenth-century poet Thomas Traherne put it), can enter the mind and heart. But the reality of contemporary American life—which often seems like a kind of collective ADHD—is that this consciousness requires a great deal of resistance, and how does one relax and resist at the same time?[37]

God is not an "answer" to anxiety or "collective ADHD." But the "anxiety of existence," as Wiman puts it, feeling one's ultimate existence within one's daily existence, is to be truly alive and is what so many great teachers in the world religious traditions urge.[38] God is not "beyond," out or up there. And God is not merely other and surely not a list of rules and tasks, rubrics and restrictions. Sarah Coakley describes the power of just being silent, keeping still. Only then can Christ "inbreak," address us, and we realize our poverty, vulnerability, and weakness.

It should not be surprising that Wiman, for years away from the church, from services, hymns, prayers, the scriptures, far from theological discourse and spiritual masters' reflections, should keep coming up with so much of what all these contain and communicate, but in less traditional forms. As you read through *My Bright Abyss* you are continually reminded that the essay writer is really a poet. Wiman keeps plucking out such beautiful stanzas and lines, from Richard Wilbur, Geoffrey Hill, Seamus Heaney, Osip Mandelstam, as well as all those others mentioned earlier (the wealth is just too great to do more than list a few names here). Their lines become his prayers and hymns.

Yet a thread keeps reappearing, one already looked at: the Christological or incarnational one. While doctrines may be doubted, miracles appear unlikely, and parables raise more questions than they answer, there is always the bridge that Christ builds, or better, *is*, between the human and the divine. Wiman seems not to realize that in speaking of "the humanity of God" in Christ, he's using a phrase that, from Soloviev and Bukharev on down to Bulgakov, Skobtsova, and Evdokimov, Russian thinkers contributed to our sense of what Incarnation is—*Bogochelovechestvo*. Often rendered as "Godmanhood," I side with Paul Valliere who insists that in English the better version is "the humanity of God."[39]

> Christ, though, is a shard in your gut. Christ is God crying I am here, and here not only in what exalts and completes and uplifts you, here in what activates and exacerbates all that you would call not-God. To walk through the fog of God toward the clarity of Christ is difficult because of how unlovely, how "ungodly" that clarity often turns out to be.... Christ abhors a vagueness. If God is love, Christ is love for this one person, this one place, this one time-bound and time-ravaged self.[40]

Silence, the Limits of Language

Along with the poet Geoffrey Hill, Wiman acknowledges his own boredom in church, though he does go. But he is anything but "religiously secure," that is, content with the "secondary edifice" of religion, church, all that is there in public and in history, necessarily even, but secondary to encounter of God in "the everyday voices of other people, other sufferings and celebrations, or simply in the cellular soul of what is."[41]

Contemplating Paul Celan's experience of the Holocaust, the loss of family, the indescribable evil and destruction of which human beings showed themselves capable, Wiman, with his own terror and pain in mind, wonders about the need for less God-talk, more silence. He finds support in Meister Eckhart, Marguerite Porete, and George Herbert, as well as in Moltmann's *The Crucified God* and in Sufism's *fanā* or annihilation (as Merton did). His persistent intuition is that God is not above or immune to human suffering, but in the very midst of it, intimately with us in our sorrow, our sense of abandonment, our hellish astonishment at finding ourselves utterly alone, utterly helpless.[42]

As a poet, Wiman admits the limitations of language to capture faith, grace, and mercy except in very basic ways, not connected to the terrors with which we live.[43] Bonaventure, from the thirteenth century, provides, in an account of the various passages or crossings made in the spiritual life, a threesome that connects to Wiman's experience: the "sea of contrition," the "desert of religion," and the "Jordan of death." It is not necessary to rehearse these once more from Wiman's narrative, for we have heard enough of the West Texas rites of initiation, the asceticism of the artist/poet, and the journey with death he experienced.[44]

In the graphic accounts of his hospitalization, the miserable effects of treatment, the pain that separated him from everyone, cutting him off from the land of the living, Wiman uses his passage through sickness and likely death to speak to the deeper anxieties in which people of the twenty-first century exist. It's not a projection of the metaphor of disease to everything and everybody. That would be absurd. Yet, looking back now to what happened a decade ago, he can more objectively notice some important moments.

He observes that conversions seem linked to intense, traumatic experiences, and that these are not to be thought of as just the most momentous ones. The unbelievable pain of bones expanded by cancer in the marrow is on the next page from his vision of the twin daughters and their explosive energy. The memory of seeing the sculptor Lee Bontecou with the woman with whom he was falling in love, who would become his wife—now the sculptor's work makes sense. The spaces, the holes between life and death, reveal themselves, as does the flow between them. Wiman's long dead grandmother, almost as in dreaming, crisscrosses into view, a woman of simplicity and substance he did not appreciate back then. Once more his little girls, their vitality and glee, bounding, are the proof of joy, of hope, of life even as the poet deals with sickness and the death "smoldering" in his body even after remission.

Christ as Focus

Wiman's essays come to an end with reflections on Christ, and they are provocative, intriguing. The resurrection, he realizes, is crucial, central, unavoidable, if one is at all interested in Christ—and he passionately is. But it is all too easily reduced to a concept, a claim or bit of history to which all should give a nod before moving on. This is where religion becomes itself deadly. The poet sees it clearly. "He rose from the dead two thousand years ago because he is alive right now."[45] Not a mere moral exemplar, nor a theological concept either.

After such serious reflection, it was stunning for me to learn that an editor had gotten very nervous about how many times "Christ" appeared in the text of *My Bright Abyss*. I know exactly the tone, I can hear it, including the urban and literary professionalism and anxiety. But, after all, consider the essays Wiman crafted, the death and life struggle from which he wove them, and the subtitle: "Meditation of a Modern Believer"! Seriously, what did the editor sense she or he was editing?

In the end, Wiman offers neither a comprehensive, convincing argument about life as spiritual struggle nor a blueprint for how to get through it. As much of a figure in American poetry as Wiman has become, his work about the sometimes embarrassing realities of faith ring true. I cannot help but think that the strangeness of anything religious or spiritual in the top drawer of writers makes for an angle, an edge. The publications of Barbara Brown Taylor's *Learning to Walk in the Dark* and of Marilynne Robinson's *Lila*, both the completions of trilogies dealing with persons and issues of faith, provoked considerable media coverage like Wiman's—feature articles, author profiles, interviews.

Even in a doubting age, things spiritual still seem to have a niche. While not all the writers we are listening to would be in the guild, it is worth noticing that many stand high up among American writers of profile. Interviewers even beyond Krista Tippett and Bill Moyers take them seriously. And so do I. That's why they are conversation partners, even teachers here.

Christian Wiman forces us to think about prayer outside church, services, scriptures, prayer books, and the like. He accounts for a second experience of faith, a conversion, I think he would not object to calling it that, after one strong exposure in childhood and the now proverbial drift away later in life. It is telling that the intensity of his West Texas upbringing in the church is never a target of scorn or ridicule. He can no longer live in that vision and way, yet neither does he ever reject it. In an aside he cites the theologian George Lindbeck on the force that original spiritual experience has over us. It's our "native tongue," I suppose, the language in which we dream and curse and more.

Both the Christ focus of Wiman's much later, second experience, and, closely connected, his incarnational fix on the "humanity of God," have roots back where he came from. Yet he also allows us to accompany the complicated journey he did not choose, the one his cancer put him through. When at the very end of his reflections, he can say the following, it rings amazingly true.

> *Grace.* It is—not at all coincidentally, I now think—the name of the street where my wife and I first lived together. It is the middle name of our firstborn child, who with her twin sister has taught us so much about how to accept God's immanent presence. And it is, I am absolutely sure, the fearful and hopeful state in which my wife and I lay the first night I was home from the hospital after the transplant, feeling like a holy fever that bright defiance of, not death exactly, and not suffering, but meaningless death and suffering—which surely warrants, if anything does, the name of faith.[46]

"Call it self-hypnosis, prayer, whatever": Mary Karr and Prayer in Difficult Times

A Tough Life

Finally among the poets whose experience of prayer we are listening to is Mary Karr, who teaches at Syracuse University. In addition to her poetry, exquisite and powerful, for which she has won Pushcart Prizes and which has appeared in major venues, Karr has published three extremely well-received memoirs. One dealt with her child-hood, *The Liars' Club*. Another followed her adolescence and young adulthood, *Cherry*. The third, *Lit*, tracked her later adult life.[47] All have been *New York Times* best sellers.

That she survived to adulthood, Karr observes on occasion, is a kind of miracle. She reports readers expressing wonder that she is still alive, this not just due to her childhood but to her own struggles with depression and drinking. Her mother suffered from severe emotional illness and was prone to violent, often life-threatening behavior. Her father, while caring for her and her sister, suffered from alcoholism. The accounts of her family life are beyond dramatic, often very dis-turbing, though told in a droll, very matter-of-fact manner, as if we all grew up this way.

Karr's description of her gifted but tortured mother's numerous marriages, violent outbursts, and unintentionally hilarious perfor-mances stand out. One in particular is her mother's behavior at Mary Karr's wedding to a man from a very upper-crust New England family.

Mary Karr

Karr's narratives of her former in-laws polite but bizarre antics are equally over the top.

Karr has been spectacularly open and extremely honest about her life, especially her drinking and depression. It is not just her parents and friends that she has showcased in her memoirs. There is a whole lot of Mary Karr. She has also been open, probably painfully and problematically for many, about discovering her absolute dependency on and need for God. Her faith, attending Mass, reading the scriptures, praying through struggles—this has all become not just part of but central to her persona, both as a poet and as an individual.

She has written and talked about her relationship to the brilliant and also tortured late David Foster Wallace. He was but one of a number of brilliant, up-and-coming writers with whom she was connected in the early '90s, Jonathan Franzen, Jeffrey Eugenides, and Mark Costello among them.[48] She not only writes but says, in several interviews, how she was drinking daily, with a small child and becoming her mother. The forthright talk about all of this does not sound like her hilarious self-deprecation or her stranger-than-fiction stories of her parents.

Karr was a gifted though not always high-achieving student. She however was fortunate to have a faculty sponsor and almost guardian and was thus able to complete both undergraduate work and a graduate writing degree. Yet both depression and drinking became major issues in her adult life. She was able, after great struggle, to come to grips with both. Her upbringing, despite taking place in the Bible Belt, was completely devoid of any church membership or religious experience. Only at her young son's insistence did she start experimenting with various houses of worship, eventually being baptized and finding a home in the Catholic Church.

Pronouncements on Prayer

Even so, her prayer and religious experience was most uncommon in not being rooted in any specific tradition until she entered the church. And thereafter, her intuition of Christianity as that of an outsider is insightful. Here is an extended excerpt of an interview in which Karr is asked explicitly about prayer. When speaking about matters as serious as faith, prayer, addiction, and depression, she often comes off in a very disarming way, wise-cracking her way through not only the wreckage of life but some most sublime realities as well.

INTERVIEWER: When did you start praying?

KARR: When I got sober, in 1989—twenty years ago now. Only with prayer could I stop drinking for more than a day or two. Once I made three months clean, but it was a white-knuckled horror show. Call it self-hypnosis, prayer, whatever. To skeptics I say, Just try it. Pray every day for thirty days. See if your life gets better. If it doesn't, tell me I'm an asshole. People tend to judge a faith's value based on its dogma, which ignores religion in practice. It's like believing if you watch enough porn or read enough gynecology books, you'll know about pussy. For me, being a Catholic is a set of activities. Certain dogma seems nuts to me too. I'm not the Pope's favorite Catholic.

INTERVIEWER: Do you pray before you write, or during?

KARR: Both. I try to pray formally morning and night starting with breathing exercises or centering prayer. Then the Lord's Prayer or the Prayer of St. Francis: "Lord, make me an instrument of your peace…" Sometimes I listen to the daily liturgy on my iPod from Pray-As-You-Go.com, or I go online at Sacred Space—both Jesuit sites. I say thank you a lot. This morning I walked out saying, Thank you for the wind, thank you for the blue sky. Really dumb, puerile stuff. At night I do what Jesuits call an examen of conscience, plus I keep a list of people to pray for.

In times of pressure or anxiety—like when Mother was dying—I'll do a daily rosary for everybody. Or I'll light candles and climb in the bathtub, try to put my mind where my body is—the best prayers are completely silent. Otherwise, I do a lot of begging. I just beg, beg, beg, beg like a dog, for myself and those I love. And I do the cursory, "If it's your will…" but God knows that I want everything when I want it. He knows I'm selfish and want a zillion bucks and big tits and to be five-ten. So I'm not fooling him with that "If it's your will" shit. The real prayer happens when I'm really desperate, like when I was going through a period of illness last year. Amazing what power there is in surrender to suffering. Most of my life I dodged it, or tried to drink it away—"it" being any reality that discomfited me.

I turned down the earliest offers from publishers for *Lit* years ago because I had a sense that it was what God wanted me to do. In prayer, I felt steered to write a book of poems. There was all this quiet energy around the poetry, though it meant flushing down the drain this big pile of memoir money I needed to pay for my son's private school tuition and college. That was scary, but writing's always scary. The prospect of failure after a big success is scary—the page is very blank, and you feel conspicuous, and plenty of detractors want you to fail from sheer spite. I'm a fearful person by nature.

INTERVIEWER: What are you afraid of?

KARR: Failure. I keep Beckett's motto above my desk: Fail better. A priest once asked me a very smart question, which I've yet to answer, or have only answered in small increments: What would you write if you weren't afraid? Prayer lessens fear. It reduces self-consciousness, so I attend to the work and kind of forget myself. It's strange, though—I know praying a steady hour a day would make me a happier human unit, but I don't do it. Do you know why?

Me neither. It's like, Why not floss every day? I think it's because my big smart mind likes the idea that it's running the show, and any conscious contact with God plugs me into my own radical powerlessness.

INTERVIEWER: What do you feel when you pray?

KARR: When I feel God, it's quiet. I can't hear anything—it's like balancing in air in some vast, windless space. If I'm trying to discern God's will, I'll feel a leaning sensation toward what I'm supposed to do. Like a dowser's wand. It's a solid tug. Even if that direction is scary for me—like refusing the first offers for *Lit*, or like the writing of it was. There'll be quiet around it. This takes days, sometimes weeks. The trick is not to act until you have a solid leaning, and not to obsess until you get that—really give the problem up, in a way. You might say you leave it to your intuition. I say I leave it to the Holy Spirit. The God-centered choices tend to stay solidly quiet. I never regret or recant.

I prayed when I threw out most of the manuscript of *Lit*—both times. The first time, four years ago, I tossed almost five hundred pages, leaving just eighty—the early chapters. Then, in August of 2008, I threw out another five hundred pages, and I was left with only about a hundred and twenty. I was nearing my deadline, and my tit was in a wringer, timewise. A sane person might've bargained with my publisher for more time, but I didn't. It was as if God were saying, You're in this now: do it. Which, by the way, my publisher said too. Yet the book felt impossible. I had to surrender the outcome. But surrender is hard for me. I'm a willful little beast.[49]

Prayer and Surviving

There is a lot of diversity among the writers and others to whom we have listened here, but Mary Karr is an original. There's simply no one like her. Perhaps the streetwise Sara Miles comes closest but she really minds her manners much better. Perhaps it's the addiction and the depression talking in Karr. She is, in just a little of the interview above, uncensored, a mix of truly off-the-wall humor and deep conviction. You could label her smart-mouthed, and potty-mouthed too. The tone is very much like that in the three memoirs, and it is not just the small details of how she prays, but the attitude, the way of being you sense when you hear it all that is most important for us here. The bulk of this interview has a great deal more confessional material as well as some poignant reflections about needing to get over the thick bitterness and anger she had—toward her mother, her ex-husband in particular, and, of course, herself. She notes that it is crucial to get at motives in memoir and autobiographical writing, otherwise the product is, in her words, "crap."

Karr summarizes much of her conversion—it really can be called that—in the essay "Facing Altars: Poetry and Faith," in a poetry collection titled *Sinners Welcome*.[50] The Catholic parish she attended in Syracuse had a banner with this invitation hanging outside. As in *Lit*, she also describes in disturbing detail how she reluctantly but doggedly started praying every day, morning and night, on the insistence of a recovering heroin addict named Janice.[51] "You don't do it for God! You do it for yourself. All this is for you," Janice counsels. "And how does getting on your knees do anything for you," Karr asks. Janice says, "It makes you the right size."

A fellow poet, Thomas Lux, tells Karr that his prayer consisted largely of saying thanks. Along the way toward sobriety, Karr cites gorgeous lines from Hopkins, Knott, Milosz, and others, bits and pieces of prayer. And again in *Lit*, there is the riveting image of her, all glammed up, gorgeous but down on her knees in a bathroom stall at a party with other writers and literary agents, desperately trying not to have a drink.[52] And all of this before hospitalization for severe depression and suicidal ideation.[53]

Later, after stabilizing, taking a teaching position, she goes "God-shopping" with her now-adult son, Dev, who wants to visit churches to "see if God's there."[54] Eventually they find their way, after a parade of visits, to the Catholic parish that university colleague and fellow writer Tobias Wolff attended. The liturgy, the Eucharist, the priest, the prayers soon become a welcome part of existence, and, along with her son, she's baptized.

She remained her inquiring, critical self but has also noted the deep humanity of ritual, as well as her opposition to the past pope Benedict XVI.[55] I imagine she is much more a fan of the "pope of mercy," Francis. While she can make you laugh, as with a friend's near sacrilegious lines about traditional representations of the Sacred Heart of Jesus on Mass and holy cards, she is a discerning observer of the carnality of Christ on the cross and of the broken bread of the Eucharist.

As with the other wonderful writers and poets sampled here, Mary Karr deserves to be read, both in her poems and memoirs. There while sitting in the now empty room of her son, gone off to school, she remembers,

> the sarcophagus
> my drinking boxed me in when he was a baby whose cry
> ripped through the swathe of ether I hid in,
> and the certain, struggling
> substance of him helped to my shoulder
> did birth me to this flesh,
> each luminous dawn
> he grinned up and eventually down

to me from his towering height—each breath
that filled freed me
from my own ribcage.[56]

In *Sinners Welcome* there are also several poems entitled "Descending Theology," with subtitles of the nativity, Christ human, the garden, the crucifixion, the resurrection—Christ poems.[57] And while these are beautiful, the real vision, the lived prayer Karr shares with us comes forward much more powerfully in the gritty details of her Texas childhood, in the desperation of her as a young adult falling through drinking and depression, in the hard-to-believe portraits of her parents, and in some of the literary and academic worlds around her. Largely, though, the Incarnation is most tangible in her own swirling consciousness, freely doled out to us, her readers. I cringe at the scenes of her efforts to deny and hide the drinking and at the rituals of personal degradation and disempowerment that are essential parts of a detox center, a psych ward, a twelve-step group prior to steps toward healing. Karr embodies the shell of denial and delusion that addicts build. Her wise-cracking tone might get abrasive for some, but I take it as her own self-knowledge, really an ascetical tool.

The most luminous visions are subtle. In the lines just above, the nostalgic savoring of her son's absence but also his life on his own, Karr remembers her own death and resurrection, how the drinking did in some ways deaden her and how the child to whom she'd given birth made life come back to her. Compare with the last lines of "Descending Theology: The Resurrection."

In the corpse's core, the stone fist of his heart
Began to bang on the stiff chest's door,
And breath spilled back into that battered shape. Now
It's your limbs he longs to flow into—
From the sunflower center in your chest
Outward—as warm water
Shatters at birth, rivering every way.[58]

The Incarnation and Resurrection are close to the bone, there where skin meets skin. It has been important for us to hear this, in Mary Karr, but also in Merton, Wiman, and Mary Oliver, as we will from others.

CHAPTER FIVE

The Prayer of Forgetting and Remembering

A List and a Map

Do you pray on any sort of regular basis? How many of us do, other than in church on Sunday? Does a pastor pray? One would think so. Hope so. Yet every day as I read the names on a tattered card in my prayer book, I am reminded of how the card came to be. It was the result of my being asked to pray for a family member by a parishioner many years ago. It was a sincere request, an affectionate one too, as the parishioner said she was sure my prayers would help. The next Sunday in church, she came up and, beaming, said the prayers had been successful. Her mother was greatly improved. The reality, however, was that I had forgotten. I had not remembered to pray for her. And I realized that I had lost the practice and discipline of daily prayer. This is the origin of my prayer list.

The list has become for me a kind of journal as well as a map of the last several decades of my life. But it is not just about me. It is very much about those with whom I have been connected—teachers, friends, family, a few enemies, parishioners, students, and colleagues. Because the list is about the web of persons in my life, because it is about what I have done and where, because it is about what I was once and have turned into, it is very much about prayer. Prayer is listening as well as talking to God. Prayer is also about everything that happens in every day of my life—another way of fulfilling the mandate to "pray always." We forget those who have asked us to pray, but in prayer we also remember.

I look at the prayer list most every day, run down through the names, often with my finger, to remember them, thereby to pray for them. However, as time has gone on, I find I cannot always recall much about some of the people now. Too much time has passed. It is only first names on this list. Sometimes I look back over old parish pictorial directories. This helped a great deal to add a last name and some memories of a person I'd forgotten about. Even with this kind of digging, in some cases the details are sparse. In other instances, though, the memories are intense, vivid. I remember a particular visit, a specific interaction, the accent and tone of a voice.

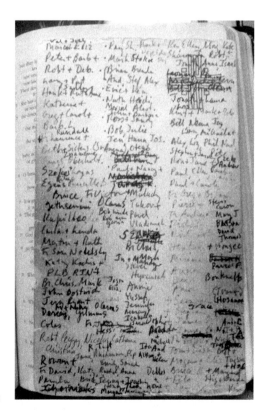

Author's prayer list

Trying to recall and narrate the past also triggers memory retrieval, at least to some extent. I know that in writing a chapter in an earlier book about my time in the Carmelite order, I ended up dreaming in startling detail about the interior of the minor seminary high school buildings in Middletown, New York, where I was a student from fall of 1961 till spring of 1965. The same held true for the novitiate in Williamstown, Massachusetts, and the houses of study in Niagara Falls, Ontario, and Washington, DC, and the priory in Pottsville, Pennsylvania, where I was a student friar and teacher.

That prayer list has become a map of the last thirty years of my life. The list covers a lot of territory and a great deal of living and all that comes with it. There are four different parish communities, and that requires remembering what came before, how I got to be a pastor in those parishes. The list also connects to my teaching all that time and longer at the City University of New York. Mapping that many years, the prayer list names many who have died, some with whom I have lost contact, others who remain part of my everyday life. The list and the life it charts affirm that remembering is prayer. Networks of parish members, neighbors, colleagues, relatives, friends, and even those with whom we don't get along, enemies — these are connections for prayer, not just people for whom to recite prayers from books or even send off a "Lord have mercy." Like a vine, prayer twists, wraps around, insinuates itself into our experiences, until it is completely tied up with what we do, those with whom we live and work, and, in the end, who we really are or, better, who we have become. In some cases, only much later on, do we remember what actually happened, how we were, how we changed. In sharing those memories below, I hope to show the manner in which prayer in everyday experience is like a rich tapestry or mosaic. All the small details of failure and satisfaction, joy and sadness, work together, eventually come to be remembered, to be seen as forming the whole of one's life with God and others, all the turns and twists life brings.

Moving, Settling

We moved to Holmes in Dutchess County, New York, in spring of 1981, Jeanne and I. This was after a National Endowment for the

Humanities Fellowship and other grants had enabled us to study in Copenhagen for almost two years. After apartment living on the upper Westside of Manhattan, a fixer-upper Cape Cod was our very first house. Pawling was a small Hudson valley township with decent schools and, very fortunately, with the Harlem line of the Metro-North commuter railroad close by. I would start what is now almost forty years of commuting to my work as a professor at the City University of New York's Baruch College, and Jeanne would commute by car to *Reader's Digest*'s now-former expansive campus in Pleasantville, in northern Westchester County.

Relocating to the Hudson valley meant great change for us—the end of graduate student days, a house of our own, and our having children. But it also lacked something important to us. Where we had lived previously, we hopped around to various churches in New York City and Copenhagen. Those we attended most were Riverside Church and the Cathedral of St. John the Divine, and a number of Copenhagen parishes of the Church of Denmark. My connections with the Lutheran Campus Ministry grew out of worshipping with the Lutheran student community at St. Paul's Chapel at Columbia University with Pastor Albert Ahlstrom. Not far from our Holmes house we found Trinity, a parish of the Lutheran Church in America (LCA), and H. Henry Maertens, its pastor. We were welcomed and joined and were there most Sundays.

Toward a New Path: Pastoral Ministry

During my alternative service as a conscientious objector, I was the head teacher and administrator of a Headstart Center in the Lutheran Church of the Good Shepherd in Old Bridge, New Jersey, not far from the Rutgers campuses in New Brunswick. Pastor William Mitschke of that parish befriended me, welcomed me into the community, and, on learning of my previous training, invited me to be a reader, lay communion assistant, and occasional preacher. And he began encouraging me to approach the bishop about ordination. He was convinced I should serve in the ministry alongside my academic profession. When Jeanne and I moved to New York after our wedding, there was simply too much dissertation writing, course work, and papers and then what appeared to be a very discouraging job search for me. Church vocation was put on the backburner, though we still continued to be regulars at local churches.

After our son Paul was born in 1982, I began the process with the Metropolitan New York Synod of the LCA, with endorsement from Pastor Maertens and Trinity parish, to seek ordination. The candidacy committee assigned me several members as contacts. In turn I was sent for colloquies, that is, interviews and oral examinations with several faculty members at the Lutheran Theological Seminary in Philadelphia. They found me more than adequately theologically trained, as a Ph.D. in religion and sociology with specialization in Kierkegaard and modern theology. What remained was an internship under Maertens's supervision, with regular opportunities to preach, assist in liturgy, do pastoral work, and teach.

I was one of three ordained by Bishop James Graefe at Fordham University Church in the Bronx at the annual assembly of the Metro New York Synod. Ecumenical history was made as we were the first non–Roman Catholics to be ordained in the chapel's more than a century of service. It was also June 3, the commemoration of John XXIII, the pope and bishop of Rome, in the Lutheran calendar, who had opened the doors and windows of the church to the world in convening the Second Vatican Council in 1961 and has since been canonized.

After ordination I began at Trinity Church. I also served at parishes in Red Hook and New Paltz for another fourteen years—all this alongside my full-time work as a professor at CUNY—and later moved to St. Gregory, where I have been for more than twenty years.

Jeanne and I were part of the building of a new church in Brewster, consecrated in 1988. Trinity was then a sizeable community, approaching five hundred members when I was there. As an associate pastor I shared the ministry. We alternated preaching and presiding. When needed, I did other pastoral acts such as baptisms, weddings, and funerals. Pastoral visiting, as will become clear, was a major activity for me. I participated in church council meetings, taught Sunday school, helped with youth retreats, and participated in deanery and synod gatherings. My principal pastoral assignment was visiting inactive members and the elderly home-bound for communion, anointing, prayer, and conversation. Pastor Maertens was glad to have help considering the size of the congregation and the demands on him. He completed a D.Min. thesis on team ministry at Drew University and now was seeing it take shape in our cooperative pastoral work. These were years of intense learning for me.

Rediscovering, Recovering Prayer in Life

What does this personal journey have to do with prayer? It might seem obvious that one who had been through a high school minor seminary, a Carmelite novitiate and house of studies, and who had been a regular Sunday worshipper and then a pastor would be no stranger to prayer. So it would seem. I am sure that by the time I was ordained at thirty-five I must have spent hundreds of hours in liturgical services and in a truly ecumenically diverse collection of churches. For years I had prayed the daily office as a friar, sat or walked through hours of meditation, quiet prayer, and *lectio divina*— prayerful reflective scripture reading. I presided at all kinds of services from ordinary Sundays to the great feasts and rites of passage: outdoor services at church camps, retreat worship with other clergy, attendance at monastery services when visiting, and communion in hospitals, nursing facilities, and private homes. Pastoral ministry in a parish soaks up enormous amounts of time and energy.

Did I experience something in all these liturgical moments, solemn and small? Yes. I remember many powerful moments—during the chanting of the great Easter canticle during the Easter Vigil in a church lit only by candles, or the mesmerizing drama of the holy week services from the foot washing and mass of the Last Supper on Holy Thursday through the singing of the Passion of St. John and the Reproaches and veneration of the cross on Good Friday to the passage/Passover from dark to light of the Easter Vigil. I remember the crush of dozens of presbyters joining the bishop in the laying on of hands at ordinations. I was at the first ever joint Episcopal-Lutheran service in the great cathedral of St. John the Divine. I watched our firstborn baptized, and then baptized our daughter myself. Many years later, I preached at my own mother's funeral and then led the interment at the cemetery. I will never forget lying prostrate alongside my friar-classmates with the hood of the white Carmelite mantle over my head when I completed novitiate and made first vows. Nor will I forget raising the bread and the cup after saying the Lord's words over them for the first time: "Take and eat, this is my body broken for you. . . . Take and drink, this is the cup of the New Covenant poured out for the forgiveness of sins." Or the baptism and anointing of a very vocal infant for the first time, or watching a coffin lowered into the grave in sub-zero temperatures in a driving snow storm in a tiny rural cemetery. I also was launched into a laughing fit when Bishop Seraphim Sigrist, before re-ordaining me, bent over and reassured me: "Father Michael, ah, now your holy orders have been rebooted."

I would be dishonest if I said, after all these moments just noted, and numerous others, that I never experienced prayer. I could have been granted an advanced degree in it by the time I was thirty. Yet the now-tattered card with many names scrawled on it, some crossed out, a few rewritten because the ink faded—this prayer list, which probably would make sense to few others, was a great lesson in prayer for me and remains, inside the small bible I use for daily prayers, an enduring map of prayer for me.

I do not remember the name or even the face of the parishioner who came up to me after the Sunday service many years ago at Trinity. She was upset and told me of the urgent need for my prayers for her elderly mother who was seriously ill. I assured her I would remember her, this without writing down the name. So the week passed.

Those were hectic days. During Lent there were evening services and classes. There were also regular monthly evening meetings of the parish council and other committees. When we look back on those days, when we were younger, but with so much to do—little kids in constant need of supervision, a change of diapers, feeding, bathing, chasing—we do not know how we carried it off. It seems impossible now, the tasks that would line up in the course of virtually every day, even with the help of wonderful child-care providers, who took care of the kids at their homes when we were both at work. I started leaving for the city around 5:30 am in order to start teaching before 8:00 am and then be done with classes, office hours, and meetings by early afternoon, to commute back home, about an hour and a half, to pick the kids up in the early evening so they could have dinner at home. On the days I did not teach, the children would go to the sitter a little later, and then I would get to church after 9:00 am to then go out visiting till around 3:00 pm, then to the child-care givers for pickup and home.

When the rector of the parish asked me about his plan to organize a weekday evening special class plus social get-together for younger parents in our parish, I burst out laughing. What an absurd thing, asking already stressed younger parents to fit yet one more church event into their lives. The evening for young parents never happened!

With every week so harried and with my own immaturity, it was no surprise that I simply forgot to pray for this much loved and suffering family member. But I do not put forward the pace of our lives as an excuse. The next Sunday, as reported, the same parish member who had so wholeheartedly asked my prayers for her mother returned, sought me out, and hugged me hard as she shared the great good news that my prayers had worked. Her mother was much better and out of the hospital. She insisted that God had specially listened to *my* prayers—those of a pastor, and answered them rapidly and effectively.

I was mortified. I felt like a fool—worse, like some kind of liar or cheat, for I had never uttered one syllable of prayer, not even a wordless sigh or glance to heaven for this sick person unless you count the moment I was asked for prayers. And there I was being profusely thanked, almost congratulated for accomplishing a healing through my fervent prayer for a sick parent.

Learning to Pray, Again

But through this humiliating experience I came to realize that prayer was something I did only at certain times. Prayer was not integrated into my daily life. It was crowded out by teaching, research, writing, child care, home chores, commuting, and pastoral work. As I look back on this, I recognize I was no different than most everyone else in my parish then and now.

If you are expecting some moment of conversion as a result of this parishioner's return the next Sunday with the good news of answered prayers, I am sad to say I cannot report this. I simply felt terrible.

However, that's when I did a few things. I returned to the daily office, the prayer of the hours that I had known as a friar. So many of our best spiritual writers these days, like Esther de Waal and Kathleen Norris, recognize the importance of the monastic life's patterns for ordering one's own spiritual existence.[1] The commitment to the daily office or prayer of the hours is a particularly significant instance. It is a commitment to make prayer a consistent element of one's daily living. It leads to a certain persistence at and in prayer.

There are numerous versions. *The Lutheran Book of Worship* had one model shared by the Episcopal *Book of Common Prayer* and many other Catholic and Protestant worship books. It was a greatly simplified but essential version of the order of daily prayer, morning and evening, from the Western church tradition. The Eastern church prayer of the hours, as all its other liturgies, was more monastically shaped, was longer, more complicated in the number and kinds of texts used, but there are now more accessible, simplified versions. In most versions there is no attempt, as for the ancient monastics, evidenced in Benedict's Rule, to recite all 150 psalms in a week, every week. There are lectionaries, year-long daily selections of readings from the Hebrew Bible, the New Testament epistles, and the gospels for each day. There is also usually some hymnody, often scriptural canticles, most especially the songs of Mary, Zechariah, and Simeon from the Gospel of Luke. The hymns are from the ancient church and down the centuries. Lastly there is some form of litany or prayer of intercession. I chose the more portable, accessible *Book of Common Prayer* for my daily prayer, following the readings and the placement of psalms that covered several weeks for all of them. I still have that book with lots of finger stains on the most used pages.

I also found a large index card and started a list of people to remember every day. Up in the left corner I started a column of those whom I visited in that parish. These were elderly people, in some cases physically badly off but some more emotionally handicapped. In not too much time this column became a communion of saints both living and departed into the heavenly kingdom. Given the years since I started writing out the list, all now are in the latter category.

Next to those I visited I placed the names of family: Jeanne, our grandparents, all deceased, and then our parents, siblings, and eventually the names of our children, and in time their partners. I listed my tutor at the University of Copenhagen, a priest of the Danish Church who died very young, as well as academic colleagues close to me—the anthropologist hired along with me whose wedding was the first at which I officiated when ordained. Also there is the name of my tutor and friend from the Kierkegaard Institute in Copenhagen, who died young. And I listed my rector and colleague at that first parish, along with some council members with whom I worked closely. There were names of simply tragic deaths—one an undergraduate from the first parish, murdered for no apparent reason, sitting in his car, parked in front of his home. Another was a seminarian intern at my later and present parish who, suffering from profound and seemingly untreatable depression, ended his own life. Even with the deaths of some on the list, the list has always been growing. Prayer is not only remembering but the linking of many faces and lives with my own, a continuing circle of friendship.

Remembering to Pray Leads to Prayer as Remembering

I remember that, at first, the list was still short, covering only part of the front of the card. Time has added so many names that there is little space left now. As I scan the list every day, the last almost forty years of my life opens up in front me.

On the list I eventually placed the names of many friends who were clergy colleagues. The list thus is not only a chart on the state of parishes and the churches more generally but also a map of where life and work have taken people I love. Sadly, many, actually most, of my clergy colleagues and friends' names remind me of a great deal of suffering—harassment by parishioners, by deans, even by fellow clergy. One was criticized for not wearing enough clerical attire to lunch at a restaurant. The clergy shirt and collar were insufficient. Cassocks were the new traditional garb even for lunch out at Denny's! The name of another pastor friend reminds me of how many marriages are battered, in this case, ended, by the uncertainties and the demands of church life. One name, a colleague of thirty years, is a painful reminder of parish members using their pastor for target practice.

There are so many names on this list, faded as some are. Some of them still bring up a face, a last name—most are first names only. Here and there a whole story, the troubles, bits of happiness. I can hear Willy's North German accent as he pronounced the city of his birth, so soft the final "g" of Leipzig disappeared. There is Jan. I can think back from the interment of her ashes all the way through many visits as she struggled with cancer. Somewhere in the middle of these, to our mutual astonishment, we found that we grew up within blocks of each other, a close relative's home almost within view of my childhood house. She had been a cancer survivor, even passing the five-year point in remission, only to experience it return, and with a vengeance. She was so strong. She fought it, grimaced through chemotherapy and radiation, with all the side effects. But eventually she came to terms with dying. When she died I was away and could not be at her funeral. Yet months later, her husband asked me to lead a service for family and friends. Her ashes were to be interred in the middle of her beloved backyard garden. It was still fairly early in the spring and Al had opened a spot where the daffodils would soon emerge. We prayed inside the house, with signs of Jan and memories everywhere—so much so Al said he had to move, he could not stay there with so many memories and now her departure. When we went out to the garden, the hole had filled up with water from the thawing earth surrounding it. After several unsuccessful efforts to drain it, Al placed a large stone on the top of the box to secure it, telling Jan, "It's just like you, Jan, you'd never listen or stop moving!" At this service there was more laughter than tears, for one whose faith was truly resurrectional.

My own faith was strengthened and deepened by the people I cared for as a pastor. When I remember Jan and our seminarian interns, when I recall how the people I encountered lived the cross and resurrection, I have to acknowledge that they increased my faith, renewed my hope. And this is still the case: that the reality of the prayer and lives of ordinary people in the "local church" of the parish is where I go for encouragement. As for being able to actually see Christ incarnate, it is among those with whom I share coffee every Sunday after the liturgy, with whom I make pirogi and then work at the Christmas food fair, with whom I share the meals after weddings and funerals. Here the New Testament comes alive again for me.

The Church—A Mixed Bag

"It's not all peace and love, the church." I heard those words long ago, as a very young seminarian, from a worldly wise priest. Surely, it would be wrong to suggest that the names on my list conjure up only pleasant memories. Some bring up real difficulties and struggle. One name is a kind of witness of resurrection—and in several ways. It is of a pastor who survived a "clergy-killer" parishioner, survived a kind of spiritual and emotional crisis and the death of a parent, all the while continuing to help raise his children, teach, and write alongside pastoral work. As if these "ordinary resurrections" were not enough, he saw his congregation decline, due to the 2007 recession and the generous gift of a number of families to a new mission. Rather than support and encourage him, church officials actually threatened to remove and replace him, particularly if the parish did not make good on its regular assessment obligations to the diocese and national church. This pastor faced his descent, struggled with all his shadows and demons, and experienced a real resurrection. Eventually, his parish also experienced a remarkable revival. I find myself using the Easter greeting of the Eastern Church when I come to his name: "Christ is risen! Indeed, he is risen!"

Add to this the normal pattern of those passing along, finishing up studies, starting professions. One name evokes enormous pride and, frankly, amazement on my part—a former student and intern recently tenured and promoted at a major university. His gifts in administering an important institute based at his school were not the first indication of his capabilities. Before that, there was his persistence in a horrible employment market, then a first rate tenure-track appointment, then tenure and promotion. This scholar and teacher does not cease to amaze. Along with all this is a most impressive publication record—dozens of articles in refereed journals, papers at conferences, books and contracts for more books, all within just a few years. There were also clouds and storms in his sky, not just the frustrations that are part of the academic profession—incessant demands from administrators and collegial conflicts. There were numerous collisions with the toxicity of the institutional church in which he served as a member of the clergy.

It is not all sweetness and light, not in life generally, not in the church specifically. Despite the emergence of the darker side of ecclesiastical professionals and life in recent years, there is still a dogged resistance in the minds of many to the toxic, destructive possibilities of religion. One reviewer of an earlier book of mine objected to the focus on this. And I know firsthand that many people of immense goodwill want to think and act as if the nastiness never happened or did not exist. But it is as much a part of the ecology and the economy of the people of God as heroic sacrifice or compassion for those suffering. This, I think, is one of the great gifts of prayer in everyday experience. When we become mindful that everything is God's, that all our actions and thoughts are part of life with God, then even the ugly, painful, and destructive things appear in their place. These difficult experiences, just as the beautiful ones, are moments of encounter with God.

The List Grows and Keeps Growing

My prayer list does not make me think only of our early years of marriage, in our first and only house, or of the birth of our children and our parish and my pastoral ministry there. While a good deal of the front side of the prayer list is taken up with names of both deceased and living members of that first parish of Trinity Church, Brewster, there are many other names there and on the other side that follow where the last twenty or more years have taken me.

A number of other characteristics of the parish were attractive. It welcomed interns and their families. There was a modest but decent monthly stipend, many invitations to brunch and dinner. One year, we had three student priests and their spouses and children, adding almost a dozen new members to the parish. That year we raised over thirty thousand dollars, completely off the parish budget, to help support these families. Looking back, working with the interns was one of the happiest of all activities I ever had. Preaching was an important part of the training, even before ordination. When they were ordained priests, our interns took their places on a regular rotation for presiding at the Sunday liturgy. While very difficult to extract from seminary weekdays full of classes, daily services, and parenting responsibilities, especially when spouses worked, we were occasionally able to have ordained interns come to assist at funerals, weddings, and memorial services. Our sense was that because there were only rare opportunities to actually preside at seminary services, the internship would give at least several months of hands-on experience for this important component of ministry. Most of the interns were the age of graduate students, in their mid to late twenties, although occasionally we did have older interns, one a former Protestant pastor. Some of the interns stayed a second year, either as an intern or attached as a priest to the parish. Thus, a few of them were able to engage in pastoral work more intensively and in turn became greatly beloved by the parish community.

On the list, in the interns' names, are now almost twenty years of hopes, disappointments, dramatic changes in life, and one death. Once fresh, hopeful, youthful faces, these pastors and their spouses are now in their forties. Each family now has a trail of stories. Some are of bitter discouragement in failing parishes that even their idealism and youth could not resurrect. One, a professional in nonprofit work, learned how fragile pastoral life can be, being asked to step down from a mission-planning project after his family had relocated and purchased a home. Then, after several successful years in a church-related but independent coalition of non-profit organizations, he found himself passed over for a younger director with deeper ties to benefactors. And throughout he collided with ordained leaders and their all-too-human prejudices and aggressions.

Still others had equally difficult experiences after leaving our parish. One headed off to a small parish in a declining area of northeast Pennsylvania, a former center of the mining industry. I knew this region well: it will reappear in another chapter because several members of our parish long ago relocated from there in order to find more stable employment. My own father's family settled there as immigrants from western Ukraine and an uncle served throughout the area as a priest in the Ukrainian Greek Catholic Church. I myself worked there in education for almost two years. My last year as a friar, I taught at a regional Catholic high school and after leaving the Carmelites, I taught in Project HeadStart there. I knew life in that region could be trying.

The former intern was able to take on the parish composed mainly of retirees largely due to his wife's salary. It made it possible for them to be there, since what the parish could provide would not have made ministry possible, even with food stamps and other entitlement benefits. I was impressed by his thorough familiarity with the area after a number of months. He had mastered median income, ages, educational attainment, employment numbers, and a lot more demographic data, described who were picking properties, where they were working, even some long-range hopes for development and jobs — a freight airport that could take the pressure off major airports like Newark and Philadelphia, the proximity of the interstate making shipping easy.

I recall we wished him well but also alerted him to the dismal economic history of the area in the last half-century, as well as the massive out-migration of young people for employment. The numerous vacant storefronts on the main street were a grim reminder of a healthy economy long since gone with the end of the anthracite coal industry. Their remarkable skyline of Eastern church "onion domes" and Western church steeples witnessed to a well-churched past. Now the Roman Catholic diocese would be closing several of the parishes, with a number of other mainline Protestant congregations also closing or merging. There were four or five Eastern Church parishes, at least three of which were Orthodox, and none having more than a couple dozen elderly members.

Our intern, now a new parish priest, served valiantly for almost three years there and then moved on to a struggling inner-city congregation that had some chance of revival. Visiting him, keeping in contact by calls, I was able to follow his early years of parish experience. New children came into their family. They eventually bought one house and then another, and the former seminarian intern and spouse were forty-somethings. They were but one set of names on the list, but had become a whole story of disappointments, joys, persistence, and cumulative experience, in every dimension — marriage, parenting, pastoral care. In almost a decade, I do not think this pastor could ever rest easy, knowing that the parish he was serving was secure. The future remains hopeful but also questionable. Demographic realities beyond his control or influence are affecting all congregations. Younger people do not stay around after they leave for college. They do not marry within the same ethnic or church bodies. And even the few adult children of a parish who remain in the area do not attend or contribute on any regular basis. Thus, the majority of mainstream American churches' parish membership is aging, and given the "greatest generation" and their children, the young adults of the early 1960s, the main pillars of many parishes will be gone.

Another intern has gone from bad to worse until finding, after more than five years, some temporary stability. Unable to find any parish placement, like other seminary graduates, he and his wife and children served a parish for no salary but with housing and the agreement he would work full-time. Given the disastrous employment picture from 2008 onward, they were forced to move from a very high unemployment location to one with better prospects. But once again, he was able to find only a mission parish that already had been struggling for a decade and had less than thirty members. Despite moving the parish to a much better location, he was unable in a few years to double or triple membership as local church leaders hoped. Blamed for failing to grow the mission, as well as for other things, this harassment pushed the family out and back to where they had previously lived, but this time with a parish that could provide some compensation though no housing. And there he remains, trying to keep together an aging community.

Yet another former intern, after years of trying to secure some kind of pastoral position, simply left our church body for another. When church leaders refused to answer his letters, return his calls, or meet with him, he concluded his training and status as a young ordained priest was neither desired nor needed in our denomination. Several of our interns, when they saw the bleak future ahead — declining parishes, classmates on food stamps while serving in such congregations — simply did not request to be ordained. They work in a variety of professions and serve in whatever positions their parishes need them.

One of our interns opted out of parish ministry for an academic career and performed brilliantly as a teacher and scholar. But his volunteering to serve in parishes was for the most part an abominable experience. Both he and his spouse and child were criticized because they did not meet parish expectations for participation, though they lived an hour's drive from the parish location. A couple of our interns struggled but stabilized and even saw the growth of their mission congregations to the point that in one, the construction of a new church building became possible.

These stories of interns and parishioners—I do not share them simply to reminisce. I share them because I have learned that prayer is not just reciting the names of those in need, sickness, trouble, or even great joy. I have learned that the names and stories take me back to earlier situations in my life, ones from which I have moved on but from which I also learned a great deal. The names and stories remembered and shared keep me connected to former interns, students, parish members, family, and friends, even when they are long relocated, even passed from this life. Prayer is remembering. Prayer constantly shows me that I am never alone, always part of a community, a communion of saints in the church and in my life. I am reminded to think about their situations and needs, not just my own. I am also shown that, while time with them may have passed, we all live in an eternal now, with God.

Living Icons

Despite the disheartening stories of the previous section, I can also say that almost everywhere I look on the list there are names that bring me joy. It brings such peace to see the names of our children and think of their partners who love them, good relationships, satisfaction in their work, giving back in ways large and small. Peace too now comes from the list of our grandparents, parents, and a number of relatives who have died and are with God. Several of my former bishops, including the one who first ordained me, are in this list of the departed. Here too is a substantial series of names of people with whom I used to regularly visit and commune. I never tried to write down, as one might in a diary, the names of all those I visited, buried, or, for that matter, baptized or married. The list would be a book, given thirty years or more of such ministry.

With many names there is a face, a voice, often the usual concerns or gripes, even the décor of the house. One name and face is that of an always-laughing Scandinavian lady who was in her mid-nineties when I visited her thirty years ago—Elvira. She had a very hard life, lost her husband young, also a couple of her children before their time. Even though she had a tough history and was crippled with arthritis, I usually felt I was being visited, entertained rather than the other way around. There was always tea, some cookies or cake, questions about my wife, my own very young children, back then. Not only did I learn to pray for these elderly people I was tasked with paying pastoral visits. They taught me what prayer looks like, lived out, in their patience, in the capacity to look back over lives that were always a mix of sorrow and happiness, be pleased, and thankful to God for having been able to work, raise a family, live. Really, I was the one who was gifted in the project of visiting them. I learned not to fear aging, sickness, or death by accompanying them, seeing them move along with grace and gratitude.

Another set of names is that of one of the first couples at whose wedding I officiated, in their case at a local Catholic church, sharing the rite with the parish pastor. This was possible under a protocol that had been approved for such ecumenical occasions between the churches at the national level and locally accepted by most but not all clergy. As the associate pastor at the Brewster parish, normally I did not preside at most baptisms, weddings, or funerals, this being the prerogative of the senior pastor. From time to time, though, a family might ask for me or the rector might be unavailable. I am not sure but I think that in the case of this couple—I had talked with the bride—that I was requested by her to take part in the service. She belonged to the Lutheran parish, the groom to the Catholic one.

This particular couple, of all the others at whose marriage I officiated, stand out for me as a kind of "miracle." In order to protect their privacy, I will not describe all the details of the history of their marriage. However, despite a series of very disruptive, difficult events, ranging from serious medical conditions, periods of unemployment for both with attendant financial pressures, profound problems with families of origin and siblings, serious emotional illness and suffering, almost thirty years later, they remain together. I will admit that during one of the most pressing times of their years together, despite my efforts and that of other counselors, I did not expect the marriage to last much longer. I also have to say that even with personal experience of many dysfunctional families and marriages, this particular couple has endured more challenges and threats to their staying together than any other I have known. I call them a "miracle" because it must be by grace, as well as mutual forgiveness and commitment, that they have stayed together. Seeing them from time to time, I have watched them go from twenty-somethings to middle-aged, and, when crises arise, I have seen them both flounder but eventually, somehow, come to terms with the challenge and continue on together. They sometimes tell me that it is only my concern, my prayers, that accomplished this, but I know they do not believe or understand that to be the reason for their endurance as a couple.

Throughout the Hebrew Bible and the New Testament and then in the liturgy, to remember was to pray. Over and over, the fathers and mothers, the judges and prophets, and later the apostles recalled the great acts of God that saved the Israelites from Pharaoh, that sent them prophets, and in time called on them to return to the One who loved and saved them. Many of the psalms recount the kings slain—Oreb, Zeb, Zalmon—as Israel entered the Promised Land. The great antiphon of Psalm 136 is the reminder that is also a confession: "Great is God's love, love without end." The Passover liturgy, or Haggadah, is one continuous remembering, celebrating, praising, and giving thanks, along with the breaking and sharing of the unleavened bread and drinking of the cups of wine. The song sung after the meal is what later Christians would intend in their Eucharist—*Dayenu,* "it would have been enough." For fifteen verses, this is the response for all that God did, from assaulting Pharaoh and the country with plague after plague to bringing the people out of Egypt, leading them by pillars of cloud and fire and feeding them with manna to giving the Sabbath.

Christian liturgy follows this pattern. The word of God, the scriptures, are read, prayed, preached. The whole world, the government, state, churches, the dead, and the living are remembered in intercession. The great acts of God in creation, in the Exodus, the prophets, the Incarnation, and lastly, the suffering, death, burial, resurrection, ascension to heaven, even the second, glorious coming yet to happen are remembered—anamnesis—and as at the Shabbat supper and Seder, the bread and wine are offered and shared. Remembering contains within it giving praise, confessing what God has done, is doing, and will do, giving thanks for it all while asking forgiveness and recalling the admonition to bring before God everyone and everything.

Other Maps of Other Years: Prayer, Community, and Identity

It is really not possible here to describe and reflect on all the other places and names that the list encompasses. Though I long ago left monastic life, my list contains the names of sisters and brothers from a half-dozen monastic communities to which I have been connected over the years. These include Thomas Merton's monastery in Kentucky, Gethsemani Abbey, where I have been friends with his secretary, Brother Patrick Hart, as well as several other monks. There are the communities of New Skete in Cambridge, New York — sisters, brothers, and companions. These communities were among the efforts in the 1960s to return to a simpler monastic life. Having known them for thirty years, the names reflect those who have died or left as well as more recent members. I have kept in contact with a few Carmelites who were in formation in the decade that I was in the order. Also, there are a few small communities I have visited: Carthusian hermit sisters and Orthodox nuns in upstate New York, Ukrainian monks at Univ monastery outside Lviv, another small skete now in British Columbia. Common to all of these is the natural wish for mutual remembrance in prayer.

I remember names of people from the four parishes in which I have served, three Lutheran, one Orthodox. There are also names from abroad, quite a few from a number of trips to Lviv, in western Ukraine, to teach, lead retreats, or give talks at one or another part of the Ukrainian Catholic University there. There are academic and clergy colleagues, former students and staff who made me welcome on my trips there.

I have spent all my adult life as a teacher and scholar as well as a priest. (I reflect on this elsewhere in this book, each of those vocations being, in fact, ways to pray and put prayer into action.) Thus, the prayer list reflects this in colleagues, students, and even some of the writers I discuss in this volume. I consider as saints quite a few of those about whom I have written or translated. I mean Elisabeth Behr-Sigel, Dorothy Day, Thomas Merton, Sergius Bulgakov, Nicholas Afanasiev, Alexander Men, Alexander Schmemann, amd Mother Maria Skobtsova (one of the few actually canonized!). When commemorating the saints of each day, I have my own litany of "favorites" I name, and these last mentioned are among them. Is this not a smaller version of the "communion of saints" we confess in the Creed, that we believe encircles us at the Eucharist? Looking back on all the webs of relationships and connections I have described—and there are still more—Tertullian's words ring true: *"Solus christianus, nullus christianus."* You cannot be a Christian solo, by yourself. You received the faith, were baptized by the confession and witness of others, were raised in it in your family, and probably nightly remembered them all in your bedtime prayers: "Bless Daddy, Mommy . . ." If baptism is in Christ and receiving the Spirit, then it also mean's entering the household of the Father, becoming sister or brother innumerable times in our lives.

This little card with names, then, says a great deal about what faith looks like lived out—a constant stream of relationships, each one a link to me, each one also linked to God. Thus, in going over these names as I have here, I have a map of my life displayed for me, not just my family, where I live, what I do for work, but person after person from this parish or that, from school, from places I have traveled to for work, yes, even my neighbors. When I do not have the card before me, for example, when I am praying while walking, I try to imagine the columns and then remember the names. Eventually this always breaks down, and I end up going back to times and places in my life and the people clustered in them.

All these names, some with only faint images of faces, some with none at all, others extremely vivid, urgent, because of their situation, because they are part of the present—all these names that have come to comprise a life, my life. And therefore, it is not just lifting up these names in intercession that happens when I look at the list. It is also the prayer of thanksgiving and gratitude for all these individuals, those who have come into my life as gifts. And in remembering them, which is itself prayer, I not only give thanks but rejoice in them, feel compassion for those who are struggling, ask forgiveness for those who have been wronged or neglected by me. And yes there are some I must continually forgive, especially as they are no longer among the living.

That raises for me one more aspect of prayer, one that Jim Forest dwells on with great care and humanity in his recent book, *Loving Our Enemies*.[2] I must confess that for many years, really only till this past year, I have not included on my list, by name, people who I have distrusted, disliked, or kept distant from, and who, in some cases, I remember were enemies or in some ways at present are. These are not opponents in a political race. Nor are they Yankee fans or supporters of professional sports teams other than my own beloved New York Mets. The conflicts run deeper than that.

Because the conflict was so volatile, I have to include here my former superior, the prior of the Carmelite student house, now long closed, in Washington, DC, Charles Haggerty. He too is long deceased and from what I learned of his later years it likely could not have come off very well, given his afflictions. There was never a chance to encounter him and settle the grief that existed between us, all of which he caused, when I was a student friar in my early twenties and had my share of vocational crises, my doubts about staying in the Carmelite order. On stops at the former Carmelite minor seminary, now a pilgrimage and administrative center for the province to which I once belonged, I always visit the cemetery where the priests and brothers of the province are buried. With each passing year, there is another gravestone of a former teacher or colleague. Several friars in the class ahead of me are there, so too two members of the last Carmelite house I lived in, as well as all the superiors of every place where I was stationed. Yes, also the beloved Vinnie McDonald, who challenged my immaturity once, in his high pitched Queens accent, "So . . . you wanna be HAPPY?"[3]

I walk through the rows of graves, making the sign of the cross, saying a brief "Memory eternal" at all the names of those I knew—the number scares me! I need to say that the first time I returned to this cemetery some years back, when I came upon Charlie Haggerty's stone, my feelings were so intense, decades later, was my resentment and anger so profound at how he treated me. Though outwardly I didn't so indulge, I thought about it enough to have done so inwardly.

But, through no strength or goodness of my own, I have placed a small pebble on his gravestone and made the sign of the cross myself now as I pass by it. As Forest notes, the thought of how much suffering and pain this once miserable superior must have himself undergone melted me just a little.

So when I come to the Carmelites on the prayer list, I call up his name. Also that of my last superior, still alive though aged, who could not talk to me, look at me, or otherwise bid farewell when I left the priory in Pottsville in May 1971. A Carmelite colleague reminded me of the life of loneliness this elderly friar has endured.

On the list there are clergy colleagues, fellow pastors, whose kids grew up into young adults as did mine. Other clergy on the list, as noted, are not my peers but much younger, the seminarian interns who spent a year or more at our parish. It is startling now on Facebook to see their children becoming adolescents, children who were infants or toddlers when with us, or not even yet born. It is also the case, with most, that we drift out of regular contact, and so when I come across the names I wonder how their lives and work have gone.

All of these names I have written down and treasure as members of my own communion of saints. Again, I have to admit that only very recently have I added to them the names of those whose only relationship to me was negative, connection full of conflict and anger. This included the senior pastor, whose own personal turmoil ended in his distancing and tightly controlling me in what were my last weeks in the parish; the bishop, now deceased, who told me to resign and leave that first parish; and the memory of our small children, scared and sad, asking why are we going, the last Sunday when we left. I rejoice in having reconciled and reestablished connections with my former senior pastor, now retired. Time, forgiveness, and remembrance helped me realize how grateful I was for his mentoring.

Just as with describing the other, less than pleasant sides of "communion of community," so too when it comes to remembering as prayer—not every memory is joyful or treasured. The rector of my first parish and the bishop back then, over twenty years ago—these are faces and names from the distant past. It is much harder for me to name those from the present who I know dislike me or disapprove of my ideas, my work, my perspectives, and my behavior. For good reasons, I cannot name them here or do much by way of identifying them. It is a personal struggle to remember them, I must honestly say. To think of them, name them, is to evoke hurt at being ignored in professional life, criticized, ridiculed, marginalized for my views either in conversation or in writing.

The memory then reminds me of how small and vulnerable I allow myself to be, how important my ideas or advice are, especially to me! Thinking of those who have forgotten my hospitality, support, gifts, should remind me of my very own behavior in just such ways. And here, as with thinking of the negative personalities in a congregation, there is the unattended other side of remembering. Back when I was in the Carmelite order, a wise older friar told me to be kind to those under me on the way up, so that they could remember and treat me kindly on my way down. Another senior Carmelite assured me—better, warned me—that if I did *not* speak out and act when bad things were being done in the church, I would become an accomplice to them and have no justification for opposing such wrongdoing. Powerful thought, but when speaking out especially in the institutional church means attack, criticism, even sanctions, such noble and prophetic action appears costly—as it always is. I am not proud that I have not consistently spoken out when things were wrong.

Writing a few posts on a website seeking to inform, document, and seek reform of financial and other abuses in my church body placed me into the categories of malcontent and critic. Asking, privately, about the extent of official efforts to stop protest and investigation produced my shunning by a senior member of the clergy at gatherings. Privately protesting the treatment of another colleague earned the reprimand that if I defended him, I was as much to blame as he was. As in the military, so in the church, one does not step out of line.

Still, it is not easy to remember and recommend to God those you believe to have treated you wrongly, badly. Yet prayer reverses this enmity. "Love your enemies, pray for those who persecute you" (Matt. 5:44–45).[4] It is overly dramatic, I think, for me to even label those I am describing now as "enemies" in the strict sense. I doubt they gave serious thought to me as a threat or danger and thus an "enemy." More likely, no matter the depth of my hurt feelings, most of these people fall into the category of personal collisions, dislike, or even unintended ignorance. Particularly with those in the more distant past, as the superior of the Carmelite student house in Washington, DC, my last prior in Pottsville, Pennsylvania, the first rector under whom I served, and the timid bishop—in hindsight it is much easier for me to see the issues that created the personal and official dysfunctionality I experienced in dealings with them.

I do not follow the line that realizing the weaknesses of others and forgiving whatever I experienced as wrong done to me should then lead to realization of my own imperfection and misdeeds. Both are real, true, but for me, not connected that way. It is neither honest nor purposeful to deny wrong and wrongdoing, truly destructive personalities and their behavior. To do so, in the name of humility or forgiveness is indeed, as the friar told me, to become an accomplice unwittingly, unintentionally, but an accomplice nonetheless.

I think this is where not just my prayer list but prayer becomes a necessary mirror for each of us. I include here the prayer contained in the scriptures and other liturgical and spiritual texts we read. But I also include, as all this reflection attests, to the life together with others, the interactions with them, constructive and destructive.

Remembering, mapping my work, my relationships, where my life has taken me—a lot for a small card, stained, faded, with many names. Prayer as we have seen here and elsewhere, is so many things: community, work, thanksgiving, forgiveness, intercession. But as crowded as the columns of names on my prayer list are, for all the years and places and people recorded there, the list also, like a mirror, reflects me, tells me about myself, things I have forgotten or chosen to ignore.

CHAPTER SIX

The Prayer of Darkness

Barbara Brown Taylor

"I would rather show someone my checkbook stubs than talk about my prayer life."

As a writer, preacher, and pastor, Barbara Brown Taylor has a gift for being able to open up many corners of the spiritual life. She starts, as it were, a conversation at the beginning of a book, and pages later, at the end, you wish it could continue. Now a professor of religion at Piedmont College, she is an Episcopal priest and served in parish ministry for almost twenty years. She has been a well-known figure in American church life for some time. She has been among the ten top preachers numerous times, and there are almost a dozen volumes of her collected sermons and lectures in print. To these she has added a powerful memoir of her exit from parish ministry — *Leaving Church*.[1] Equally important is a companion volume she did after *Leaving Church*. It is a remarkable reflection about recovering the sacred in ordinary, everyday life, an antidote to toxic religion, *An Altar in the World*.[2] And it was a *New York Times* best seller. (Her other recent books have won numerous awards.)

A third volume now makes for a trilogy, something she notes in the opening part of the new book. This most recent book is about the *via negativa*, the path to God through the dark side and moments of

Barbara Brown Taylor.
Photo by Kenny Simmons.

life—*Learning to Walk in the Dark*.³ In 2014 she was judged among *Time* magazine's top one hundred most influential people, and this newest book was profiled in the April 17 issue.

All these marks of success aside, there is a great deal that Taylor gives us, especially in this most recent book. She is particularly adept at describing the possibilities of prayer and finding God in the most difficult of circumstances. As a pastor, she was especially gifted in charting the struggle of those to whom she ministered. Yet in her books she also allows us to track her own insecurities, weaknesses, bad choices, and defeats. In another of my books I listened to her as a most eloquent voice on the destructive possibilities of religion, not only the institutional church but in personal piety as well. With her we can learn how loss, failure, mistakes, discouragement, and sadness are among the most powerful encounters with God, really, schools of prayer.

[I]t is enough to say that "darkness" is shorthand for anything that scares me—that I want no part of—either because I am sure that I do not have the resources to survive it or because I do not want to find out. The absence of God is in there, along with the fear of dementia and the loss of those nearest and dearest to me. So is the melting of polar ice caps, the suffering of children, and the nagging question of what it will feel like to die. If I had my way I would eliminate everything from chronic back pain to the fear of the devil from my life and the lives of those I love—if I could just find the right night-lights to leave on.

At least I think I would. The problem is this: when, despite all my best efforts, the lights have gone off in my life (literally or figuratively, take your pick), plunging me into the kind of darkness that turns my knees to water, nonetheless I have not died. The monsters have not dragged me out of bed and taken me back to their lair. The witches have not turned me into a bat. Instead, I have learned things in the dark that I could never have learned in the light, things that have saved my life over and over again, so that there is really only one logical conclusion. I need darkness as much as I need light.[4]

This is Barbara Brown Taylor's voice, one of good discernment, depth, common sense, and wonderfully good humor as well. She is self-deprecating in a most integral way, yet, at the same time, serious. Just before the passage above, she makes clear that "darkness" is no laughing matter, and everyone will have their own lists of what it means for them. It is not just physical or material darkness, though that figures importantly in her book, from the darkness of night and lunar light so often polluted by light sources of civilization to the more foreboding darkness of caves—she tries a spelunking expedition.

Adventures in Darkness

She already faced darkness in the narrative of her experiences in pastoral ministry, first in the path through postulancy and seminary that led to ordination, then in the assignments of a large urban parish and then a small-town parish of her dreams. As she notes, for the most part both Judaism and Christianity are "solar" or light based. "Let there be light" is God's command in Genesis. Jesus Christ is the "light of the world," the "light no darkness can overcome." Even her much beloved *Book of Common Prayer* asks: "Deliver us, O Lord, from the powers of darkness. Shine into our hearts the brightness of your Holy Spirit, and protect us from all perils and dangers of the night."[5] Also, again the scriptures, "God is light and in him there is no darkness at all" (1 John 1:15).[6]

Most would be familiar with this luminosity kind of religion and spirituality. As the old country hymn goes, "Keep on the sunny side, always on the sunny side . . . of life." But even a most "solar" spirituality does recognize the inevitability and omnipresence of darkness and night. Even in Genesis, there is morning and evening for each day of creation.

It is not just the subtle beauty of the moon that we are missing, nor the delicate fading of the daylight or its perhaps even more miraculous and mysterious dawning, even on the cloudiest of days. I think of those rare nights of insomnia, where the ability to see my hand and the vaguest outlines of the room are welcome signs that the night is finally over. However, dark and light are not just correlates of night and day. As Taylor emphasizes, they are but one of a number of dualisms with which believers have long been familiar: good/evil, church/world, spirit/flesh, sacred/profane, among others. And, of course, these are not equal in value. Normally the first is perceived as more important, godly, and right than the second.

Taylor is by no means the only one to question our familiarity and contentment with such dualisms. Richard Rohr, Mary Oliver, really all the writers we listen to here in this book raise similar and related questions. Cutting reality up into good and evil, light and dark, obscures and impedes us more than anything else. The very foundational texts, the scriptures, upon closer, more careful inspection, do not support such dualism. The historical books but also the Torah of the Hebrew Bible hardly divide human beings into the good and the evil, for the possibilities of both are found everywhere, in everybody. How many kings, priests, and prophets end up walking in some way other than that of God? Jesus associates with those often rejected, tax collectors, outsiders.

Taylor is alarming in her honesty about her own path. She documents her failures in ministry in excruciating detail in *Leaving Church*. I know just how painful is the experience of not being able to live up to your own ideals, as well as the unreal image of the priest who can do it all. I too had to leave a parish, at the orders of the bishop, with hardly any farewells, and then found that after leaving, it was as if I never existed, had never been there for almost a decade. There is also the experience of being the assistant or associate pastor, something I have been now for almost thirty-five years. It is often a joy to serve in ministry with a colleague and friend. It is also the case that, in such a role, one is often overlooked, not informed or consulted, put in one's place, and made the punching bag for another's aggressions and insecurities. Being called and ordained to serve in the church is a wonderful gift, but it is also a vocation of continuous self-scrutiny. As I wrote of at great length earlier, one is invited into so many lives, allowed to share in great joy as well as sorrow. Deeper is the nagging questions of one's own abilities and worth, of how the community responds to us. Deeper still is the inevitable questioning of the theological language, symbols, and rituals that we long have known and used and which support our work, especially preaching, teaching, and believing.

Stepping down from active parish ministry into teaching enabled Taylor to reflect on just how much church is able to consume the world and reality or, better, how church people construct a version of church and faith that excludes so much. Thus, she wrote an exquisitely beautiful reflection on the reality that Abraham Joshua Heschel and Thomas Merton recognized, that everything is holy—*An Altar in the World*. I have looked at it in some detail before and will not repeat that here. Suffice it to say that she lifts up spiritual practices "rooted in ordinary, physical human life on earth, like going for a walk, paying attention to a tree, hanging a load of laundry on the line, and treating people like peepholes into God."[7]

"One does not become enlightened by imagining figures of light," Carl Jung wrote, "but by making the darkness conscious." Reading this I realize that in a whole lifetime spent with seekers of enlightenment, I have never once heard anyone speak in hushed tones about the value of *endarkenment*. The great mystics of the

Christian tradition all describe it as part of the journey into God, but it has been a long time since *The Cloud of Unknowing* was on anyone's bestseller list. Today's seekers seem more interested in getting God to turn the lights *on* than in allowing God to turn them *off*. Full solar spirituality strikes again.[8]

But in turning to all that "darkness" can mean, Taylor joins several of the other writers we are listening to in this volume. She shows us how prayer and the spiritual life are not just celebrations of light and joy and peace. Darkness is not just an anomaly, the default of light. Darkness is at least half of life.[9] All too often, we limit the time and extent of grief, depression, and despair. We seek medication and treatment of all kinds, including talk therapy, even judging there to be supposedly normal, healthy time periods for these afflictions, rather than acknowledging them as inherent in our lives, even necessary elements in our growth.

In stressing this she is, of course, joining ranks with not just prophets like Moses and Elijah who had to experience the darkness of caves, of doubt, of the cloud of presence. She reminds us of the great classic writers like Augustine, John of the Cross, Teresa of Avila, Nicholas of Cusa, and then, closer to us, Jung, James Fowler, Gerald May, Pema Chödrön, and Ken Wilber who want us to end dualistic thinking, to appreciate silence, solitude, and the darkness.

Augustine documented a prolonged spiritual crisis, a journey of depression and breakdown. His coming to faith never obliterated the memory of his suffering. John of the Cross gave us the language to speak of the life of faith involving darkness and night, of necessity. Richard Rohr, as we will hear, constantly holds up the pattern of falling and rising throughout his writing. While poets like Karr and Oliver rarely use traditional theological language, they nevertheless show us addiction and loss, grief and despair, as more than horrors to be feared. Wiman more explicitly leans on traditional religious imagery and language, all the while questioning whether it is possible to believe, to pray, to think of God when health has been replaced by pain and sickness and hope tossed aside by prognosis.

In facing darkness and all that it can mean, Taylor notes that we find the transformative power of faith. Ken Wilber, who does not locate himself primarily in the Christian tradition, stresses this.[10] But then, as so many writers here will also remind us, we recall that Jesus's first words have to do with transforming, converting, turning around—*metanoite*—for the kingdom is here, among us. Our relationship with God, faith, prayer—these are no medications for suffering or antidotes for darkness.

Experiencing the Darkness

Taylor is most inventive in taking us through a diversity of darkness experiences. The homiest and most delightful are variations on her lying out on a summer night, with her siblings and father, gazing up at the stars. She repeats this with her husband and their beloved arthritic dog on a hill at their farm, completely swept away by the moon's rising.[11] She also spends the night in silence and darkness, a twelve-hour meditation retreat in a small cabin on her property. This stretch of time, including twilight and the dawn at either end of a night that happened to be the summer solstice, reintroduces longer periods of semi-awake awareness. During this stay, she remembers vividly a terrifying night of insomniac darkness in her youth, though now comforted by the soft darkness surrounding her.[12]

She participates in a very striking experiment of experiencing total blindness.[13] She does a cave exploration with experienced guides, encountering not only darkness but the powerful enclosure of caves.[14] This adventure was almost too much for my claustrophobia. Yet I was struck by connections she made to the frequency with which caves are meeting places with God in the scriptures—the caves the prophets are sent into, caves in which Saul and David find each other, the cave of Bethlehem, the cave of the new tomb of the resurrection. Caves are full of darkness, sometimes danger, but are also places of life.

The sixteenth-century Spanish Carmelite mystic John of the Cross, a poet himself, has given the most vivid, beautiful, and enduring account of how darkness, absence, and being lost in one's life of faith is, paradoxically, the path to greater intimacy with God. John did not invent these insights. They are to be found much, much earlier, in the sayings of desert mothers and fathers from the Jordan and Egypt, in the fourth and fifth centuries. Diarmaid MacCulloch documents this in his 2006 Gifford Lectures.[15]

Barbara Brown Taylor uses John of the Cross as a point of departure for reflecting on her own darkness with respect to the language of faith. That she, a pastor for over two decades, judged among the ten top preachers in America, the author of numerous collections of sermons, meditations, and her own memoirs, should hit a wall with theological language, with words like "sin," "salvation," "repentence," and "grace," among many others, is startling.[16] Yet to be too shocked or to deny that this could happen to a religious professional or to search for satisfying explanations would be the worst avoidance of authentic darkness in the spiritual life. Something of this happened when Mother Teresa of Calcutta's letters and diaries were published, texts in which she described years of feeling so distant from God that God might as well have not existed for her! Likewise, the publication of Thomas Merton's journals, disclosing his falling in love with a student nurse, was unacceptable for some earlier devotees of his spiritual publications. The inability to accept the imperfections, the fallibility, in short, the humanity of persons of faith is what I have devoted a good part of two earlier books to disputing.

Taylor actually started a truly remarkable confessional narrative in *Leaving Church.* A former student and later clergy colleague introduced me to this troubling, provocative, yet most important book, one he's been required to read in a clergy rehabilitation center. It is a most courageous, honest, and therefore moving account of Taylor's breakdown from overwork in ministry. Perhaps "breakdown" is too strong a word. But recognizing from personal experience and the experience of other colleagues what over-identification with priestly status and over-involvement in pastoral activity looks like, the toxicity of religion these contain, and the destructive emotional, physical, spiritual, and personal consequences, I do not think the term is inappropriate. There have been plenty of very public meltdowns of clergy, not to mention abusive and self-abusive behavior. The resignation of Mark Driscoll from Mars Hill church in fall 2014 is one recent example. The forced resignation of a German bishop by the Vatican for financial improprieties in grandiosely refurbishing his residence is another, and there are many more cases of clergy misbehavior, as Donald Cozzens documents.[17]

Living with the Provisional

Taylor does not think of what she experiences as a loss of faith in God but a loss of faith in the system of language, symbols, ritual, rules, and more, the structure of church in the twenty-first century. Religious writers such as Hans Küng, Karen Armstrong, Phyllis Tickle, Diana Butler Bass, and Harvey Cox have in different ways argued that we are experiencing a historical moment of change for traditions of faith, the Christian one for sure. Others, like Rob Bell, Brian MacLaren, and still others in the "emerging church" movement, have called for serious reassessment not only of church structure and operation but of the ways in which the fundamental sources of the tradition are interpreted and practiced. MacLaren has spoken of a more "generous" orthodoxy that allows for adaptation, accommodation, the welcoming of those excluded and condemned. Pope Francis has called for more openness to LGBT people by the church, and his theological spokesman Walter Kasper called for the use of mercy rather than only doctrinal rigor in dealing with reconciliation and communion for divorced and remarried people. Not surprisingly, these more "generous" suggestions have been attacked as "confusion" where there should be certainty and order, and the church therefore "rudderless" and tilting toward schism. But one can also hear the church as mercy echoed by many other voices, both from the rank and file of the people of God and church leadership, slowly but surely.

Taylor is not so much focused on the larger trends of faith and church, aware of them as she surely is. Rather, she wants to affirm that even in the sense of God's absence, even with lack of earlier clarity and conviction, it remains possible to continue.

> At this stage of my life, this sounds like a fifth Gospel, in which the good news is that dark and light, faith and doubt, divine absence and presence, do not exist at opposite poles. Instead, they exist with and within each other, like distinct waves that roll out of the same ocean and roll back into it again. As different as they are, they come from and return to the same source. If I can trust that—if I can give my heart to it and remain conscious of it—then

faith becomes a verb, my active response to the sacred reality that the best religions in the world can only point to. This faith will not offer me much to hold on to. It will not give me a safe place to settle. Practicing it will require me to celebrate the sacraments of defeat and loss, but since the religion I know best has a lot to say about losing as the precondition for finding, I can live with that. I think I can even live inside this cloudy evening of the soul for a while longer, where even my sense of God's absence can be a token of God's presence if I let it be.[18]

Throughout this book there is a strong sense of our faith and spiritual life always being tentative, this in the face of a culture that is obsessed with security and order but also full of mobility and change—a paradoxical pairing. To hear that doubt, one of the many forms of darkness, is all right, is a part of the journey, is most encouraging. It does not mean the end of faith. It should not exclude anyone from the community of faith. It is possible to not only doubt but also to protest, to talk back to God, as numerous friends of God have done, from prophets of the Hebrew Bible to Teresa of Avila and our contemporaries, Mary Oliver and Mary Karr. There are moments when grief and loss are so searing that we have to cry out, asking why this has happened. Christian Wiman speaks to this. But there also are the many times of frustration with the never-ending stream of misery of those around us and the seeming impossibility of making a difference. Those who served the hungry, homeless, and poor like Mother Maria Skobtsova, Dorothy Day, and Sara Miles give voice to sheer exhaustion and discouragement. Darkness takes many forms.

Taylor discovers other fascinating things in her multidisciplinary study of darkness. She learns that our assumed "full night's sleep" of eight hours is a fairly recent phenomenon, linked largely to the invention of the lightbulb, a dependable light source that needed no tending, refilling, or watching. Being no longer dependent on the length of daytime and nighttime, human activity patterns radically changed, and now, more than a century after the incandescent lightbulb and with the information revolution, 24/7 has become a new "normal" for work, investing, entertainment, and more.

Our Lady of Darkness

Barbara Brown Taylor's engagement with darkness closes with a beautiful narrative of her encounter with "Our Lady of the Underground," *Notre Dame de Sous-Terre*, the ancient dark/black Mother of God image in the crypt of the cathedral of Chartres, best known for its stunning stained glass and its medieval labyrinth.[19] This is one of many dark Madonnas, most of them from the middle ages, in churches across Europe. Another notable one is in the Spanish abbey of Montserrat and of course the Black Madonna whose icon is in the monastery church at Jasna Góra, Częstochwa, Poland. Thomas Merton commissioned a dark statue of the Mother of God for the novices' chapel at Gethsemani abbey when he was novice master there, between 1955 and 1965.

Taylor is deeply ecumenical, so there is no resistance to the figure of Mary, far from it. She recognizes that the Mother of God is linked to deeper spiritual instincts, the magna mater, also to feminine figures of maternity, fecundity, protection, and consolation. At the Chartres cathedral gift shop she discovers a silver medal of the Lady of the Underground, the dark Virgin. On it are the words, "All must come through me in order to live in the light."

This connects to the place of Mary in the New Testament. She is present before the plan of salvation begins, is herself intrinsic to it. The angel greets her as "full of grace," announces the good news that the son she will bear will be the savior of the people—Yehoshua, Joshua, Jesus. Her fear and confusion at how this could happen, not yet married, is supplanted with a resounding "yes"—"I am the slave/servant of the Lord. Let it happen according to his word."

Asking for her son's intervention at the wedding in Cana, Mary's presence is subtle. She mostly is in the shadows, to the side. She worries about the child separated from her on pilgrimage in Jerusalem at the Temple. She is identified not just as the birth-giver but more importantly as one who hears God's word and keeps it, lives it. She is explicitly located at the foot of the cross and in the upper room when the Spirit descends. She likely is one of those who come to the empty tomb.

Mary is an essential figure in the Christian narrative, but Taylor insightfully recognizes that she represents so much of what Taylor's study sought to emphasize. Contrary to a stereotype of robust faith, Mary at the outset is young, small, and powerless. She is in no position to comprehend what will happen to her or her child. Is this not the great gift of the prayer of darkness, that though unable to see clearly or understand comprehensively, nevertheless we continue on? The gospel writer affirms this by putting into Mary's heart her song, the *Magnificat*: "My soul proclaims the greatness of the Lord, my spirit rejoices in God my savior." It is an echo of the song of praise and of faith in the dark from the woman who likewise did not understand what God was doing with and through her, Hannah, the mother of the great judge and prophet, Samuel. Hannah is even accused of being drunk, seen as silently praying in the shrine at Shiloh (1 Sam. 2:1–11).

Taylor does not just direct our attention toward the ways in which faith consoles during dark days of suffering and confusion. As in her other recent books, she is well aware both of the toxic possibilities of religion and the transformative power of faith. Even without extensive references to the scriptures, something she very easily could have done, the reader is reminded, many times, that it is hardly all light, joy, and exaltation in the life with God. The prophets' despair is seen, from Moses and Elijah to Jonah and Jeremiah. The parade of wicked kings and false prophets, the destruction of the Temple, the deportation, so much that is terrible. She recalls, at the end, that Jesus hears the Father's voice aloud but once. All the rest of their communication was out in solitude, silence, and the dark. Seemingly, it all came to a devastating end on the cross, a corpse placed in a dark tomb. The disciples are scattered, terrified, unable to recognize what an empty tomb meant or the one who came through the walls and across the water and down the road to Emmaus with them.

The Darkness of Faith

At the conclusion of her study, Taylor invokes the famous prayer of Thomas Merton.

My Lord God, I have no idea where I am going. I do not see the road ahead of me. I cannot know for certain how it will end. Nor do I really know myself, and the fact that I think I am following your will does not mean that I am actually doing so.[20]

It is startling that such a supposedly gifted teacher of the spiritual life and such a brilliant mind could really feel this way! There is a great discomfort when those we revere and trust reveal their humanity, their weakness, their doubts. Merton surely did this, as did Mother Teresa and Dorothy Day, among so many others. Perhaps it is one of the striking characteristics of persons of faith in our time, namely, that they are able not only to express their own difficulties in faith but, thereby, allow us who read them, listen to them, to find some resonance and some encouragement. I would not want to make too much of this modern ability to acknowledge what is hard, a struggle, in the spiritual life, make of it a necessity for all of us looking for God these days. But I would also affirm how much it means to hear of the difficulties of others. It immediately establishes a connection with them, a true communion of those trying to hear God and do God's work. That I learn of the humanity of fellow travelers, fellow saints-in-the-making, not only consoles but also impels me, pushes me on.

While Taylor does not emphasize it, there is something very significant about the incarnational reality of the Christian vision that this sensibility of the weak, the imperfect, the fallible also brings to mind. Richard Rohr has more to say about this. Merton, in his own way, seems to have constantly been surprised and lifted by the remembering of God's mercy, something Pope Francis will not allow even his critics to forget.

The other voice Taylor echoes, the Buddhist nun Pema Chödrön, puts it very simply. "The real problem has far less to do with what is really out there than it does with our resistance to finding out what is really out there. The suffering comes from our reluctance to learn how to walk in the dark."[21] When we venture out, in our prayer and action, we end up with Merton, in the last part of the prayer.

But I believe that the desire to please you does in fact please you. And I hope I have that desire in all I am doing. I hope that I will never do anything apart from that desire. And I know that if I do this you will lead me by the right road, though I may know nothing about it. Therefore I will trust you always though I may seem to be lost and in the shadow of death. I will not fear, for you are ever with me, and you will never leave me to face my perils alone.[22]

I think here of Psalm 139:11–12.

If I say, "Surely the darkness shall cover me, and the light around me become night," even the darkness is not dark to you; the night is as bright as the day, for darkness is as light to you. (NRSV)

It is important that in attempting to see how prayer looks in the lives of people, in the experiences of the writers to whom we have been listening, we have come to learn that prayer is no stranger to adversity. At the same time, it is no mere solution to suffering either. Mary Karr surely prayed through her depression and addiction, not just the Lord's Prayer or Jesus's prayer or the rosary or favorite lines from the scriptures but real cries of the heart. In the face of unbearable pain, Christian Wiman too could protest against the God who seemed distant, indifferent to his suffering. Sara Miles prayed, encountering many faces who hungered for attention as well as food. Sarah Coakley faced her inner emptiness and the many challenges of gender, body, and culture in opening herself, quite vulnerably too, to God in silence. Later, we will have Richard Rohr remind us of the pattern of falling and rising that is not only Christ's paschal mystery, but the map for each of us in following Christ, in living out his gospel. Barbara Brown Taylor laid out for us the profound challenge we all face in whatever forms of darkness our lives bring us into. I also think of the people from the places of my own pastoral ministry, and before that, in my own experience of formation in the Carmelites.

So many different forms of prayer, so many situations in which to pray and live.

CHAPTER SEVEN

The Prayer of Care for Those in Need

Dorothy Day and Maria Skobtsova

A perennial issue in the Christian tradition is the Mary-Martha conflict, called such because of Lazarus's sisters' differing modes of bustling busy-ness and quiet reflection. Jesus's claim that Mary, the contemplative, the spiritual one, had chosen the one thing necessary, "the better part," contrasted with Martha, "distracted by her many tasks" (Luke 10:38–42), has been taken by generations to mean that prayer trumps action and that faith is more crucial than service. At root, the question is whether loving God and observing the commandments, attending services, and saying prayers was more important than, has priority over, activity, that is, feeding the hungry, clothing the naked, housing the homeless, standing up for justice for the oppressed. But this is a false opposition, a problem that does not arise in the New Testament itself. "Truly I tell you, just as you did it to one of the least of those who are members of my family, you did it to me" (Matt. 25:40).

The example of Jesus himself shows there is no true contrast, no real opposition, certainly no hierarchy of value. Rather, Jesus becomes what he teaches. Jesus lives what he preaches. Jesus does not only talk about healing and the bread of life, he heals and he feeds people with that bread. So many friends of God have exemplified Jesus's integration of action and contemplation over the centuries: Francis of Assisi,

Sergius of Radonezh, Margaret of Hungary, and Juliana the Merciful in the medieval era, for example. Closer to our time there are two remarkable women disciples of the Lord who also, both in their writings and their lives, witness to the integrity of the prayer that is care for those in need.

Dorothy Day was entered into the official process for canonization in the Roman Catholic Church in February 2002 by Cardinal John O'Connor, despite her saying she did not want to be thought of as a "saint." She believed that would make her irrelevant and likely to be dismissed or ignored.[1] Hers was hardly the typical life of holiness. From a family of origin indifferent to religious upbringing, her life kept taking turns not thought of as pious. She had a first marriage that ended very quickly. She had an abortion and a child out of marriage. She held radical political perspectives as a young journalist and equally radical social and political views for most of her adult life as an activist and writer, one of the founders of the Catholic Worker movement. Her witness of feeding the hungry and sheltering the homeless was paralleled by incessant calls for social justice and spirited criticism of war-making as policy and extravagant defense spending. While she followed the daily prayer of the hours, was a regular at the liturgy and communion, her prayer extended far beyond the traditional modalities, as her columns for the *Catholic Worker* newspaper, her letters, and her diaries attest.

Almost exactly a contemporary of Dorothy Day, although across the Atlantic in Paris, Liza Pilenko had a startling similar path in life.[2] Her words, "The way to God lies through love of people," could be a motto or a description for the lives of both women. Liza, later Mother Maria Skobtsova, had a life so rich, so nonconformist that, along with Dorothy Day, it still seems a challenge to think of them in terms of spiritual existence, service to the neighbor, and living out prayer. Dorothy Day struggled during the Great Depression, through WWII and then the Cold War, and at the end in the years of the civil rights and anti-war movements. Her prayer was that of engagement—intellectual and spiritual combat, it could be said, in an era when American dreams and hopes were severely challenged. Through those difficult times, she remained in the Worker houses, serving meals, finding bedding and medical care for the smallest of society, the invisible poor. Maria Skobtsova's engagement was not only in the dy-namic arena of ideas among the writers and thinkers of her "Russian Paris" but, as with Dorothy, in direct action, in feeding, sheltering, and protecting those in need, as well as speaking out, in lectures and essays, on their behalf. Both she and Dorothy Day witness to prayer and advocacy, prayer and work, liturgy and life being seamless.

The Poet in the Monastery of the World: Maria Skobtsova

In those years I personally knew Mother Maria, and often visited her. An old house on a poor and run-down Paris lane, a tiny courtyard, a few scraggly trees, an old garage in the back turned into a chapel. . . . In the house day and night: crowds, activity, the poor, ragged, unemployed, forgotten and abandoned. Everyone is being fed, attempts made to find work for all, and mainly—everyone is received with love and brotherliness. In the middle of everything, a large red-cheeked, always smiling woman in monastic garb, flitting about in some unstoppable, seamless action. She is making soup in the kitchen, sweeping stairs, painting icons on the damp walls of the garage-chapel, embroidering vestments, and in the evenings sitting in the half-lit sparse living room, greedily absorbs a passionately debated lecture.

What a panoply of stars met on those evenings: that's where I will always recall the Assyrian head of Berdyaev, the scraping voice—he had throat cancer—of Father Sergius Bulgakov, the fragile, tender, kind countenance of Constantine Vasilievich Mochulsky. Soup, the poor, hospitality—all this was during the daytime, but at evening—the deep problems of life, poetry, and culture. She sits embroidering under a lamp, and her vestments are always bright, paschal, radiant with flowers. There was not one iota here of anything formal or sanctimonious, or rigoristic, but always the lightness and joy of love, the freedom of faith.[3]

Years after its closing, this is the memory Father Alexander Schmemann had of the house of hospitality on the Rue de Lourmel in Paris that Mother Maria Skobtsova had established. Very much like the Catholic Worker houses of hospitality on the Lower East Side of New York City, it had at its heart a chapel, and daily prayer was part of the schedule, for whichever residents could make it. Another fascinating memoir, by recently deceased writer Dominique DeSantis, who met Maria as a teenager herself, is vivid in its description of the warmth amid chaos of this place.[4]

Dominique and her boyfriend, themselves political radicals, went to the house for an evening of tea and lively discussion with some refreshments. They brought a large pastry and were heartily welcomed by this larger than life woman in a nun's habit, with thick glasses and strands of her hair falling out of the veil on her head. Embraced by her, they were swept into the evening gathering, a salon being held with well-known intellectuals and academics of the Russian Paris. Present was the already mentioned philosopher Nicholas Berdyaev, editor of one of the major Russian periodicals, *Put'*, "The Way." There were also literary critic and professor Constantine Mochulsky as well as theologian Fr. Sergius Bulgakov, the dean of the St. Sergius Theological School. Other St. Sergius faculty often present at these salons were historian George Fedotov, theologian Lev Zander, and philosophy professor Basil Zenkovsky. The treasurer of the house, himself editor of the radical journal *Novy Grad*, "The New City," Ilya Fundaminsky, was frequently present, as was Feodor Pianov, also a staffer at the house, and Yuri Skobtsov, in his twenties, a seminarian and on the house staff. There were others of varied backgrounds too: chaplain Fr. Dmitri Klepinin, his brilliant wife, Tamara, the American YMCA head in Paris, Paul Anderson.[5] Others included board members of the organization called "Orthodox Action," which oversaw and sought funds for her.

This lively ménage of creative thinkers and writers, clergy, the politically engaged, none of whom really agreed on things, made for a real cross-fertilization of ideas. It was, in many ways, a reflection of the intense laboratory of thought Paris was for the emigrés, as Antoine Arjakovsky's magnificent study shows.[6] Maria Skobtsova learned much, not only from her spiritual father, Bulgakov, but from numerous others—it is there in her essays easily identified without any footnotes. Despite the Russian church experience she must have had growing up, very much on view in her "Types of Religious Lives," she broke through the formalism and near superstitious aspects of this piety. She was able to rediscover the human, the everyday, in worship and faith. Thus, she was able to criticize the fanaticism and extremism of Russian piety. Positively, she was able to see the world around her in Paris as the location for doing the work of compassion. She was able to call all the people of God "living icons."[7] She linked this to liturgy. The deacon or priest at Eastern Church services censes first the icons of Christ, the Virgin, the angels and saints on the church walls, and then the people gathered there, for they are the kingdom of heaven walking and talking. They are saints in the making.

And this vision of her neighbors as saints-in-process carries on into the most basic commandment of Christ, that of love. One cannot just keep the rules, the fasts and feasts without loving the neighbor and God. She spent much of her writing elucidating this crucial con-

Mother Maria
Skobtsova

nection. It is telling as well that the Eucharist ends up at the center of the worshipping life of the community, both the local parish and the greater church. This she received from Bulgakov, Afanasiev, Lev Gillet, who was her first chaplain, and others. And she made it her own. It is striking too that she argues that faith must fulfill itself in action, that there must be a "liturgy after the liturgy," "outside the church building." The idea that sanctity is to be found in different shapes and lives in different times she must have acquired from George Fedotov who created a new kind of hagiography, a thoroughly historical, socially realistic understanding of holy women and men.[8]

Maria's life was colorful, really almost too colorful for what she later became—nun, social activist, protector of those hunted by the Nazis, and eventually a concentration camp victim and martyr. Her family was affluent, with a winter, "in-town" apartment in St. Petersburg and a summer estate in the almost Mediterranean Black Sea town of Anapa. She was especially beloved of the last great high procurator of the church, the reactionary Pobedonostsev. Liza Pilenko, as her own memoirs make clear, dabbled in many artistic media. She drew, drafted plays, and sat in on lectures at the Petersburg Theological Academy, one of the first women to do so. Poetry became her principal addiction, and she made herself a protégé of the noted Alexander Blok, actually described herself as stalking him all over the city, at once both comforting him in his depressive disillusionment while at the same time trying to push him into political and social action. She and her first spouse, Dmitri Kuzmin-Karavaev, attended the all-night Wednesday readings and debates at the famous tower apartment of Vyacheslav Ivanov, culminating in fried eggs and tea at the break of dawn for breakfast. She is surrounded by a who's who of Russian Symbolism and the Silver Age. In addition to Berdyaev, Blok, and Ivanov, there were Akhmatova, Mandelshtam, Gumilev, Merezhkovsky and Gippius, and Bely, among others. She eventually leaves husband number one, other relationships emerge, and two daughters are born from the series of connections.

The color continued in her wild life. Liza became politically active in the Socialist Revolutionary party. Once, when hauled off a train by the Bolsheviks, she feigned friendship with Lenin's wife to save herself from arrest and likely execution. She was elected the first woman mayor of Anapa, and then was arrested by the White Army and put on trial for being a Bolshevik—how else could she be elected mayor? Adept at administration of the town, she was able to talk her way out of further punishment, a friend's intercession with the military tribunal also of great help. Friend becomes lover becomes husband. Daniel Skobtsov falls in love with her, marries her, and before long they are migrating toward Europe through Istanbul. The last child, Yuri, is Daniel and Liza's only son. Both daughters tragically die young, the eldest, Gaiana, of a botched abortion back in Russia, where she relocated with her lover. The younger daughter, Nastia, died of meningitis.

With the marriage in tatters in not too many years and her life a nightmare of loss, Liza makes a radical move for one not terribly close to the church. She asks the archbishop of the Russian Orthodox Church in Paris to be allowed to end the marriage with a divorce ecclesiastically accepted and then be received as a nun by tonsure. In the Eastern Church at this time, women monastics lived in monasteries, not in cities, their works of love done within those confines. Metropolitan Evlogy, a remarkable, visionary pastor, agreed to her monastic reception only if she made the world, or at least the city, her monastery.

> At the Last Judgment I will not be asked whether I satisfactorily practiced asceticism, nor how many prostrations and bows I have made before the holy table. I will be asked whether I fed the hungry, clothed the naked, visited the sick and the prisoner in jail. That is all I will be asked.[9]

So Liza became Mother Maria, but it was not just peace and joy thereafter, not at all! She was criticized all of her life for her very different way of following Christ and the gospel. One chaplain, Fr. Cyprian Kern, a very traditional monastic priest, asked to be transferred from the chaplaincy of her house, as did several of the sisters she had welcomed to join her. Too many people, too much noise, not enough monastic life. Maria was not always at services. When challenged she argued that foraging food at the markets at Les Halles was her morning prayer! Not long ago, a leading voice in the Moscow patriarchate dismissed her as one who did not understand either the church or monastic life, a not-so-subtle though unofficial rejection of her canonization.

Later himself an archbishop and sought-after speaker on the spiritual life, then–medical student Anthony Bloom admitted being embarrassed at Mother Maria out and about in the streets and bistros of Paris. Later in life he realized his narrowness and lack of discernment, calling her "a saint of our day and for our day, a woman of flesh and blood possessed by the love of god, who stood fearlessly face to face with the problems of this century."[10]

Her Bohemian, nontraditional ways rankled some in her Russian émigré community. How could a nun be out in a bar, asking customers if they had a place to spend the night? Even her good friend Berdyaev wondered what really she was trying to accomplish in running a homeless shelter and soup kitchen. But he supported her, as did those who saw the clarity of her essays about the love of God and love of neighbor requiring each other, the life of Christ bearing witness to this "mystery of community."

In describing the authentic gospel type of faith, the only really Christ-like "religion," Mother Maria sounds what is the theme of many of her essays, published at the same time as she's putting together soups and stews from food she'd foraged from greengrocers, butchers, and bakers at the Paris Les Halles markets.

> Christ gave us two commandments: to love God and to love our fellow man. Everything else, even the commandments contained in the Beatitudes, is merely an elaboration of these two commandments, which contain within themselves the totality of Christ's "Good News." Furthermore, Christ's earthly life is nothing other than the revelation of the mystery of love of God and love of the neighbor. These are, in sum, not only the true but the only measure of all things. And it is remarkable that their truth is found only in the way they are linked together. Love for man alone leads us into the blind alley of an anti-Christian humanism, out of which the only exit is, at times, the rejection of the individual human being and love toward him in the name of all mankind. Love for God without love for man, however, is condemned: "You hypocrite, how can you love God whom you have not seen,

if you hate your brother whom you have seen" (1 Jn 4:20). Their linkage is not simply a combination of two great truths taken from two spiritual worlds. Their linkage is the union of two parts of a single whole. These two commandments are two aspects of a single truth. Destroy either one of them and you destroy truth as a whole.[11]

In a number of periodicals, including Berdyaev's, she waged a publicity campaign not just for her house of hospitality but for her vision of liturgy meeting life, faith active in the world, or, in the term we have heard in this book, "becoming what you pray." She called her movement "Orthodox Action," a not-so-subtle knock on the typical obsession of Eastern Orthodoxy with liturgy, iconography, and church rules. She knew where to aim her criticism as well as how to mount her arguments about what is central to Christianity. Understanding the enormous popularity of the Mother of God to Eastern as well as Western Christians, she wrote several essays on the "motherhood of God." This was not, as we might think after the emergence of feminism, an argument about gender and God or the inclusive language that should be used in theology and liturgy. As Natalia Ermolaev has shown brilliantly, Mother Maria puts forward the Virgin Mary as an image of how to love as God loves. It is a love that is selfless, that is willing to suffer along with others, love very much like a mother's love.

> Only that maternal love is truly Christian which sees in her child a real image of God inherent not only in him but in all people, given to her in trust, as her responsibility, which she must develop and strengthen in him in preparation for the unavoidable life of sacrifice along the Christian path, for that challenge of bearing the cross facing all Christians. With this kind of love the mother will be more aware of other children's misfortunes, she will be more attentive to their neglect. Her relationship with the rest of humanity will be in Christ as the result of the presence of Christian love in her heart. This, of course, is the most radical example.[12]

Among the last things Mother Maria made in the Ravensbrück camp were two embroideries. One has been saved and I have seen it myself, through the kindness of Helene Klepinin-Arjakovsky, daughter of Fr. Dmitri Klepinin, Mother Maria's chaplain, who died in the camps as she did. It is a copy of the famous Bayeux tapestry, the invasion of Normandy in 1066, but clearly what the camp internees knew had happened in June 1944 with the Allies again invading to end the war and save Europe from the Nazis. The other embroidery, lost but recreated in a painted version, was a distinctive type of Marian icon, one that Mother Maria had also seen in a fresco, namely, of the Mother of God holding not the child Jesus but the God-Man on the cross.[13] As any icon, this is not an attempt to capture reality as in a photograph but rather to express the truth of what the Gospels describe. The prophet Simeon describes, in the Gospel of Luke, at the presentation of the child Jesus in the Temple, a sword as piercing the Virgin Mary's heart. Maria Skobtsova sees this sword as the cross on which the Virgin's son is tortured and killed.[14]

The Mother of God is one of the very few of his disciples who stand beneath the cross in the hours in which he suffered and died. Mary is there, just as she was in the cave at Bethlehem, at the marriage celebration in Cana, numerous times as Jesus preached and healed. And she will again be there when the tomb is found empty, when he ascends, and when the Spirit comes down to make the disciples the community, the church. The Mother of God is one of the most profound and ancient images not just of the church, there always with Jesus, but of each Christian, loving in compassion.

> If a person is not only the image of God but also the image of the Mother of God, then he should also be able to see the image of God and the image of the Mother of God in every other person. In our God-motherly soul not only is the birth of the Son of God announced and Christ born, but there also develops the keen perception of Christ's image in other souls. And in this sense, the God-motherly part of the human soul begins to see other people as its children; it adopts them for itself. . . . But insofar as we must strive to follow her path, and as her image is the image of our human soul, so we must also perceive God and the Son in every person. God, because each person is the image and likeness of God; the Son, because as it gives birth to Christ within itself, the

human soul thereby adopts the whole Body of Christ for itself, the whole of God's humanity, and every person individually.[15]

A critical spirit is characteristic of Mother Maria's approach to all aspects of the life of faith, to liturgy, prayer, church teachings and history, also monasticism, of which she became a part. What is more, there is a powerful realization of experience in her vision and a demand to see how an idea, belief, or even liturgical text works out in practice, how it makes a difference in a person's life. Very much a woman of the twentieth century, of the Russian Revolution, of the emigration, of the Great Depression, and of both world wars, she assimilated these perspectives from all the intellectual sources at work in her experience. She drew from the poetry of the Silver Age giants and the political ferment that led to the Revolution, as well as the great minds in the Russian emigration in Paris. Her essays probing the work of early monastics in reaching out to those in need is a vivid example of the critical historical method not just arguing her claims for more service to the poor but of a more accurate view of the evolution of monasticism itself. Much more of this illuminating inquiry will be seen below in her still riveting analysis of different psychological orientations to religion, the diverse motivations, visions, and behaviors she presents as different religious "types."

But as the lines from her essay on the imitation of the Mother of God also make clear, Skobtsova was far from being just a careful, objective historian. Not only was the fire of a poet in her, there was also the wild, passionate love that marked her relationships and her zeal for the neighbor in need. There was also the authentic political and social activist who was mayor of Anapa, a participant in the politics of the Russian Revolution. Especially during the occupation of Paris, but before it during the Depression as well, she applied for her hostel's cafeteria to be recognized as a municipal canteen for emergency feeding, thus enabling the house to receive public support for meals, medical treatment, and shelter. She also used her essays to raise serious questions about state propaganda and official silence. With the rise of fascism, and the dehumanizing rhetoric and destructive forces being implemented on Nazi territory, she spoke against the tendency to distance oneself from these forces, to find ways to live around them. She must have been convinced they would come to devour the rest of Europe in time, and she was right.

The essay on imitating the Mother of God echoes the point of view Mother Maria consistently presents in her writing throughout the 1930s and into the 1940s, namely, the impossibility of the Christian or any moral person avoiding engagement and responsibility for the suffering unleashed in the world around her. This is the recurring theme of Dorothy Day's writing too. One need not despair at the heroic feats of the saints of centuries gone by, their fasting, miracles, and extreme behavior. Look around you and you will find everything that is in the pages of the gospels—the sick, the despairing, the hungry and confused. You are to be there with them, "co-suffering" as did Christ and his mother.[16] Skobtsova dug into church history and high-lighted the monastics who communed with God in the daily prayer of the hours, the psalms, and the scriptures, but who then went and enacted these prayers in the prayer of loving the neighbor, the "sacrament of the brother/sister."[17] Prayer is not restricted to the esthetic beauty of church architecture, sacred music, the gaze of the holy ones from the icons, or the texts of power and consolation. Prayer also importantly consists in filling the sacks with day-old bread, the day's reminders of produce and fish, the steaming pots and the bowls that hungry hands clutch, warmth of food but also of care and companionship making a weekday supper a feast.

Sorting out Types of Religion

An essay from 1937, "Types of Religious Lives," was only redis-covered in 1996 in the papers of Maria Skobtsova's mother, Sophia Pilenko, in the Bahkmatiev archives at Columbia University by He-lene Klepinin-Arjakovsky and her son, Antoine Arjakovsky, an his-torian, and published posthumously in the 1990s. Outside the culture and community of traditional Russian Orthodoxy, some of the vari-eties or types do not immediately appear relevant or lucid. The first, the "synodal," refers to that period when Peter the Great reformed the Russian church, removing the historical patriarch at its head, plac-ing over it instead a Minister of Cult or Religion, and making what used to be the gathering or synod of bishops a much smaller, tightly controlled legislative group. There was in this supposedly Lutheran model little sense of the church as conciliar, a council of all members of the church or at least, as in the historical councils, a council composed of the bishops and other clerical and lay members.

There had been a truly groundbreaking, reformative Council of Moscow in 1917–18, which restored not only the patriarchate but also much of the conciliar shape of the church, a gathering of bishops, clergy, monastics, and laity to actually deliberate and administer the church.[18] Despite this, religion in the "synodal" type is all about the externals—making sure that even in the tiniest garage church there is some kind of icon screen, some kind of censer for incensing, some version of the seven-branched candle on the altar, and of course the vestments and the sacrosanct Slavonic text understood by very few even among the clergy. This is religion that is "business as usual," something bedrock in Russian national identity, such as communion once a year after confession because this is the rule, otherwise no communing. Children are dutifully baptized, taught essentially the rules of the church, some basics. The various ranks and awards of the clergy and of the bishops are of enormous importance in what is at root an "official," state approved and controlled and supporting cult. Some chalices are so huge it takes several deacons to lift them. The covers on the Gospel book are heavy and ornate, the performance of the services stylized and overly dramatic, the chanting style obscuring rather than communicating the texts of the lessons at the liturgy. The fasts and feasts of the church year are laid out in scrupulous detail, though the majority of people do not observe them in practice. This is, in short, religion of the most elaborate, operatic, dramatic style, with huge cathedrals and long processions and services that consume hours. And yet, as Sara Miles would put it, such religion or church is very, very small and quite empty of humanity and feeling. Thus, in actual data, few attend services or observe the rest of the rules on any regular basis.

The "ritual" type is another very typically Russian and Orthodox way of experiencing and doing religion, one in which, again, externals are everything. In reality, the ritual type is that practiced in the synodal style of religion. There is an absolute character, a supreme order to doing things "by the book," according to the most precise rubrics. The church calendar, what one can and cannot do in various seasons of it, the intricate order of the services, the fanatical devotion to the Church language, Slavonic that is not accessible or understandable to most worshippers. There is debate, even conflict, over small details of ritual practice and doctrine. Creativity is taboo, following the rules and rubrics paramount. Nothing can be changed in the church because it is believed, wholly inaccurately, that nothing ever has changed. But, Mother Maria writes,

> Christ, who approached prostitutes, tax collectors and sinners, can hardly be the teacher of those who are afraid to soil their pristine garments, who are completely devoted to the letter, who live only by the rules, and who govern their whole life according to the rules.[19]

She even names the two great monastic centers, Valaam in Russia and Mount Athos in Greece, as the pinnacles of ritual correctness. These are the monastic idealists to which ritualists model themselves. But it is, to use the New Testament lines, the Sabbath that triumphs over and rules humanity in this ritual form, not the Sabbath/ritual that exists for the good of us all.

The "esthetic" type is religion as art, whether in images, architecture, music, texts, or even history. Not surprisingly, it is the externals that again dominate, that define correct religiosity. An artist herself, Skobtsova surely does not reject beauty in expression, particularly in the service of God, lifting the minds and hearts of people to heaven, to God's peace and joy. In a passage that is profoundly moving, she sees,

> Christ Himself departs, quietly and invisibly, from the sanctuary that is protected by a splendid iconostasis. The singing will continue to resound, clouds of incense will still rise, the faithful will be overcome by the ecstatic beauty of the services. But Christ will go out onto the church steps and mingle with the crowd: the poor, lepers, the desperate, embittered, the holy fools. Christ will go out into the streets, the prisons, the hospitals, the low haunts and dives. Again and again Christ lays down his life for his friends . . . those who study and understand the world's beauty, will not comprehend Christ's beauty, and will not let Him into the church because behind Him there will follow a crowd of people deformed

by sin, by ugliness, drunkenness, depravity, and hate. Then their chant will fade away in the air, the smell of incense will disperse, and someone will say to them: "I was hungry and you gave me no food. I was thirsty and you gave me no drink. I was a stranger and you did not welcome me, naked and you did not clothe me, sick and in prison and you did not visit me."[20]

The "ascetical" type of religion comes easily to those in the Eastern church, as it does for Catholics, given the very important place of monasticism in these traditions and the prominence of fasting and the downplaying of the material, the physical, the sexual, also, sadly, of the feminine and often the human. Always plagued by the Christological union of the divine and the human, Christianity, as Diarmaid MacCulloch has noted, has waffled back and forth between both, not only in defining Christ's identity but in spelling out how the Christian life should be enacted.[21]

Skobtsova once more is the discerning thinker in talking about devotion to past tradition and the details of ritual and ascetical practice. Asceticism is absolutely part of the great traditions of Judaism and Christianity, rooted in human nature, the human condition after the Fall. In itself, asceticism is transformative, and the consciousness of needing to change, to be transformed, is omnipresent in the scriptures, alive in movements like monasticism. But when asceticism becomes turned in on itself, becomes an end in itself and the primary end of faith, distortion has come to rule. A passage with dramatic attention to everyday life reveals Mother Maria's insight.

Today, in a time of plague [1937] as a rule one counts one's daily earnings and in the evening goes to the cinema. There is no talk of the courage of despair because there is no despair. There is only utter contentment and total spiritual quiescence. The tragic nature of the psychology of the contemporary person is self-evident. And every fiery prophet, every preacher will be in a quandary: on which side of the café table should he sit? How can he cast light on the nature of today's stock market gains? How can he break through, trample, and destroy this sticky, gooey mass that surrounds the soul of today's philistine? How can he set the people's hearts on fire with his words?[22]

Of course there is need for an asceticism far more relevant than what kind of oil was used in this dish, can one have an egg, cheese, or olive oil today? One can still hear such debate and concern among many devout keepers of the fasting rules! Authentic asceticism will not be legalistic or sectarian but truly catholic and really practical. As Dorothy Day would often argue, working for economic and political change so that inequality and the suffering of poverty could be removed—this was as important as saying many prayers and avoiding meat on Fridays.

In concluding the essay, Maria Skobtsova saves her greatest enthusiasm and best lines for describing the "gospel," literally "evangelical," type of religious life as that closest to the heart and actions of Christ himself. It's not the usual meaning of "evangelical" as a Reformation or revival-based movement. Rather, the emphasis is on the gospel and, even deeper, on Christ. Skobtsova speaks of a "christification" as the translation has it. As awkward as this sounds, the vision is basic: "It is no longer I who live but Christ who lives in me" (Gal. 2:20). Every one of us is an image, an icon of Christ. We are, again as she put it, "living icons" or, one could say, "walking sacraments," who do what Christ did and, by our lives, say what Christ said. This is no simplistic "imitation." Just as "churching" the world, a leading goal of the younger people in Skobtsova's Russian emigration, was more than hanging crosses and icons in your home and lighting candles before them, more than constructing more church buildings, having more services, reading more religious books, the same is true for becoming more Christ-like.

And essential to this is the two-fold commitment Christ himself repeatedly emphasized. You love God with all your being. You likewise love your neighbor. Mother Maria draws on many of the other themes she has written about, following the model of the Mother of God, recognizing the neighbor is Christ come to us as a guest, stranger, hungry, thirsty, and so on. One never loses by giving or by loving: one only and always gains, is gifted with even more. Emptying oneself is not destructive. Rather this is God's essential orientation toward all creation, and thus to so act is to act in a most godly fashion.

Mother Maria argues that love for the neighbor is an essential outgrowth of the Eucharist. The sacrament of the altar must then be celebrated on the altar that is the heart of the sister or brother in need.

It is the liturgy "outside church walls," the "liturgy after the liturgy," as John Chrysostom described it.

> But if at the center the Church's life there is this sacrificial, self-giving Eucharistic love, then where are the Church's boundaries, where is the periphery of this center? Here it is possible to speak of the whole of Christianity as an eternal offering of the divine liturgy beyond church walls. . . . It means that we must offer the bloodless sacrifice, the sacrifice of self-surrendering love not only in a specific place, upon the altar of a particular temple; the whole world becomes the one altar of a single temple; and for this universal liturgy we must offer our hearts, like bread and wine, in order that they may be transformed into Christ's love, that He may be born in them, and that they may become hearts of God's humanity, and that He may give these hearts of ours as food for the world, that he bring the whole world into communion with these hearts of ours that have been offered up, so that in this way we may be one with Him. . . . Then truly in all ways Christ will be in all.[23]

Sara Miles found church too small; so did Barbara Brown Taylor. We know this all too well. Congregations turned in on themselves, tribal, isolated from the rest of their neighborhoods. Liturgy becomes an end, esthetic or otherwise, in itself. Maria Skobtsova wanted to push the liturgy out of the walls of the church. She clearly also wanted to push out the church walls in another sense, urging merciful care to the world and those suffering there.

The Prayer of Solidarity and Witness, Caring for the Persecuted

Mother Maria argued for a kind of spiritual formula that seemed to contradict mathematics. If I give — a piece of bread, a ruble, my love — I should be now in deficit of that bread, money, or compassion. But no: in the realm of the Spirit, in God who, as she learned from Bulgakov, is constantly emptying himself out and giving himself away, one never loses! One only gains. It defies our math and contradicts our will to self-preservation, our inherent egoism.[24]

Defiant in her rejection of the Bolshevism she saw dominate in Russia, Mother Maria also turned on capitalism in the West. All around her in Depression Paris, she saw what happened to what we call the 99 percent today, while the privileged 1 percent flourished. One cannot claim freedom and virtue for such an inhumane system that values profit before everything else. Even before September 1, 1939, she saw in the rise of fascism the future as one of destruction and war. Her teacher and confessor, Father Bulgakov, likewise saw the fascist future, the persecution of the Jews and any others defined as threats to the state. The Paris in which they had worked to educate and inspire Russian and other refugees to shelter, feed, and clothe the victims of exile and the depression, this became the Paris of the Nazi Occupation. Mother Maria would bring water and food to the French Jews gathered and held at the cycling stadium Vel d'Hiver in July 1942. She would smuggle several children out in trash cans.[25] She and Father Dmitri Klepinin would create cover papers for Jews and others targeted by the Gestapo for roundup and extermination. Baptismal certificates were produced, making them members of the parish of the Mother of God's Protection located in the Rue de Lourmel chapel, for which Mother Maria had sewn and woven tapestries, icons, and vestments.

> [T]he laws of spiritual life are the exact opposite of the laws of the material world. According to spiritual law, every spiritual treasure given away not only returns to the giver like a whole and unbroken ruble given to a beggar, but it grows and becomes more valuable. He who gives, acquires, and he who becomes poor, becomes rich. We give away our human riches and in return we receive much greater gifts from God, while he who gives away his human soul receives in return eternal bliss, the divine gift of possessing the Kingdom of heaven. How does he receive that gift? By absenting himself from Christ in an act of the uttermost self-renunciation and love, he offers himself to others. . . . [T]hen he meets Christ himself face to face in the one to whom he offers himself. And in communion with him he communes with Christ himself. . . . Thus the mystery of union with man becomes the mystery of union with God. What was given away returns,

for the love that is poured out never diminishes the source of that love, for the source of love in our hearts is Love itself. It is Christ.[26]

Mother Maria and several of the house staff were eventually taken into custody by the Gestapo. She, her son, Yuri, Father Dmitri, and Ilya Fundaminsky were sent off to concentration camps. She survived the longest, volunteering to take the place of another inmate in the truck to the gas chambers on March 31, 1945, just weeks before the liberation of Ravensbrück.

That such a gifted though unusual woman with so colorful a life could become such an atypical nun, that she could become an important voice in the Russian intellectual circles in Paris and do such good for so many marginalized people—all of this was both improbable and remarkable. That she along with her companions became the first "new saints" of the twenty-first century outside Russia is even more astounding. The Moscow patriarchate ignored the documents collected on her life and writings by Helene Klepinin-Arjakovsky and Antoine Arjakovsky. In May of 2004, after the decision had been made by the synod of the Ecumenical Patriarchate in Istanbul, at the home cathedral of Mother Maria's home diocese/church in Paris, she, her son, Yuri, Fr. Dmitri and Ilya Fundaminsky, all of whom died in the camps, were made saints. Like Christ, as the canonization document said, they gave their lives for their friends, trying to save those the Nazis determined unworthy of life. They became what they prayed.

In her time, and this would also be true of Dorothy Day, Mother Maria was known for her action, for somehow locating those who, in turn, find the funding for not only the house of hospitality in the city but also for a residence for the elderly in the suburbs. This was done during the Great Depression, by Russians of the emigration themselves challenged by poverty and displacement. But, also like Dorothy Day, Maria Skobtsova knew the importance of public relations, of effectively communicating the ideas behind her work, the goals of her outreach, of the "sacrament of the brother/sister" she argued had to follow the sacrament of the altar. She was writing and speaking at gatherings in the middle of the century, the time of fascism, the Great Depression, the Holocaust.

She did not live to see the Cold War and nuclear proliferation, which became major targets of Dorothy Day's writing. She was able to identify the inhumanity not only of the Soviets but of the Nazis. She spoke out against the Depression's greatest destruction—on immigrants, the elderly, children, workers, and their families. And she was not too pious to absolve the church from its ignorance of suffering in favor of ritual, nationalism, or esthetic attachment. She knew all too well the identification of services with Russian belonging, of the esthetic fixation on the beauty of the liturgy and its music, and other misdirected forms of piety. She contrasted all these tendencies with the straightforward living out what one prayed and received in service of the neighbor, an approach she termed "evangelical," simply "of the gospel."

All the Way to Heaven: Dorothy Day's Path

We were just sitting there talking when Peter Maurin came in. We were just sitting there talking when lines of people began to form, saying, "We need bread." We could not say, "Go, be thou filled." If there were six small loaves and a few fishes, we had to divide them. There was always bread.

We were just sitting there talking and people moved in on us. Let those who can take it, take it. Some moved out and that made room for more.

And somehow the walls expanded.

We were just sitting there talking and someone said, "Let's all go live on a farm."

It was all as casual as that, I often think. It just came about. It just happened.

I found myself, a barren woman, the joyful mother of children. It is not easy always to be joyful, to keep in mind the duty of delight.

The most significant thing about *The Catholic Worker* is poverty, some say.

The most significant thing is community, others say. We are not alone anymore.

But the final word is love. At times it has been, in the words of Father Zossima, a harsh and dreadful thing, and our faith in love has been tried through fire.

We cannot love God unless we love each other. We know Him in the breaking of bread, and we know each other in the breaking of bread, and we are not alone anymore. Heaven is a banquet and life is a banquet, too, even with a crust, where there is companionship.

We have all known the long loneliness and we have learned that the only solution is love and that love comes with community.

It all happened while we sat there talking, and it is still going on.[27]

A Young Radical, A Radical All Her Life

Thus did Dorothy Day conclude her autobiography, summarizing in a few very beautiful, powerfully packed lines what was for her a lifetime of prayer and work in the community of the Catholic Worker movement. Dorothy was such a good writer! The phrasing, the cadence, just the right words, the core leaps out at you in these lines, and you know exactly what she is feeling. You feel it too. An artist and activist, she hungered for love but also justice. She followed all the radicals in the first decades of the last century, was one with them in the calls for unions, just wages, decent health care, better education, and support for families. War was a monster she never was able to justify, hence even when it cost the movement, her stance was that the gospel was about pacifism, the rejection of war, and the seeking of peace.

If you think that "love is the measure" throughout her writings and life, you have listened well, but food, eating, and feeding those in need is just as much a principal theme. Bread was always there, and there was always something that could be shared with the hungry: coffee, cheese or apple butter sandwiches, soup. But there was another bread always present, Christ, the bread of life. She communed every day, tried to have a chapel with the sacrament in every house if at all possible and, if not, then prayers in community, the omnipresent cross, and images of the virgin and saints.

Dorothy Day at
Maryfarm, Easton,
Pennsylvania, ca. 1938.
Photo courtesy of
Department of Special
Collections and
University Archives,
Marquette University
Libraries.

She was not a wannabe monastic, though she was in fact a Benedictine associate who prayed the daily prayer of the hours in addition
to daily communion, retreats, meditation, and readings from scripture
and other spiritual materials. The liturgy and prayer were inseparable
from the movement and its communities, even if individual members
were less than believing or devout. And while her spiritual practice
and frequently her attitude toward the church were quite traditional,
she was not imprisoned in the least by unquestioning loyalty. Numerous times, explicit in letters and diary entries and columns, she was
openly, rigorously critical of the institutional church, its clergy, and
its policies.[28] She once told a disillusioned colleague that the church
had always been full of corrupt, dysfunctional popes, bishops, abbots,
and other leaders from the very beginning.[29]

"All the way to heaven, is heaven. . . ." So went Teresa of Avila's line, concluding, "all the way to hell is hell." Dorothy Day was very fond of this saying, and the enormous collection of writings she created echoes both sides of the proverb. Robert Ellsberg used it as the title of the edition of her letters.[30] Her voice was strident—demanding political and social change for a more just society. Then she would record in her columns, not just in her journal and private letters, her deep discouragement, frustration, and exhaustion with the endless stream of those in misery who surrounded her in the Worker houses.

Dorothy, a convert, became a model of faithful Catholic practice in daily prayer and communion, regular retreats and confession, respect for the bishops and clergy. Yet she was at the same time ruthless in identifying their dysfunctionality, ineptitude, and corruption. She realized that she would have to work around the institutional church and opposed any official status or relation of either the Worker movement or the houses to the Catholic Church. She insisted on dedication and loyalty from Worker resident members, yet she could react in exasperation at the lives, actions, and values of young people, despite the experimentation and extreme nonconformity of her own youth. Her wild youth perhaps made her rigid and puritanical when it came to sex, divorce, and other moral questions. She used to cut off communications with Worker members or ex-members who divorced. She was surprisingly traditional with younger women in the 1960s and '70s given her own liberated style of life in her twenties.

She opposed war even when it was hugely popular, during World War II. She refused to participate in air raid drills and was arrested several times between 1955 and 1958. Once, she appeared before a judge who called the protestors "murderers." She was arrested numerous times in her life, the last time in 1973 for protests in California for Cesar Chavez and the United Farm Workers. For all this public persona as a person of radical conscience and action, she was intensely knit into the Worker communities, those in which she lived as well as others. The complexity of relationships and the challenges of living in community have been documented by Worker members over the years.[31]

In the more frequently viewed and used photographs, Dorothy looks like a sweet and affectionate grandmother. There are numerous images of her surrounded by her own grandchildren, and late in life great-grandchildren and younger members of the *Catholic Worker* paper or one of the houses. One shows her gingerly walking along a path at the house the movement then had in Tivoli, New York.

In some of the videos of interviews with her, and in older film footage, the mantle of dignified age and sweetness is blown off almost instantly. Even in her last years she was articulate, outspoken, feisty—even combative. Her responses were never considered or delayed. She had opinions and very decided, strong ones on everything, particularly political questions and issues of social justice. Now her letters and her diary have been published, edited by writer and publisher Robert Ellsberg, who worked with her the last years of her life. There is also a new biography utilizing these sources, by Jim Forest, who also worked with her.[32]

It is impossible to pretty up what was also, as in Maria Skobtsova's case, a complex, colorful, even wild life. Born in Brooklyn in 1897, her father's profession as a sportswriter took the family to the west coast, to Oakland, California, and then to Chicago. Her childhood and adolescence were upper middle class. The family was not at all religious, but she did attend an Episcopal church along with her siblings and was exposed through Sunday school to the bible. She started studies at the University of Illinois, Urbana-Champaign, but left after two years, impatient with college life, enthusiastic about socialism, and itching to work as a journalist. When the family returned to New York for her father to work at the *Telegraph,* she was able to find a job after much hunting with the socialist paper *The Call.* This was really the beginning of her vocation and profession.

She absorbed the ethnic diversity of the Lower East Side, the wretched poverty and miserable working conditions of immigrants. She sampled through conversations and connections much of the radical left spectrum in the city at that time, from the anarchists and socialists to the IWW, the Industrial Workers of the World, or Wobblies.[33] She wasn't yet twenty and was hanging out with beat cops and at saloons with labor organizers and political operatives. She counted among her friends and mentors communist party members, eventually including leaders Elizabeth Gurley Flynn and Mike Gold. She was clubbed at a demonstration but came to know much about the Russian Revolution, the socialist vision, and the ongoing battle for workers' and women's rights, covering demonstration after rally after protest march. Photos of her from this period demolish the grandmother image. She's tall, beautiful, stunningly so, and with a face so intense you are immediately drawn to her gaze. She left *The Call* and moved on to *The Masses*, a monthly magazine edited by Max Eastman and the gathering place for politically left writers and thinkers. But the magazine was raided and shut down by the feds, and Dorothy moved on again to cover suffragist demonstrations and was jailed with participants for the first time after a march in front of the White House protesting involvement in World War I. The jail experience, with a hunger strike and poor treatment even in a women's detention center, was deeply disturbing yet a transformation for her.

Dorothy's life was hardly just political protest and radical journalism. She became a regular at a tavern frequented by lowlife locals, writers, and political activists. She became a drinking pal of Eugene O'Neill, actually more a friend. Later she fell for Lionel Moise, moved in with him, got pregnant, and had an abortion, only to be abandoned. She would relocate to Chicago to be with him later on. There was a brief marriage to an older man, Berkeley Tobey, who she knew from *The Masses*. There was work at *The Liberator* in Chicago, and at the *Chicago Post*, and the experience of being locked up after a raid on what feds thought was a house of prostitution. She published *The Eleventh Virgin*, a disguised autobiographical piece turned into fiction, and made money from it and from its screen rights.

With some of her money from the sale of the piece, she bought a cottage on Staten Island that would become a home to her, her companion Forster Batterham, and their daughter. Numerous photos of the couple show a radiant, happy relationship, a singularly attractive twenty-something with a bob haircut. But the relationship, deep and passionate as it was, would not last. Dorothy's only child, Tamar Theresa, came from this relationship. In the years leading up to Tamar's birth, Dorothy was reading, inquiring, and finding herself drawn into religion, specifically the Catholic Church. Batterham was not able to deal with much of what Dorothy threw at him—neither parenthood nor a child, and decidedly not religion. Day wrote an essay, "Having a Baby," that *The New Masses* published, and excerpts from it in her anthologies are today still striking, moving. As a single parent, she continued freelance work for the Anti-Imperialism League, for the Fellowship of Reconciliation, as well as for MGM and briefly for Pathé, which took her and Tamar to Hollywood. Letters to Forster continued for years. They express Dorothy's need and passion for him, truly the love of her life, and her grief at the end of the relationship.[34]

Something New: The *Catholic Worker*

After covering a trip to Washington, DC, the police brutality against protestors, and finally, after delays, the Hunger March on December 8, 1932, Day met Peter Maurin, an enigmatic French activist, almost a holy fool. Yet there was something profound in the simplicity, power, and radicalism of his thinking about direct engagement with the poor, war, and many other issues of social justice. He must have intuited that Dorothy, with her writing gifts, was the one to begin the newspaper that would get out the message, would incite readers to reflect on injustice and then act. She felt Maurin's efforts to educate her were almost harassment, yet she also recognized some kind of spiritual genius. She insisted the name of the paper grasp something of the class inequality that the Great Depression, with its unemployment and the loss of savings and homes, made a national catastrophe. The vision of FDR's "New Deal" was just forming. On May 1, 1933, the first issue of the *Catholic Worker* was published and offered for a penny on Union Square.

Space does not permit elaboration of Maurin's unusual, utopian, almost anarchic Christian vision. He distrusted government and most social movements and groups. His conviction was that real economic, social, and spiritual change would occur simply if people saw the needs of the neighbor and met them. Hospitality houses were part of this vision, and soon the space rented by Dorothy for her and Tamar and to house the paper's volunteers became such a place. While Peter remained for the rest of his life a kind of sage to the movement, a mystic and teacher with a constant stream of aphoristic sayings, his vision was really incapable of being put into practice. Unable and unwilling to use the language that radicals had for years, to demand better wages, working conditions, more action of the government for those in need, Maurin disdained protests or politics of any kind, as well as government and its programs such as those of the New Deal that he saw as displacing the works of mercy that could and should be done by individuals.

While many of his ideals would remain part of the Catholic Worker movement, clearly it was Dorothy who was able to begin an actual organization, one that could both publish the paper as well as acquire, staff with volunteer members, and run the houses of hospitality. In the winter of 1933, on December 11, the first house of hospitality, a rented apartment, was open to women with no place to stay. Soon other apartments were also rented on East 15th and East 7th Streets for men as well as for women, and then a house at 144 Charles Street. The pattern of the Worker soon was established — young, idealistic, and generous volunteers to staff the houses and get out the paper, receiving in return room and board. Artist Ade Bethune came in those early days. Her art would adorn the paper's masthead from that time on. Some of those who came at the start would spend the better part of their lives with the Worker, such as Stanley Vishnewski, for one. Most came for a time, moving on in their lives. Dorothy relied on priests like Pacifique Roy and John Hugo, both rigorous in their understanding of how to live the gospel, in sync with Peter Maurin's demanding views of Christian life.

Dorothy created a literature through her regular columns in the paper. She later called it "On Pilgrimage," but titled it earlier as "Day after Day." She pulled together a number of columns into *House of Hospitality* in 1939, then a collection of them as *On Pilgrimage* in 1948. She published an account of her own journey to the church in the form of a letter to her skeptical brother, *From Union Square to Rome* (1938). Eventually she would publish an autobiography, *The Long Loneliness* (1952), but many aspects of her earlier life would be left out. Following Maurin's ideas about getting back to the land, growing food for the community and those who visited, Worker members bought and ran a farm in Easton, Pennsylvania, later closing and selling it, relocating to Newburgh, New York.

Houses of hospitality spread throughout the country. Many different locations in Manhattan would be used as houses of hospitality, also for some years a dilapidated old mansion in Tivoli, upstate. By the time of Dorothy's death in 1980, there were over eighty houses. There were notable members, many of whom had profound yet complicated relationships with her—Ammon Hennacy, Michael Harrington, Tom Cornell, Jim Forest, Robert Ellsberg. There are so many it is impossible to list them all. She corresponded with Thomas Merton, worked with Cesar Chavez and Dan Berrigan, and was arrested with A. J. Muste, later with actor Judith Malina, and for the last time in 1973 in California, in protests for the UFW.

In many ways, Dorothy became the heart of the movement. Individual Worker houses and members would take on their own character, their specific work and place in their own community. There was, however, a pattern she established. There was a central place for prayer and the sacraments. There was hands-on care for those in need who came to the houses, feeding, clothing, getting them to medical care. But she was also most importantly the voice of the movement, through her lectures all around the country for decades and her many articles in periodicals like *America* and *Commonweal*. But most especially her voice rang through the *Catholic Worker* newspaper. There are quite literally volumes worth of her writings just from the paper, not including, as mentioned here, correspondence and her diary. Quotations from a few selected texts will give us a sense of Dorothy's vision of how prayer permeated all her work and life.

> Our lives are made up of little miracles day by day. That splendid globe of sun, one street wide, framed by the foot of East Fourteenth Street in early-morning mists that greeted me on my way to Mass was a miracle that lifted up my heart. . . . Sunshine in the middle of January is indeed a present. We get presents, lots of them, around *The Catholic Worker* office. During the holidays a turkey, a ham, baskets of groceries, five pounds of butter, plum puddings, flannel nightgowns and doll-babies, sheets, washrags, and blankets descended on us. . . . We appealed in our last issue for beds, and eight beds came. . . . A great many of our friends urge us to put our paper on a businesslike basis. But this isn't business, it's a movement. And we don't know anything about

business here anyway. Well-meaning friends say, "But people get tired of appeals." We don't believe it. Probably most of our friends live as we do, from day to day and from hand to mouth, and as they get, they are willing to give. So we shall continue to appeal and we know that the paper will go on.[35]

Today we are not content with little achievements, with small beginnings. . . . We should look to St. Teresa of Avila, who was not content to be like those people who proceeded with the pace of hens about God's business, but like those people who on their own account were greatly daring in what they wished to do for God. It is we ourselves that we have to think about, no one else. . . . Do what comes to hand. . . . After all, God is with us. It shows too much conceit to trust to ourselves, to be discouraged at what we ourselves can accomplish. It is lacking faith in God to be discouraged. After all, we are going to proceed with His help. We offer Him what we are going to do. If He wishes it to prosper, it will. We must depend solely on Him. Work as though everything depended on ourselves, and pray as though everything depended on God, as St. Ignatius says. . . . In what time I have my impulse is to self-criticism and examination of conscience, and I am constantly humiliated at my own imperfections and at my halting progress. Perhaps I deceive myself here, too, and excuse my lack of recollection. But I do know how small I am and how little I can do and I beg You, Lord, to help me, for I cannot help myself.[36]

In the columns of the paper, there are graphic descriptions of daily life at the houses of hospitality, of absolutely bizarre behavior by residents, one of whom bathes and medicates the house cat, other scenes of the long lines of hungry people in the cold, before sunrise, waiting for a cup of coffee and a couple slices of bread. Residents steal and fight, and, despite the prayerful commitment to never be discouraged, Dorothy is beside herself with frustration and sadness. So many in misery, and all that they do to provide food, clothing, and shelter is a drop in the bucket. What destruction poverty brings to the lives of decent people! She shares that praying about it helped her to see that losing her temper helps no one, that it is monstrous to be harsh to

someone who is so down and dependent and that it was good to realize that the miseries of those who come to the houses do not completely crush them—there is leftover rage to vent on each other—not
necessarily a bad thing.

> I should know by this time that just because I feel that everything
> is useless and going to pieces and badly done and futile, it is not
> really that way at all. Everything is all right. It is in the hands
> of God.[37]

> Every morning about four hundred men come to Mott Street to
> be fed. The radio is cheerful, the smell of coffee is a good smell,
> the air of the morning is fresh and not too cold, but my heart
> bleeds as I pass the lines of men in front of the store which is our
> headquarters. . . . It is hard to say, matter-of-factly and cheerfully,
> "Good morning." . . . One felt more like taking their hands and
> saying, "Forgive us—let us forgive each other! All of us who are
> more comfortable, who have a place to sleep, three meals a day,
> work to do—we are responsible for your condition. We are guilty
> of each other's sins. We must bear each other's burdens. Forgive
> us and may God forgive us all!"[38]

This scene reminds her of the disciples with that stranger who
was Jesus at Emmaus and how they only knew it was he for sure
when he sat down and ate with them, breaking the bread. How many
loaves have they given out at the Worker? Thirteen thousand, five
hundred in the last month. Knowing the least of His children, they
are knowing Christ. In column after column, Dorothy talks about
her travels to Los Angeles, Chicago, Detroit, Cleveland, New Or-
leans, with more accounts of parents starving with small children,
homeless and desperate people. She describes the unemployed lining
up on the street outside the Catholic Worker house on Mott Street,
waiting for a cup of coffee and piece of bread. She tells of the pain of
having to listen to affluent Catholics tell how much of a tragedy the
sight of so much degradation was for them, that there was nothing
they could do to help the starving and unemployed, and that workers
beg their employers to "save" them from unions.[39] Do we not still

hear this from politicians and right-wing media people, claiming that food stamps and unemployment benefits are "hurting" the poor? And that if allowed total freedom from regulation, the market would make everyone's life better?

Dorothy's columns are full of images of suffering during the Great Depression. She describes, in February of 1940, watching a man pretty much in rags sitting in the subway car opposite her, till the last stop, South Ferry. Likely he would get back on and ride all the way to the other end of the line to the Bronx, to stay out of the cold. Once he had a home to which to return on the train, a meal, the radio to listen to.[40] We cannot live alone and we cannot go to heaven alone, for as Péguy, whom she cites, says, God will ask, "Where are the others?" It is striking to me how this virtual film of small frames of unemployment, loss, and despair from the Depression years is played out in the very *New York Times* I read on a fall day in 2014, seeing a sixty-year-old former IBM professional still sending out resumes three years after being let go, having sent out almost two thousand of them, hearing a campaign ad in which a candidate jokes in a TV interview about cutting dental coverage for Medicaid recipients, saying they can eat soup, soup is good.

The Mother of Many

So Dorothy was indeed writing up a storm every issue of the *Catholic Worker* paper to raise awareness of the Depression's consequences for ordinary people. The same with all her crisscrossing the country to give talks, all the other pieces she places in other papers and magazines. She was raising funds for the houses of hospitality, to make it possible to produce enough coffee, bread, and apple butter for hundreds of the hungry in the morning, for a handful to have soup and a warm place to sleep in the evening. She saw the immediate parallels with Francis and Clare of Assisi, only that she was operating down on Mott Street and in other Lower East Side neighborhoods, as were Catholic Workers all over the country in other houses of hospitality. As of this writing in fall of 2015, the Catholic Worker website lists 208 communities in the United States and another 28 internationally affiliated with the movement.[41]

But I think it is obvious in much of Dorothy's writing that she is also talking out loud: to God, to her readers, and especially to herself to make sense of it, to pray herself through it, and importantly, to develop a way of proceeding. Despite the very ad hoc, almost anarchic appearances of the Worker movement, the accounts by members who worked with and knew Dorothy over the years make it clear that she was gifted with inspiring others and getting funds, accomplishing much through the members of the movement. While she would often deny administrative abilities, and members would agree that her moods shifted and her gifts lay in other places, it is telling that the Worker movement, more than eighty years later, still attracts committed people and still continues to offer direct assistance, not to four hundred hungry people a day but to thousands across the country. Recent celebrations of its eightieth anniversary affirmed the radical character of Dorothy's life and witness.

What one hears in just these few quotes above is representative of what Dorothy Day would write and say and do, pretty much from 1933 till she died in 1980. It was crucial that one actually do the works of mercy, not just argue theory about economic change. While far more a realist that Peter Maurin, recognizing from her far left youth that unions are necessary, as is legislation that protects workers' health and wages, she insisted that seeing the faces, fighting back one's despair and sometimes disgust at the filth, the odors, and the attitudes, that one must actually help those in need.

And it was "a new heaven and new earth in which justice dwells" that her movement and all people of faith had to work for. The hope that could not be killed is evident even when she was no longer the long, tall, good-looking journalist of the 1920s but a gray, braided hair, grandmother type, seen in many photos with her grandchildren but also seated with those eating dinner at the houses, with both members and guests.

In the early 1950s, after two decades of struggling to be the movement's radical voice, she wrote at length about the difficulty of writing about poverty. This was the case because while one could, like St. Francis of Assisi, decide to simplify one's life, be voluntarily poorer, the plight of poor people was not freely chosen and was always horrible. Dorothy never tried to glamorize the actual lives of the poor she knew and helped. Frida Berrigan, the daughter of radical priest Philip Berrigan and niece of the Jesuit poet and activist priest Dan Berrigan, very matter of factly described her own decision to leave a position, salary, health insurance, and apartment for a much simpler situation in Dorothy's own residence for many years, the Catholic Worker Maryhouse on Third Street in the East Village, formerly the Lower East Side.

> Dorothy Day talks about being pruned. In *The Long Loneliness* she writes about her Catholic Worker co-founder Peter Maurin as he nears death: "He had stripped himself throughout life: he had put off the old man in order to put on the new. . . . He had stripped himself but there remained work for God to do. We are to be pruned as this vine is pruned so that it can bear fruit, and this we cannot do ourselves. God did it for him."
>
> Moving into the Catholic Worker, I pruned away some things that I had thought I needed: a steady paycheck, health insurance, privacy, the security that comes with the presumption that tomorrow will more or less look like today and yesterday. And I have added a critical gift—one I grew up with, but needed to be an adult to embrace on my own—community. Community is fertile ground—for the seeds of conscience, for deep roots of faith and practice. Out of this fertile ground and with these seeds—what grows? Acts of goodness, resistance, generosity, creativity, a new vision of the world—one that feels possible and close and ready to be born.[42]

So here we have the experience of a, perhaps not as devout traditionally speaking as Dorothy, yet wholly engaged woman in the twenty-first century. Like countless others who come in and out of the Worker movement and numerous other groups, the restlessness and the fire of a Dorothy, of a Maria Skobtsova, are evident. And what is also importantly here for our topic, without any excess piety or self-consciousness, is the presence that is prayer in ordinary living, prayer incarnate.

Richard Rohr, to whom we will listen, notes that Christianity is full of dualisms and none of them helpful. Thus, the task of growing in faith and life will mean recognizing these and undoing them, at least in the beginning, for ourselves. Divine versus human, flesh versus spirit, the virtuous versus the evil, heaven versus earth, sacred versus profane. Mother Maria cut through many such dualisms, but at the same time, and in much the same vein as Dorothy Day, restored a primal unity. It takes an unusual soul to do this, and I think it significant, that in the case of both it was the wisdom of strong women, women of great passion, lovers and mothers, who could bring back together the two great loves of the "new commandment" of Christ, love of God and love of the neighbor. For all their attendance at the liturgy and love for it, all their discourse in print on religion needing to be lived out, made flesh and blood in the care of others, they offer still today extraordinary witness to prayer enacted.

CHAPTER EIGHT

The Prayer of Pirogi Making and Other Food Adventures

The Communion of Community

Communion and Community

"Communion" within the context of prayer immediately suggests the sacrament at the heart of the church's liturgical life. Perhaps the single most noticeable change in the worship of Christian communities in the last century has been the restoration of the Eucharist—the Lord's Supper or Holy Communion—to the center of the liturgical life of Christians. This is a reality spreading across the churches, even to those of "low" liturgical backgrounds and within the "emergent church" movement. St. Lydia's "dinner church" in Brooklyn, an outreach to young adults, gathers around shared supper in which the Eucharist is set, complete with readings, homily, prayer, and the breaking of the bread and sharing of the cup. Many emergent church communities have restored the Eucharist to their gatherings each Sunday.[1] Mainline Protestant denominations, in their new worship books, have made the complete service of Word and Sacrament/Communion the norm for the Lord's Day. While the eucharistic restoration is far from universal, most pastors say they are aiming at it in their communities. While there remains enormous diversity in the style of celebration, from the use of ancient liturgical forms to very informal styles, two aspects of the Eucharist as prayer stand out—that material food and drink are the heart of the action and that the action is decisively and powerfully communal.

Now, this book was to be a look at uncommon, that is, nontraditional, informal prayer, prayer in everyday experience. Why the invocation of clearly the most liturgically central and formalized rite, that of the Eucharist? After all, one speaks of "high mass," the elaborate liturgy of the Eastern Orthodox, Catholic, and Anglican Churches, the vestments, icons, candles, incense, and chant. The communion and community we shall examine here are related to liturgy. They are, I will argue, not just outgrowths of parish liturgy but liturgy in themselves.

Holy Communion implies community, really requires it, communion among those who pray and celebrate the liturgy and share the bread and cup. Communion exists, further, in that they share life together, talk to each other, eat together, share. Here I will look at a parish activity of food production, the making of pirogi, but also several other parish communal activities, all of them connected with food, with a shared meal. Almost all of them could be seen as fund-raising ventures. But each, as it turns out, is truly a liturgy, obviously connected to the liturgy that the parish celebrates upstairs from the hall where the work of food prep or sharing takes place. It is the same people who worship upstairs.

Pirogi production is hardly the only food and communion-filled activity of our community. I have experienced the activities I shall describe below through working side-by-side with parish members, as does the parish's rector, though neither of us wears anything to distinguish us as clergy. Like everyone else, I am a "concelebrant" in this liturgy of food and friendship. There are places for years of expertise in this project and for real leadership skills. But beyond these, there is no hierarchy. Each one of us is needed. Too many at one task and not enough at another means the production breaks down.

We work all day, even share a meal, and I often head the cleanup crew. But this liturgy has no candles, incense, vestments, or holy books. There are no icons on the walls but only the sacred images, what we saw Maria Skobtsova called "living icons." These are the women and men of the community, saints already by baptism and on the way to further holiness. Upstairs we all celebrate the liturgy together, most often that of the Eucharist, on Sunday mornings. We also gather on feast days and for special seasonal services such as those of Lent, Holy Week, and Easter night.

The same Mother Maria Skobtsova also wrote about the "gospel" or "evangelical" mode of Christian living, which made its hallmark the "liturgy outside the church," sometimes also described as the "liturgy after the liturgy" and as "the sacrament of the brother/sister," the service of the neighbor just we have been served by Christ from the holy table.[2] Mother Maria made this theme of the indissolubility of the love of the neighbor and of God the central one of her writing. It was the driving rationale of her running houses of hospitality in Paris between the wars for the poor, homeless, and marginalized. The idea of feeding the hungry in close connection with prayer and the liturgy was, as we also saw, the vision of the Catholic Worker houses of hospitality and service, the joint creation of Peter Maurin and Dorothy Day. Catherine DeHueck Doherty aimed for much the same in her Harlem house of hospitality in the same time period, and later in Madonna House in Combermere, Ontario.

There are many other quasi-sacramental gatherings in parish communities. In Lutheran circles, the ubiquitous, absolutely necessary coffee hour is referred to as the "third sacrament" or "sacrament after the sacrament," as well it is—a time of conversation, the word, and sharing, not of the bread and cup but of whatever baked goods and other dishes are set out. There are also meals after funerals, "repasts," and receptions after weddings and baptisms and anniversaries. At this parish there are also parish picnics, with people bringing salads, sides, and desserts, and council members grilling, one in the fall and the other around or on Pentecost, in the spring. And there is a celebration of the parish's patron saint, Gregory the Theologian, whose feast day is January 25, most often celebrated on the closest Sunday. There are gatherings to bake Easter breads and other delicacies like poppy seed and nut and prune rolls for sale. Along with pirogi making, all of these are occasions of "communion."

Making Pirogi

The unusual kind of communion in community I am talking about is the assembly of members of the parish, a couple of times a year, to make a staple of Eastern European cuisine—*pirogi, pirohy, piro-heh, varenycky*—ravioli-like dumplings filled with potatoes, cheese, onions, or other stuffings. These have been, for many congregations, substantial means of fund-raising, not just during holidays or Lent but year round. I do not know precisely how many years our parish has been making pirogi as a community activity. I have heard stories about the sheer, exhausting physical exertion needed years ago, before the roller machine was purchased to roll out all the sheets needed.

Pirogi making. Photos courtesy of Gary McCarthy and Tania Metz.

Originally, this was purely an internal fund-raising activity, the finished products being sold in order to raise money for the parish. Our parish now has been using the proceeds of sales for outreach, especially to the local soup kitchen, The Lunch Box, as well as other local service providers and houses of hospitality. These have included Emmaus House, Harlem, St. Basil's Academy, the monastic communities of New Skete, and Sister Vassa Larin's online programs, among others. The pirogi are sold along with many other ethnic foods at a Christmas Fair in December and with special Easter baked goods in the springtime. So right from the start, this community work is liturgical, but not just because it is done by members of a parish or in the church hall. It is liturgical because, like the actual liturgy, it has many layers of meaning and different levels of motive. Some come out of a sense of obligation. In the past this had to do with needed revenue for the upkeep of the rectory and other projects at church as well as the general parish budget. It was also part of other actions such as personal generosity in giving that made a parish, with all its expenses, possible. Not the least of these expenses, nowadays often the single largest cluster of them, are the support of the pastor and his family.

But a genuine "conversion" or transformation of attitudes with respect to fund-raising took place in our parish several years ago. The experience of serving meals at the local soup kitchen was pivotal. A number of our families prepared and then served the main meal at The Lunch Box in Poughkeepsie and were deeply moved by those who came to get a hot meal and expressed tremendous gratitude for this. The many needs of this center became a target for our giving, our sharing of what we took in from the sale of pirogi and the other homemade foods and baked goods. Rather than keep the proceeds of the Christmas and Easter food fairs for our own expenses, these proceeds have been designated for support of outreach elsewhere, both locally and in the city. This has been a huge step in the spiritual lives of our parish members, even though there has been some vocal opposition to it.

The point here is that in addition to being "community building" events, that is, group activities that strengthen and solidify the sense of community, the pirogi making and related work has been a powerful and transformative spiritual experience for us in the parish. Spending so many hours with each other, talking about so much while making the pirogi or baked goods, was a form of Eucharist, a feeding of each other with life and hope. As exhausted as one was at day's end, back aching from so much standing, joints worn out from pinching the circles of dough closed around the filling, there was yet real exhilaration, a bounce in one's step. You forgot about your own problems for a few hours, listening to those of others. You got to know a little better someone with whom you'd sat in church for years. In introducing some longtime parish members to each other at these pirogi days, I came to realize that even in a modest Sunday assembly of no more than a hundred, there were still circles that did not intersect with each other, people, perhaps of different age brackets or backgrounds, who had yet to have a conversation with each other. Doing so while pinching the dough was a great icebreaker.

Pirogi and Parishes

Observing what happened to our seminarian interns when they left us over the past twenty years, I gave a paper at a Huntington Ecumenical Institute conference. It was entitled, "The Church Has Left the Building."[3]

We live in a time when a constellation of demographic changes, none of them specifically having to do with religion, is nonetheless radically changing the life of congregations. In some cases the departure from the building is quite precise. Aging structures become incapable of repair after years of deferred maintenance. Beautiful, cathedral-like buildings cannot be sustained by a handful of senior citizens on fixed incomes. Generations of children and grandchildren have moved away to where the jobs are. Pew and other surveys find almost 20 percent of millennials are "religious nones," perhaps believing in God but belonging to no religious body or congregation.[4] Mills and mines that brought immigrants and others to work and thus gave rise to the opening of parishes have long since closed. Many of the same have married out of the ethnic and church groups in which they were raised. Some attend other churches, practice other faiths or none at all. The communities that established and constructed houses of worship, from urban brick basilicas to small-town clapboard chapels, have changed, in some cases have dispersed or disappeared.

So, while the church endures—the communion of saints, the body of Christ—parishes can and do die, congregations slowly go out of existence. Now and again an entire parish "plant" of buildings can be repurposed, not for a restaurant or antique store but as home to a community without a permanent location. A Bronx Lutheran congregation was not long ago made home by an Ethiopian Orthodox community who had rented worship space for many years in Union Theological Seminary on the Upper West Side of New York City. My own Ukrainian Greek Catholic parish of origin in Yonkers, New York, relocated and sold the first plant to an Indian Orthodox community.

One of our former seminarian interns had his first pastoral assignment in the northeast section of Pennsylvania, formerly the coal region. From the mid-nineteenth century till after World War II, this area was the center of anthracite mining. It was booming when this kind of coal was in great demand for the heating of homes and businesses. My grandfather was a miner and my father and his brothers grew up in this area, in Nanticoke, near to Wilkes-Barre. One uncle was a Ukrainian Greek Catholic priest throughout this region for over fifty years. When our intern was willing to go to one of the shrinking coal region parishes, it was only because his spouse's employment made it possible for them to survive, so minimal was the compensation from the dwindling congregation. But I remember, on a visit to him there, the group of retired seniors who assembled every Wednesday to make pirogi, stocking up their freezer in the church hall kitchen. Sales of pirogi were still a crucial source of parish income for them, as had been dinners of fried fish or chicken in previous decades. Many coals towns were meccas of Eastern European cuisine, homemade by parishioners and sold to help keep up the parish. So entwined were this little Eastern European versions of won-tons or ravioli with the parishes and peoples' lives that one could see them as "sacramental" and not at all risk irreverence.

The Mysteries of Pirogi

Even though pirogi making has become an action of outreach instead of fund-raising for our parish, it remains an important social gathering for the community a couple times a year. The fall session produces pirogi for the Christmas Food Fair, which falls on the first Saturday of December. In our part of the county, this is an annual time of parish and fire-company food and crafts fairs, mostly for support of the local organization. A second session is scheduled late in winter. The goal for this is another food fair and bake sale held close to Easter. Pirogi would also be available for purchase through Lent. And the other component of the bake sale is homemade Easter breads—*babka* and *kulichi*, both moist, yeast-based confections loaded with eggs and butter, which were not used in Lent, just as, in the *kulichi*, was candied fruit and nuts with a confectioner's sugar frosting on top. The *kulichi* resembled a snow covered silo with icing, while the *babkas* were golden brown and round, dense and with elaborate designs of braided dough, crosses too on top.

Making pirogi in the church hall, usually starting around 8:00 am—the dough maker is there even earlier—we assemble a few at a time. The word of God is heard, but not in readings from the scriptures and the choir's singing of the texts for the day. Rather the word takes voice in the nonstop conversation of all those who have come to work. You hear it in their gossip, in the latest news about their families or other members. You hear it in their tales of happiness and disappointment, their narratives of accomplishment, their expression of gratitude, their hopes.

It's not at all the wide variety of fillings or modes of serving that are of interest here. Rather, the production is a kind of "liturgy outside the church," without a fixed order of worship but certainly with the need to keep up with the production flow. Imagine controlled chaos—noise from the dough being made in an industrial mixer. Noise from the large, commercial rolling machine, churning out long sheets of thinly rolled dough. The noise of the crew in the kitchen, with steaming pots of water, cooking the prepared pirogi and then sloshing them into ice water to cool them before packaging.

Out in the main part of the church hall there are several dozen members of the parish, relatives, and friends. One team mans the rolling machine. As dough comes out of the rolling machine in sheets and is cut into circles, the thirty or more who have come proceed with filling and then pinching closed the dumplings over the course of several hours. In the church hall kitchen yet another team boils the dumplings, then cools them down and coats them with a light layer of oil to prevent them sticking together. These cooled pirogi are carried back out to the end of the hall in large trays. There yet another team packages and puts them into the commercial freezer.

All of the tasks necessitated in the pirogi production process enable conversation. While the action at the rolling machine is pretty frantic and the boiling and cooling physically intensive, the hand work of pinching and later packing easily enables all kinds of conversation— telling stories of the past, sharing family problems, asking questions about the community, getting to know newer members or ones not well known. While I have experienced most of the phases of pirogi production, I have probably spent more time around the horseshoe configuration of tables where the pinching is done.

I am sure that in more than thirty years of pastoral ministry, there is no other parish event I have experienced that matches pirogi making for community building and transformative possibilities. I also realize that coming from a Ukrainian background I am biased. There is nothing magical about these scrumptious delicacies that, except for a few rejects from the kitchen boiling crew, are not consumed in any significant way on the production day. A shared lunch makes for more time together. There are also similar gatherings to make Easter breads and a variety of other baked goods such as poppy, nut, and prune rolls. At the day-long food fairs, where all these products are sold, there is further opportunity to hang out, pick up on earlier conversations, encounter new friends, sample even more homemade delicacies for lunch.

Because I have not been part of the Easter bread and nut/poppy seed roll baking events, I cannot speak to them. And while also very much a context for community interaction, the food fair itself involves hundreds of visitors coming to buy take-out frozen pirogi, stuffed cabbage, borscht, and many other homemade dishes from Serbian gabanitza and Greek spanakopita to Lebanese chicken kebabs and tabbouli. American favorites like hot dogs and hamburgers are also available along with homemade chili and soups. There are also some crafts, but it is primarily a food event. All day long people are sitting down to homemade foods served hot and fresh from the kitchen. Parish members serve, retrieving frozen or fresh pirogi, stuffed cabbage or soup, delivering sit-down orders from the kitchen, taking payment, conversing with shoppers. Sometimes there are tours of the church upstairs for guests. It is a very busy day! Yet, despite the greater demands of the crowds in and out of the church hall, my experience has been that this is one more opportunity for the "communion of community." In the early part of the day, before crowds arrive, there is a lot of time for conversation while setting up, pricing baked goods, and starting food prep in the kitchen. Conversation continues throughout the day and during the clean-up time after the fair has closed.

The Prayer of Conversation

There is nothing startling or unusual about people enjoying each other's company, deeply engaged in talk while working together. Barn raisings, sewing circles, quilting bees, pie and cookie baking, dinner prep, and, of course, christenings, weddings, funerals—there are numerous examples of community-building activities both at church and in more secular settings in American life. These gatherings appear endless—parents and children preparing backpacks with supplies for students in need of them before the start of school, kids themselves making cookies for a scholarship, parents of youth hockey players running a bake sale for equipment.

The very ordinary character of people working together and talking up a storm while doing so—I suspect not many would consider this prayer! But here I am claiming it very much is prayer.

As I was pinching the dough one morning at pirogi making, I listened as several members and fellow pinchers began to talk about their adult children, their spouses and kids—their grandchildren. There was the usual bragging about colleges into which grandchildren had been accepted, new homes or new jobs or moves by their children and sons- or daughters-in-law. But there was also the sharing of far less happy situations, of serious, chronic illness, of marital turmoil and endings, of truly destructive behavior by young adults. This was neither the sacrament of confession nor a pastoral counseling session. Nevertheless, a remarkable atmosphere of trust, of camaraderie, always prevails on pirogi days and the talk flows very, very freely. What is said at pirogi making stays at pirogi making.

I listened to one participant lament about how distantly her children and grandchildren now lived from her and how distant they had become to her. It wasn't that way when she was growing up. Yes, it can be more difficult nowadays, not to be living close to your extended family. But then, you're not all crammed together, not a spectator, constantly, to the spats and fights between family members. Yet my fellow pincher was expressing the real loss of seeing her own children as adults, a parent missing too the company and the accomplishments of her grandchildren. She's never going to tell a therapist about all this, but she was free to tell us, pinching the dough with her. And her account not only jogged my own memory of growing up, a bittersweet one, but also those of the others working around the table. There were plenty of other narratives like this each time we gathered for pirogi making. To be sure, not all were sad either, many were stories of good things, gratitude, joy.

Personal Stories and Journeys

I heard, on one pirogi-making day, the extremely lengthy story of how, fifty years earlier, a young man from the coal region of Eastern Pennsylvania headed for IBM country and other better paying employment possibilities not far across the New York line. I asked, out of curiosity, since I had not seen this senior citizen in a while, due to illness, how he and his wife had met and how they had gotten from "the region" to Dutchess County. Danny lived to be 94, a veritable "comeback kid" from several serious illnesses before coming off a ventilator and dying peacefully. In the scene I am describing, he was still in top form, and I was warned by his wife of over fifty years that I was in for it, would be there listening late in the afternoon unless I cut him off. I didn't need to listen that long: he was able to slice off just a small part of that half century, and in so doing recount the exact pattern one of my own uncles had followed.

Having found work with IBM in the Poughkeepsie area so many years ago, this transplant from the coal region found a living arrangement where, with several other Pennsylvania boys, an apartment in Poughkeepsie was where they stayed during the work week. Back "home" they'd drive on Friday night, most often in time to get to a church supper or dance or local tavern—this is where Danny met his wife. Then Sunday evening back to Poughkeepsie they'd drive, the carload of them, to work the week until late Friday afternoon, then home again to Pennsylvania. One of my uncles did this for almost forty years, back and forth from Nanticoke, Pennsylvania, to Mahwah, New Jersey, and a Ford plant. My storyteller settled in Dutchess County as soon as he married. He was almost a founding member of our parish, missing this by just a few years. As he is remembering all this, he and his wife are in their nineties.

Not only do I hear about what growing up in the coal region was like—poor, no future with the mines closed, few opportunities for education—I also end up getting an oral history of the parish where I have helped out as associate priest for over twenty years and where this man and his family have grown up for the last forty-five. I hear about Sunday liturgy in what was the living and dining rooms of the present rectory, with Sunday church school conducted down in the basement. I learn of all kinds of fund-raising events from these very pirogi we are making to raffles, rummage sales, and bake sales, all to get a mortgage on the building that still houses our church. It is not just hearing another version of the second generation of immigration—like my parents, he and his wife were born in the United States. It is also becoming an anthropologist with an "informant" on parish life in the last half century, from the post–WWII 1950s through the tumultuous '60s and '70s, now into the twenty-first century. Our parish was founded in order to have English-language services, preaching, and religious instruction for the third generation of immigrants' offspring. We never had Russian or Ukrainian language classes at our parish nor those ethnic adjectives "Orthodox" on the church sign out front.

One might not expect to find social history, generational evolution, and ecclesiastical ethnography while pinching dough. However, they are there for the listening. I also hear stories of remarkable determination. These are not just informal sacramental "confessions" or pastoral counseling encounters, since the narratives are shared beyond me, a priest but at that moment in a tee shirt and jeans dusted with flour, like the other nearby pinchers. There are the tales of getting through a child's struggle with substance abuse, the devastation of an adult child's divorce. There are wrenching accounts of years of familial estrangement, deep rifts over inheritance and how it was apportioned to siblings.

Just a few of the most senior participants are from "the greatest generation," others from the years right after them, "baby boomers," and I am one of them. There are virtually no lifelong residents of the Hudson valley and, sadly, very few younger members of childbearing age. This is a demographic reality of many church bodies in America—the disappearance of thirty-five-year-olds and under. Almost every one of us has relocated here, many for work with IBM, though in recent years this corporation has been shrinking significantly. I would say that only a third or less are "cradle" Eastern Orthodox, the majority either having married into or converted to this tradition. Our parish, quite deliberately, never identified itself by any ethnic label as many Orthodox churches do. It is simply St. Gregory Orthodox Church, no "Russian" or "Carpatho-Rusyn" or "Ukrainian" in the title. As noted, English was agreed upon as the liturgical and communal language of the parish, though here and there, on various occasions, one does hear other languages. At Easter, the greeting "Christ is risen" is delivered in Greek, Slavic, and Arabic versions, as well as Romanian, Spanish, French, and Armenian. I would estimate there must be close to two dozen ethnic groups represented in the parish community. This is often deliciously evident at potluck dinners and picnics and particularly at the banquet after the Easter vigil service.

But I do not want to give the impression that in most of these "holy" conversations, the sacred sharing is grim, full of disappointment and pain. Not at all. Up till now I have not noted the triumphs over bad grades and addiction, the gift of seeing adult children experience deep, joyful marriages. So many other, everyday, hilarious conversations unroll. There are many tales about growing up in the Great Depression on a farm or in a mining town. The highlight of the week was an ice cream cone at the grocery store, a few cents that somehow financially pressed 1930s parents let go of to give their otherwise impoverished kids a little joy. Other tales include those of urban cold-water flats, walk-up apartments with communal toilets, heat from coal stoves and hot water made on those stoves. Into such an apartment twin sisters, prematurely born, were placed in shoeboxes and wrapped in cotton and placed on a shelf above the stove to keep them warm.

As the parish celebrated its fiftieth anniversary in 2014, there were numerous stories, not just from the several founding members still with us, but also from others who joined in the early years. We late-comers of twenty years' membership heard about how immense the work of making pirogi was without the dough roller. All the dough was hand rolled in the "good old days." And before instant potatoes were used, there was the labor intensive process of peeling, boiling, then draining and squeezing liquid to make the right consistency to be pinched into dumplings. The same was true for onions—peeling, dicing, sauteeing, until dried ones were incorporated. It was with de-light, not pride, that other narratives from the past were exchanged in the past year, not just at pirogi and baking days but at coffee hours and other gatherings. Kids going to Sunday church school in the base-ment of the residential home that served as chapel and rectory for the first assigned pastor. There were tag sales, rummage sales, sales of baked goods and pirogi, and more from 1964 till 1970, and these made it possible for the prefabricated church building we still inhabit to be purchased and erected. It almost did not happen as there were dis-putes among the out-of-state construction workers contracted to as-semble the structure.

Middle-aged adult children of founders reminisced on what it was like to grow up in this community. One's family left the Russian par-ish in Poughkeepsie decades ago and came to ours. As a teenager she was asked to leave church because her skirt, even though below the knee, was deemed inappropriate. Others who also first went to this parish explained why they decided to found a parish of their own, with English as the liturgical language enshrined in the parish con-stitution. They had asked for the gospel to be read in English after the Slavonic and for English to be used in church school—both re-quests refused. Thus the determination to form an American parish has been its history—a parish with no single ethnic identification and a wide diversity of backgrounds joining, as well as deep hospitality and tolerance.

In most of these happy as well as sometimes painful narratives, there is a freedom to speak, a sense that one will be listened to with compassion. Where else does one find this kind of trust? And this is a collection of fellow pirogi pinchers not of the same family, ethnic background, or income level, not to mention political perspective. In the parish community we indeed have a Tea Party contingent, also middle of the roaders and progressives along with many apolitical types. As Diana Butler Bass noted in her study of congregations over a decade ago, "Red" and "Blue" became "Purple" where there was strong, deep community.[5] That is, political, or for that matter other religious and cultural differences, came not to make a difference! Something else transcended these divisions that otherwise produce intense friction in our society. As students of American religious life such as Robert Putnam and David Campbell note, parishes are some of the last examples of communities still existing in our society.[6]

The Very Human Sides of Community

I am not a romantic about parish life. Over thirty years in pastoral ministry and four parishes have taught me otherwise. In recent years a number of pastors have crafted clear, honest accounts of their experience of ministry in the parish. Some years ago, Lloyd Rediger, himself a pastor and psychologist, published pioneering work on the toxic, destructive aspects of congregational life.[7] Rediger calls certain parishioners "clergy-killers," for they are bent on the personal defamation and destruction of their pastors' existence. They do great damage to clergy and their families every year, spreading slanderous accusations, calling to other congregations to "warn" them of the "bad pastor" they have just welcomed. There are also toxic cliques of members, unwilling to allow newcomers into their circle or the larger community of the parish. Add to these those who out of fear or rigidity cannot accept the neighbors who are "not our kind," folks of diverse ethnic and religious backgrounds.

Aside from these more gross and serious types, there are those possibly unaware of how their own preferences and prejudices make life in a parish difficult for fellow members and pastors. They cannot accept that years bring, rather demand, change. The so-called "seven last words," not those last words of Christ on the cross, but of a congregation, form their mantra: "We have never done that here before." From the details of the church services, or decoration of the building for feasts to more mundane items such as what is served at a potluck supper or the selection of donated homemade baked goods and other dishes for food fairs, no aspect is unworthy of comment or, better, critique.

The church, in scripture and tradition, is a net that is deep and wide. All kinds of fish are caught up in it. It is a large, spacious ark, bearing all sorts to the kingdom. It is a treasure chest containing all kinds of precious things and people. It is neither accurate nor fair to talk of the parish as either just a joyful, loving community or merely as a cantankerous, negative group. The parish in which pirogi making happens is no different from any other in having a great deal of opinions, some fairly edgy. Some are politically very conservative. Often coming from impoverished backgrounds themselves, the position of these members toward Medicaid, Affordable Health Care, SNAP (Supplemental Nutritional Assistance Programs), and food stamps is negative. Their parents and grandparents took no "relief," but suffered and worked for all they had. Often, there has been very little experience with others of different ethnic or religious backgrounds either. They criticize the hungry who come to various food pantries and other outreach centers we support with funds from the food fairs and other sales. And yet, paradoxically, they still continue to come and participate in pirogi making and other food prep. I think the value of being with others in the community outweighs whatever political perspectives they otherwise have.

Other instances of community attitudes vary considerably. The contributions of this or that baker can be scrutinized and judged severely. Or not. Or praised. Or simply accepted as such, with thanks. So too the clean-up of the hall by volunteers after a pirogi-making session. The regular cleaning crew has very high standards! These types of criticisms are not restricted to events outside of worship. Parents who do not effectively control their children, both during the service and in the hall during coffee hour, come in for constant comment. As do the hairdos, clothing, and the cars of others. Anyone with even the briefest participation in church life will be aware of the gossip and criticism that is endemic to congregational life. You cannot have community without it.

Social Change and Communities

Those who study community life in America tell us that it has not disappeared but has undergone substantial change in the last half century or so. Robert Putnam chronicled this in *Bowling Alone*, as did Robert Bellah and his associates years earlier in *Habits of the Heart*, and as Nancy Ammerman has also done in decades of studying church congregations and their communities.[8] There are still "voluntary associations," to use one sociological term for them, that function. Property owners and tenants' associations are still important in many communities, maintaining standards and enforcing community regulations on everything from lawn care to house design. The more affluent and selective the community or building, often the more demanding are the standards of the association. In some communities the school board or elected town boards meetings are still very lively forums for discussion as well as fierce debate. Likewise the associations that support athletic teams and leagues for young people. And in some cases alumni associations are particularly important.

But those who write from within the intense world of congregational life, authors such as Barbara Brown Taylor, Richard Lischer, and Lillian Daniel, to name just a few, reveal just how powerful the relationships, the love, as well as the conflict can be in the body of Christ incarnate in a local parish.[9] The kind of community found in a congregation cannot be found anywhere else. One chooses to be a member. Further, one chooses, and continues to choose, to actually be there as opposed to being simply a name on a list of inactive members. And one chooses how much of a presence to be, how often and in what ways to participate.

In interpreting parish life to visitors, seminarian interns, and a new pastor and a new bishop, my sociological training led me to emphasize some aspects not normally prominent. Substantial changes have occurred to the places where many parishes are located. As many as forty years ago, attention was focused on inner city locations, where neighborhoods had dramatically changed, where poverty had come to replace working class populations or where poverty endured among recent immigrants and people of color.

In recent years, however, we have come to see parishes challenged by demographic change in rural, small-town settings as well as in many older industrial locations. Mining, mill, and factory towns that originated from 1880 to 1920, the greatest period of immigration in America, have ceased to possess these industries. Many such communities, as those in the Northeast Pennsylvania coal region where my father's family settled and my uncle served as a priest for over fifty years, are "ghost" towns as a result. The closing of mines and factories led to population leaving, not only for work but also for education. As the pull of ethnic and religious communities on their young people loosened, and with increasing mobility for employment and schooling, later generations married out of their nationalities and denominations. Relocating to places other than their hometowns, as many studies have shown over the past several decades, those who were interested in joining churches let go of "brand loyalty." They shopped around, found congregations that were sensitive to children, were keen on social justice, had beautiful services and welcoming communities.

In the past, being from the same county or province, speaking, more or less, the same language were probably the reasons why parishes formed, why communities took shape and continued. Theologians and church leaders would like to think it was correct doctrine or liturgy, and surely familiar hymns and chants, icons and words, were treasured. However, if culture in all the small details changes over time, why not also congregations and their communities? Old parish photos show women in long dresses and huge hats, men with high collars and thick moustaches and beards. Though the technical quality of old photographs used to make me think the sun never shone very much back then, and everything was some variant of black and white, of course the world was full of color, smells, strong emotions, fierce love and anger.

We no longer live in the same grinding poverty as did many of those miners and factory workers, those toiling wives and grandmothers. We may also romanticize their church behavior. One very senior pastor, when I asked about his earliest parish memories, the very early 1950s, took the sheen off "the good old days," when supposedly all flocked to services upon hearing the church bells ring. Weekdays, he said, it was often himself at the altar, maybe an elderly man singing the responses and a few equally elderly women at the service. Sundays, ordinary ones, there was more of the congregation, though always more women than men and not many young people. The packed buildings that some imagine were only that way on the biggest of feasts, and for funerals and some weddings, not necessarily for the entire service and certainly not everyone in the community, since the building could never hold them all. Some memories of the "golden" past are more fantasy than fact.

Parish communities today still welcome new members who visit and join, and continue to baptize children. One difference is that often the number of younger families with children has markedly decreased while the proportion of aging members has grown. That is the case with us, where the pirogi are made. A scan of the hall during the pirogi production confirms this. There is surely more time for members to come and work together and share than in earlier times where work hours were longer. Retirement and longer life expectancies also free up time.

The prayer of pirogi making I have described surely was experienced decades ago when parishioners gathered for this kind of work or other activities. This prayer of shared presence and exchange is the very marrow of parish life. I have seen much smaller groups, often mainly retirees, gather for this food prep as well as for bible study or conversation. As I have portrayed it here, it is a "liturgy after the liturgy," not unlike the fellowship and sharing at post-liturgical coffee hours.

Other "Feasts" of Community

The prayer of pirogi making or the "communion of community" stretches far beyond these little dumplings and their fabrication. The parish coffee hour has been called the "eighth" or the "third" sacrament, depending on how many sacraments you believe there are. The mundane setting of a big percolator of coffee and hot water for tea, plus platters of rolls, cake, bagels, cookies, and, if fortunate, egg casseroles, cold meats, salads, and other goodies always evokes for me Jesus's multiplication of the loaves and fishes for the crowds. In our old parish hall, the low ceiling and hard surfaces helped the din of many conversations, the decibel count of noise, to become almost painful, all of this now remedied by a light-filled, more open space. Anyone who has heard those narratives of the feeding of thousands in the Gospels must have thought about the intense conversation before, during, and after the miraculous event.

A few years ago we expanded our parish hall, actually adding a new structure that is filled with light from many large windows all around the periphery and much more space in which to spread. Pirogi making now extends into this space, and it makes the food fair a veritable bazaar. The new hall also makes it possible to host wedding celebrations as well as fund-raising dinners for cancer research and post-funeral meals. A recent event, on the surface nothing extraordinary, was our parish council president's throwing a mortgage-burning party for a lot of his relatives, work colleagues, friends from the volleyball league in which he plays, and parish members, among others. Hamburgers, hot dogs, and various cold salads were served up in the early afternoon. After vespers (this was a Saturday), a dinner was catered, buffet style, from a local restaurant the church used many times before. There were wonderful desserts as well, plenty to drink. So, one might say, how long could anyone stay at such an event? I myself was among perhaps fifty or more who were there for most of the afternoon, with a pause for vespers, until 8:00 pm. And, as is the case with all of our parish events, pirogi making and the rest, it became one of those gatherings where time stands still, when your feet begin to ache from standing. Before you know it, you have been circulating around, eating way more than you intended, and having numerous conversations, some with members you are close to, some with those you hardly ever engage. I almost got into one political argument, over entitlement programs—I was ambushed, maybe better hijacked, into it but emerged without any lacerations. "Red" and "blue" people can make "purple," as noted, as long as they don't assault each other politically, try to ambush one with whom they do not agree.

Possibly it was the host of this party, someone who, in the Gospel's words, "has no guile," is known and loved by all. I think that his generosity, his tremendous reservoir of goodwill, always apparent, shaped the gathering's spirit. As I say that, I credit him, but I also remember, as I have throughout here, the similar ocean of friendship and acceptance that is the community of the parish. Surely, here and there you could turn into choppy waters, into personal issues or attitudes that would seem anything but hospitable. But for the most part, this is a community of great goodwill. And when they assemble, there is the ritual, the liturgy that begins among us, when good food is served. Such a seemingly ordinary, nonreligious celebration, this mortgage-burning picnic and dinner. Yet it is sacred indeed. The scriptures are full of feasts, banquets, people being fed. The prophet Elijah is brought bread by a raven lest he die of starvation in the desert (1 Kings 19:4–9). In turn, his disciple, Elisha, makes sure a widow does not starve and feeds the brotherhood of prophets, removing a poison from their stew and multiplying bread (2 Kings 4:1–7, 38–44). Think of the manna falling from heaven to the Israelites and then Jesus's feeding of the thousands in the fields, the banquets of the parables, the wedding feast at Cana, the supper in the Emmaus inn. Each of these was a little taste of Paradise.

The Celebration of Goodbye

Funerals are no longer what they used to be in America. A recently deceased colleague and friend, a professor in Alaska, who, with his wife from the Tlingit tribe, worked for years to preserve indigenous language, celebrations, and culture there, described once the effort to compile the funeral orations or speeches as well as the rest of the elements of saying goodbye to members of a family and a parish.[10] While it was no longer possible for survivors to offer the oration or speech in the indigenous languages, Richard and Nora Dauenhauer encouraged those they knew to have the funeral repast or meal of consolation, an important Eastern Orthodox practice, in English and with whatever food they now found appealing and obtainable. Older delicacies like dried seal and smoked fish have given way to buckets of Kentucky Fried Chicken and pizzas from Pizza Hut and Domino's.

Usually, funerals in our parish custom have an evening service, followed by refreshments that include desserts, sandwiches, other finger foods, coffee, tea, and cold drinks, and, in some more ethnically traditional events, vodka and whiskey shots are also available, though these usually are kept in the kitchen rather than being put out with the rest of the refreshments.

The former rector of our parish, of Russian background, was fond of referring to the funeral services as *otpevan'ye*, literally, the "singing away" of the departed one. My experience tells me that other kinds of funerals, in the Western churches, also perform this consoling, communal celebration of goodbye and comfort, particularly with old, beloved hymns. Ignorance breeds fear and suspicion, this we know. And with increasing distancing of death—memorial services weeks or months after a death, the body long since gone by cremation, lack of actual burial and the cemetery plot and stone—clearly many today have either forgotten the rituals of funerals or have had no experience of them.

Growing up in the 1950s, even as a child one was regularly taken to "wakes," the visiting hours at funeral homes, and then to the services in church and the interment at the cemetery and the meal afterwards. This was the way we once bid farewell to grandparents, but other relatives, neighbors, and friends as well. I still vividly remember the funerals of the pastor of my home parish and of a classmate who died in an accident.

In Russian and likely other ethnic Eastern church practice, there is sometimes a "scale" of the solemnity of funeral services. (There is also like practice in Western churches.) The amounts may be inaccurate in memory, but I heard of "fifty ruble" services, with much singing and therefore singers to be paid, not to mention the priest as well as a deacon. From there it headed downwards, not only the cost, paid out among clergy and singers, but the amount of singing and number of prayers. As elaborate as Eastern church liturgy is and contrary to rubrical purists who insist that the services are always done in their entirety, "according to the Typikon," or book of rubrics, in reality there is a great deal of variation depending on local custom and the particular circumstances. One example would be the size of the assembly for a funeral and the physical as well as emotional condition of the mourners. The worse the conditions and smaller the congregation, more likely the shorter would be the services. This might also be the case for one departed who had little or no connection to the parish, that is, one who never came to services, was virtually unknown by parish members. All clergy have done funerals and interments at the behest of funeral directors who sought them out because the family lacked ties to parish and a pastor but still had pastoral needs.

Externally observed, it would appear that the formal rites of burial are primary. In them—the hymnody, the scripture lessons, and prayers—would be found the understanding of death, heaven and hell, punishment and reward, and, of course, the importance of the life once led, now over and done forever. Scholars of Eastern liturgy Alexander Schmemann and, more recently, Robert Hutcheon have examined the funeral services and texts thoughtfully.[11] The form now employed finds remarkable variation in how and how much is used across different Eastern churches and even within them. It may not be just a question of how many rubles either, but the culture and practice of a particular church body or geographical area within that national church.

Taken as a whole, the Eastern services, modeled on those of the Great Church, Hagia Sophia of Constantinople, as well as monastic practice in the Sabbaitic typikon, are mostly within the modalities of mourning, grief, and fear of judgment and punishment. Weeping, wailing, and woe are portrayed as the human response to death. Earthly life is described as only a shadow, brief, full of vanity and deluding dreams. Here and there, other themes punctuate the flow, the most important being the prayer that repeatedly concludes litanies asking God for forgiveness of sins and rest for the departed, beginning, "O God of spirits and all flesh. . . ." This prayer explicitly asks God, "who has trampled down death," for a "place of brightness, refreshment, repose where all sickness, sighing, and sorrow have fled away" for the departed as well as pardon for all transgressions, those committed willfully or otherwise. Finally, the Lord is acknowledged, in the doxology, as "the Resurrection, the life, and the repose" of the one who has "fallen asleep." In the *kontakion*, a hymn always specific to the day, the joy of resurrection, of Easter, breaks through at the end, the funeral lamentation becoming the song, "Alleluia!"

Schmemann, in a series of lectures published in Russian translation but not as yet in the original English version, specifically criticized this overshadowing of the service by what he called the "layer" of "lamentation and grief," thus obscuring what he saw as a Holy Saturday/Paschal perspective, likely the more ancient version of the rites, which used the death and resurrection of Christ more powerfully in the death of a Christian.

But this little detour stops now, because this is not a study of formal prayer, in church services and liturgical texts. It is helpful to know that in practice and, thus, in personal experience the visiting of family and friends before the service, a kind of "wake in church," and the meal or meals afterwards are just about as important as the beautiful and lengthy services.

A Most Personal Pascha

One funeral in our parish, recent to my writing this, was of a much beloved choir director. Herself a professional musician, she taught string playing and played in both chamber groups and orchestras, as did her spouse, a professional oboist and professor in the state university system. She had battled cancer for years, always being able to halt or even regress the spread. So in addition to her ebullient personality, her omnipresence in the choir, and her leading of it, the community was praying and supporting her in the struggle. She died very quickly, having performed and taught just days earlier.

Several in the parish, including the director's husband, described the two days of visiting, services, burial, and meals as like the Triduum, the three days of Holy Week and the celebration of Easter. Of course, given the pattern of the full funeral and burial service celebrated, Holy Saturday and Pascha/Easter were much in evidence in both the structure of these rites as well as Easter music sung by the parish choir before the services and as last respects were paid both in the church and at graveside. To just hear the very familiar hymns anticipating the resurrection and then the most familiar of all, the Easter hymn to the Virgin and the often repeated paschal hymn or *troparion*, made it an experience of Valentina's own Easter: "Christ is risen from the dead, trampling down death by death, and upon those in the tombs, bestowing life."

In her honor, there was serious choir practice and the services were sung beautifully, truly uplifting and joyful, in gratitude for her life. Because of the many connections through their musical performance and teaching, there was a nonstop stream of visitors for three hours or more before the evening service, and the church was filled for both services. Val's spouse, Joel, gave an eloquent and loving tribute at the liturgy's end. As lovely as the services, singing, and preaching were, there was an equally Easter atmosphere and a really palpable presence of this wonderful woman at the meal in the evening, after the funeral service. The parish's much larger new hall was built precisely so that guests and community could gather. Gather they all did—never did I see so many assembled there—to a stunning array of foods laid out: sandwiches, desserts, fruit, a feast to which the crowd did serious damage, as far as I could see. Quite a dent had been made by the time I was able to come down, after removing vestments and extinguishing candles in the church. But, even more importantly, having much of this chapter in draft at the time, I was very much in participant observer mode, as I learned in my sociological graduate training.

What I observed was much like what I already have recorded here at pirogi making, the food fairs, coffee hours, and the like—animated, beaming faces, lively conversations, a lot of hugging and reminiscing, truly an agapé meal, a love feast, as the early Christians called their gatherings. I heard people describe knowing her as a child in a parish not far from ours. I believe I heard one of our elder members tell another she had taught Valentina in Sunday church school. Everyone I listened to had a story, a memory, also too the expression of gratitude and relief that her struggle with cancer, which was indeed visible, was over.

Once again, the "liturgy after the liturgy," when food and people and stories converge, evokes the joy and the reason why Jesus must have used so many feasts and banquets in his parables and attended so many as well. Amy-Jill Levine addresses this in her always surprising look at the Jewish context and background to Jesus's teaching in parables.[12] The meal is an encounter, a meeting of the sacred and the human. There is a congregation who first assembled for prayer, whether to celebrate a holy day or bid farewell to a beloved sister or brother or wish well to a new couple or child. Later the same assembly continues the prayer with that of conversation, a shared dinner. Scripture scholars rightly underscore the eschatological significance of meals in the scriptures. The sharing of a meal satisfies not only the material thirst and hunger of now. The meal also points beyond, to the time of messianic completion, of life after this life in God. As one contemporary liturgical hymn, paraphrasing the ancient text of the *Didaché*, the Teaching of the Apostles, puts it, we find here a "foretaste of the feast to come."

Discontent Even at the Feast

Usually I ask friends and colleagues to look at drafts of what I write and that has been the case with what you are reading. However, while working on this chapter, I had not even reached a version I felt right to circulate when a good friend emailed me, after the rather moving celebration of the life, person, and passing of our choir director just described. It immediately struck me hard. I realized that in reflecting on all of these examples of "communion in community," of not formal but nonetheless very real prayer in the relationships of members of the parish, something had been forgotten, something not pleasant but without which the entire presentation risked being seriously distorted, unreal.

In quite a few of Jesus's parables, as well as in the stream of activity in the Gospels as well as in other parts of the New Testament, all is never completely well with the people of God. I mean by this the human condition's guarantee that all will not be well with everyone at the feast. Someone will be troubled, not by anything happening at the gathering but because of conflicts or negative development in that person's family, personal, or professional existence. The sadness then, or for that matter, rage displayed through the face, voice, or body language, come from elsewhere—a sick, declining parent, child, or other relative, one's own physical lack of health, the finances of the household. It can be situational or, in some individuals, habitual—a pessimistic, depressive personality and attitude toward others and life.

Or the anger, impatience, and negativity may be occasioned by particular others present and observed, or by the reason for the gathering.

The funeral I talked about, really an Easter celebration, brought together people who might ordinarily not see each other or spend time in each other's presence. Perhaps not so obvious is the fact that a funeral, much like a wedding or possibly even a baptism, is not an event that takes place regularly. Despite what clergy would like, you cannot schedule funerals, or for that matter weddings, by yourself as a pastor! Yes, obviously, the departed is necessary, not to mention the lovebirds.

So, I was reminded of one person for whom the celebration was a misery to be endured. This was a regular member, present at services and all the events I have described here. But, as many of us, this person is very much a creature of habit, preferring the usual flow and state of people and things in life. No different with life in our parish community. If something is different, someone new appears, this member is most aware!

Thus, at the big funeral, the presence of so many strangers, outsider friends of the deceased, both to visit and pray and to come share in the meal after the evening service was a veritable "invasion" both of our elder's space and tranquility. To see so many people in church and in the parish hall, people this person did not recognize or know, was deeply disturbing. This, after all, was personal space—the church, the hall, and the community. Who were all these outsiders? Why were they here, clogging the staircase and the aisles and the hall? Instinctively, our friend sought the periphery of the hall, a seat at a table against one wall, as the crowds moved past the buffet table, the level of elated conversation high. Could they not just leave, go home? But since they were not going to do so very quickly, this member of the community simply left after a cup of coffee, asking a relative for a ride.

This scene did not occur just at the post-funeral meal. And this person's reaction was not the only one of its kind. I must admit not only have I seen it at like events but even at Sunday coffee hours. When there is a baptism during the regular Sunday morning liturgy, there often are family members and friends present, both at the service and at coffee. The spread at the coffee hour quickly becomes an impressive brunch buffet very likely hosted, the food provided by the family of the one being baptized. Thus, there will be many faces that are unfamiliar, "outsiders" or, better, guests unknown to the community. They may not even be part of our church tradition and thus not know when to stand or sit or make the sign of the cross. Some may even be so bold, as communicants in their own home congregation, to come up and receive communion.

At least in my observation, for the most part, guests who attend baptisms, weddings, and funerals at our church are respectful, well behaved, even careful not to offend. Well, all right, there is the all-too-common reality of young women wearing outfits appropriate only for clubbing and parties and not for more formal events like weddings. There are also sometimes individuals so unaccustomed to being in a house of worship that they unknowingly and, I believe, unintentionally violate standards both for dress and behavior. More than once I have watched a young man wear a baseball cap into church and keep it on until told to remove it. I have also had to ask several young men to take themselves and their lit cigarettes out of both church and narthex at wedding rehearsals. I have been ordained long enough and "around the block," to put it colloquially, to have not just smelled alcohol on the breath but seen the signs of intoxication of young people at wedding rehearsals and wedding services, as well as much older folk at funerals. At one memorable funeral, feuding sides of a family and relatives of the deceased, fortified by drinks, gave every indication of wanting a fight after the interment at the cemetery. That is a colorful story for another time.

As extreme as inappropriate dress and behavior might seem, in my experience this is rare and usually restricted to weddings. Appropriately dressed and behaving guests, however, are still perceived by some parishioners not just as family and friends of the child being baptized, the couple being wed, or the one being buried. They are experienced as intruders and are not welcome. But as strange as this might appear for believers, there it is in the New Testament—those grumbling as Jesus takes up the invitation to eat with a tax collector, Zacchaeus, an outcast in their faith and society, or with women who come to wash his feet, with Samaritan and Syro-Phoenician outsiders, and assorted other persons of low repute.

As much as people may give to a church, not only money but their time to make pirogi, to bake nut and poppy seed rolls, and sell these and other food at fairs, they may also behave as though the very folks coming to purchase the same are somehow invading their precious, clean hall, making noise, jamming up the space, and generally disturbing the peace. I can hear several members of our parish voicing exactly these feelings as they tidied up the hall at the conclusion of the food fair. Why were those hundreds of dozen of pirogi made? Why the dozens of nut rolls? To sell, of course, to sell as many as possible. This would be the rational view. Yet, I have also heard great anxiety about whether there would be enough left or set aside "for our people." And such worry centers not only on the products but on the process itself. One veteran pirogi maker regularly proclaims that if we do not get sufficient numbers of volunteers to show up in the morning for pirogi production, why, then we'd simply have to discontinue the event! Every time pirogi making is scheduled, the same pessimistic "song" is sung. So far, in my twenty years of observation, there have always been enough workers to make the planned number and then some.

You might be tempted to blame such inhospitality and general crankiness on age, as almost all who so complain are seniors. You might also think it a product of their upbringing and experience in small-town churches, with rather ethnic and socially homogenous memberships.

But it is much more difficult to find either explanations or excuses when the nastiness is directed toward others whose names and faces they have known for years! One is told to "move it," because they are not moving quickly enough down the stairs and into the hall. Another is avoided because of trouble in the family. Or yet another is turned away from in the midst of a conversation because they said the wrong thing politically or shared a sadness or difficulty from their lives!

Now looking back at the symphony of talk and sharing as the pirogis were pinched, I realize that even in that generous, tolerant atmosphere, I recall facial grimaces or mutterings to the neighbor as an account of a sickness or a troubled relative unfolded. Rare were the direct, angry confrontations, though they did occur. More often, there was the silent treatment, avoidance, behind-the-back gossiping, the knowing look, the exchange among the inner circle, "Oh there he goes again. What a mess! . . . You know she's always been like that. . . . Those kids were never any good."

Even in a society of saints and angels, there will be sinners, so the great social theorist Emile Durkheim noted. Perhaps a reader will wonder, did this presence of human weakness not figure in the very Christian tradition? So what is the surprise or shock or embarrassment or even overlooking of the human condition, the always fallible, weak, and imperfect side of ourselves?

Of course, this is a reality of life in community, any community, from one's family to the monastery to any congregation. This is why we not only have the season of return and turning around, Lent, each year. Also, this is why we have in the usual Sunday service of every tradition, East or West, some confession of sin and request for God's forgiveness and that of our neighbors. The giving of the "kiss" of peace before communion is a constant from the ancient church restored in the recent past to many liturgies. This is why there is a sacrament of confession or reconciliation in which sins can be acknowledged and God's forgiveness assured. In the prayer before communion in the Eastern church tradition we hear St. Paul's admission, now put into our own mouths, "Of sinners I am the first." Also in the funeral rite: "There is no one living who has not sinned, you, Lord alone are without sin."

Beyond words and acts that reject, revile, and hurt another, there is also a more diffuse brokenness as well. I use this here as an umbrella term or symbol for quite diverse kinds of affliction that we cannot be said to be guilty of, for the states are not of our choice. The now elderly woman or man we take for an elder, respected in their family and neighborhood. Yet some have been subject to parental, sibling, spousal, and children's domination, emotional and verbal, and sometimes also physical abuse for years. Broken, grieving, starved for appreciation, approval, caring. There are numerous variations here too. Mix into this the powerful and all too often toxic effects of religion — the stress on pleasing a vengeful God, the warnings through a lifetime on eternal punishment, pain, torture awaiting a sinner, and then the anxiety resulting from being buried beneath these relentless threats. This is the caste phenomenon of the religiously observant and those who don't get to church or scrupulously keep the rules of fasting, or even the more basic commandments.

It is my observation that we now see more clearly the effects and consequences of bad religion among church-going folk. Studies seem to indicate higher rates of divorce, addiction, and neurosis among believers, and this from impartial researchers, not professional opponents and critics of religion. I see it, sadly, not just in those who have spent all their adult lives faithfully attending and supporting the church, sometimes even depriving their own families and themselves from time together and other sources of enrichment. I also see it already in young people as they bolt from church as soon as they possibly can and will tell you just how destructive and toxic the good news can be made to sound.

So what is prayerful about the messy humanity experienced in this community of a parish, which includes such smallmindedness and lack of hospitality or generosity or understanding as described? As I likely have intimated, a great deal. It first and foremost demands patience and genuine forgiveness and understanding of us when we encounter others somehow soured or embittered in our midst. At every Sunday liturgy, we hear: "Let us love one another, that with one mind we may confess, Father, Son, and Holy Spirit, the Trinity, one in essence and undivided." This is where the greeting or "kiss" of peace is to be exchanged. Built into every service, before we come to receive Christ in communion, are these words and gestures of reconciliation, as well as the words of St. Paul in which each participant acknowledges him- or herself as the greatest of sinners and in need of forgiveness.

It is not possible nor is it necessary for us to change their situation, to improve or remove what makes them negative, insensitive, judgmental, unable to accept others. A parish may be in many ways a therapeutic community, a place of healing for all of us. Yet even the pastors are not magicians. More often than not we have to allow God to work, the Spirit to blow in and cleanse and heal.

I would say that the same most positive, nourishing, caring aspects of community activities beyond the liturgy—those I have described at length—are themselves truly therapeutic. How often have I seen someone who is unhappy be drawn with care and concern out of his or her shell, made to forget self and worries for a little while, given a real welcome into the circle of those working, eating, and conversing. There are many aspects of our lives that cannot be changed—our age and gender, our past experiences and relationships—but each time "we assemble as church," and not just for services but for coffee, for a special event, for work, it is sheer gift of the many good things being part of a community brings.

Looking Ahead, to the Table Beyond

As I have argued, all these gatherings, from the pirogi making and baking to other parish celebrations, are for me beautiful and intense experiences of "uncommon prayer." This is prayer in quite informal, ordinary surroundings and activities, not the formal "common prayer" of the Sunday services in the sanctuary upstairs. There are also many things "uncommon" about it. Some starting out to read this chapter may have been confused or even troubled by calling this activity prayer at all—lively chatter around the table, pinching dough, rolling, cooking, packaging the finished pirogi, the spirited conversation on Sundays at coffee or the shared memories, stories, and mutual comforting after funerals, the rejoicing after a wedding or baptism. Where were the lighted candles, the choir, where was the priest to start it off? Where were the familiar words, the invocation of the Holy Trinity, the Mother of God, or any of the saints?

The only formal prayer at these gatherings—and it was quite brief—was grace briefly said before the meal and *bon appetit*! Everything else is as I have described it. Good news and sad, exchanged in trust and freedom. Memories of the departed shared, gratitude for the person and the life. The raucous glee at a wedding. But is such communal merry making really prayer? We may recall from church school classes that prayer can be praise, thanksgiving, intercession for others or ourselves, asking forgiveness, among other things. Prayer as we often conceive of it can be things we say to God, things God says to us—especially in meditative reading—or silence, presence with God.

If prayer is essentially encounter and interaction, then the communal activity of Eastern church Christians making pirogi, baking nut rolls and Easter bread, celebrating anniversaries and weddings, mortgage burnings and the passing of a fellow Christian—all of these are opportunities not just for recited prayer but for lived prayer. How many times do we find Jesus at a wedding, like that in Cana, alongside a funeral cortege as that of the widow's son or the deathbed of Jairus's daughter or at Lazarus's tomb? He invites himself to Zacchaeus's house for supper and dines with Simon the Pharisee and numerous times breaks bread with his disciples and friends. He asks for something to eat after having appeared following the resurrection, and he even makes breakfast for those disciples out fishing all night—roast fish and bread over an open fire on the shore. The two companions on the road only recognize him when he blesses and breaks the bread, says grace, in the inn at Emmaus. Jesus's promise of always being present in the bread and the cup at the Last Supper was but one of many meals, many times of sharing in which he communed with his friends.

When one considers all the petitionary activity in the liturgy, all the listening to scripture and preaching, the offering of the gifts and the sharing of the bread and cup, are the many details of a community event not liturgical? A grandmother offers her worry about her grandchildren. A parent expresses profound sadness in the face of an adult child's divorce. A senior recounts the path of a life, the meeting of a beloved spouse, transition from one community to another, children raised and sent on their way. Someone cannot contain the joy of a new baby in the family, of triumph in fighting addiction or treatment for depression. Friends worry about the future. Who will be the pastor after Father, who has been with us so long a time? "Let us pray to the Lord . . . let us lift up our hearts . . . let us give thanks to the Lord . . . let us depart in peace!"

As Amy-Jill Levine observes, so much of Jesus's accepting the invitations of friends to supper, his eating and drinking with all kinds of people, even sinners, were parables enacted. Like pirogi making, the baking sessions and food fairs, like the Sunday coffee hours and post-funeral, post-wedding feasts, all were signs of the messianic banquet, the gathering of all the children of God round their Father's table in the world, the age to come, pictures of paradise, but made actual already by joy and sharing here.

CHAPTER NINE

The Prayer of the Classroom

Encounter and Listening

Teaching and Prayer

I have been a teacher in a number of different levels and contexts. As an undergraduate student I taught in religious education programs and at summer camps, and after graduation I taught high school for a year. As a graduate student I was a classroom instructor in the last three years of my doctoral program. Then I was fortunate enough to be offered a tenure track position, and I have taught at the same undergraduate school of the City University of New York since 1977.

While I have spent most of my adult life teaching, reading, writing, giving papers and sermons — after all, this is what professors do — I now understand that all of this is also very much prayer. This became clear after finishing the more than one thousand pages of theologian Hans Küng's first two volumes of memoirs.[1] From childhood in the 1930s and '40s to higher education, graduate degrees, university professorships, a veritable tsunami of publications, controversy, conflict with the Vatican, and dismissal as a Catholic theologian, it was striking how matter of fact he was, as a priest too, about prayer. There is, in both volumes' photo galleries, and I am sure deliberately, an image of him vested and celebrating the liturgy.

And for all his brashness, he notes that first thing in the morning, also at noon and last of all at night, he raises his mind to God, without many words or forms. A theologian, and a most controversial one at that, who prays! How does one then assess what Küng spent almost fifty years doing—the writings describing the basics of being a Christian, those calling for reform and renewal, the others critically examining the church's history, and then the more recent explorations of the links among the world religious traditions, and the questions about end of life issues that only an eighty-five-year-old with several serious medical conditions could raise. Would it be wrong to look on what Küng did over all those years, or for that matter, what Dominican priest and theologian Yves Congar chronicled in his diaries, or Dorothy Day and Thomas Merton in their journals, as prayer?[2] Why not?

Saint Benedict's rule, as Esther de Waal and others have taught us in recent years, is not only apt for monasteries but for all kinds of people in their lives and work.[3] In the rule, Benedict builds on the wisdom of the unnamed "Master" who earlier constructed such a guide, no doubt Pachomius as well as Basil. It is a stark and unnerving clarity that mothers and fathers of the desert achieved. They were able, removed from the whirl and turmoil of the city, to return to basics, to the sources, to perceive as did the prophets and apostles long before them. A strong theme in their comments was not to impose one's own classifications on things. The all too easy distinctions between what was sacred and what was profane, what was nearer to God and further away—their sayings, terse, shocking in simplicity and insight, tore away the curtain and the barriers put up to better order society and even the church.

Supposedly great ascetic athletes, they scandalize by saying that one should eat what's put before one, regardless of the season or one's personal ascetic standards. You do not run and hide from the woman or man who comes in pain and seeking assistance because they are the opposite sex or from "the world."[4] The time for church services—you ignore that and do what you can for the desperate person before you. Mother Maria Skobtsova, in the Great Depression's misery and the terror of the Nazi occupation of Paris, provoked criticism for not staying for the whole morning service, or even showing up, because she needed to forage leftovers and remaindered produce at the farmers' markets. Those guests in her hostel had to eat. Could they eat the psalms and antiphons sung in the chapel? Dorothy Day would get up in the quiet of the morning to read her prayers. The rest of the day her prayers were the stinking, filthy, homeless folk who staggered into the Catholic Worker houses for baths, better clothes, a meal, perhaps medical care.

Benedict makes it clear that while there is a round of activities, a diversity of work to be done, one ought to view the pots and pans of the kitchen as equal to the eucharistic vessels, the plates and cups for serving Holy Communion, the body and blood of the Lord (Rule of Benedict, chapter 31). He identifies the guest who seeks hospitality as Christ (chapter 53), but he also sees the community's leader, the abbot, as Christ and each member, from the most senior and gifted down to the newest, untrained and less skilled, also as Christ (chapter 2). Benedict's vision is best summed up in what has become the motto of all Benedictines: *pax, ora et labora*—peace, to work and pray. It is most genuine to see, as does Benedict throughout the rule, that work and prayer are entwined with each other. It is no coincidence that the most lucid spiritual writers of our time, themselves struggling always in the life with God and others, Rohr, Merton, Taylor, Day—yes, precisely those we listen to here—want to break down the wall of dualism that sorts people into good and bad, that which wants to distinguish the sacred from the profane or the spiritual from the worldly.

Related is a kind of bad faith that makes us think the problems are always out there, with others, rather than inside us. The same flawed vision drives us to turn what oppress and torment us or that drive our economy and government into impersonal powers, inanimate forces that run the universe. Paul's letters seem to admit the existence of such powers, only to smash through their supposed control over us by turning our sights toward Christ.

The point here is that the same apostle Paul's injunction to pray at all times means that all times can, in fact, be times of prayer. Individuals as diverse and as discerning as Küng and Congar, Dorothy Day and Maria Skobtsova, St. Benedict and Thomas Merton, came to see this as a revelation—prayer everywhere in experience. We have explored different places and moments in which prayer is to be found, and here we encounter yet one more—the experience of learning, of reading, discussing, even fiercely debating, both in the classroom and outside it. But then again, great spiritual minds from Teresa of Avila to Basil the Great, from Benedict of Nursia to Martin Luther King Jr., knew the encounter with God possible in teaching and learning.

Religion and Culture

Graduate school was not only work with my advisor and mentor, the sociologist and theologian Peter L. Berger. In the program at Rutgers University at that time, it was possible to not just serve as a teaching assistant but actually be responsible for entire courses. Today we have doctoral students from the CUNY Graduate Center as teaching fellows doing the same—the classroom experience is invaluable for later job hunting, and tuition remission and modest stipends help. Though previously I had taught at various levels, from Headstart to high school, it was only as an instructor at Douglass College at Rutgers that I really began to learn to be a teacher.

All of this brings me to my teaching for forty years now on the faculty of Baruch College of the City University of New York. At Baruch there is an interdisciplinary Program in Religion and Culture, not a department but a collection of professors and courses. Faculty participation is voluntary, thus the course selection varies greatly from one semester to another. Nevertheless, it is possible to both major and minor in religion and culture. Many business majors, needing a non-business liberal arts minor, choose religion and culture. In addition to courses specifically offered in religion there are usually others in various departments dealing with religion—in literature, philosophy, history. These are crosslisted and qualify for major or minor credit, along with independent study/tutorial courses. While a course in religion in American history and society has always been my responsibility, almost from the start I also participated in the religion and culture program and for many years have been its coordinator.

My contributions include comparative religious traditions, as well as introductory and overview courses in Christianity and courses on writers and activists and their spiritual journeys. As in religious study departments everywhere, other courses deal with Judaism, Islam, Buddhism, Hinduism—overviews as well as special topics, such as the diverse religious communities of New York City.

It makes no difference which way it's tracked, whether through the list of courses taught at Baruch, the papers presented at conferences, articles and books published—by both choice and professional situation, I always seem to be dealing with how the spiritual life is experienced and how religious faith affects society and culture. This has been the case, whether exploring a modern thinker of the nineteenth century such as Kierkegaard and his polemics against bourgeois, domesticated religion to later examining how émigré Russian religious thinkers sought to open conversation between Christian faith and modern culture in the twentieth century of the Russian Revolution, the Great Depression, and the world wars. Both in my writing as well as teaching, I have been led from these thinkers to quite a list of poets, writers, activists, and others struggling to find meaning and God in their lives, striving to live in the spirit and do good.

Over the years, students have produced a constant stream of questions and criticism, complaints, and challenges about faith, God, evil, suffering, goodness, and joy. It is startling to hear Muslim and Buddhist students speak after they have read the gospels in the New Testament for the first time, encountering Jesus, his words and actions, rather than right-wing religion in American politicized form. I have heard a number of heartbreaking experiences of what only can be called "toxic" religion from students who grew up in church, attended not just Sunday school but full-time private religious school. But also I have heard marvelous accounts of how faith enabled students and their families to weather the trauma of immigration, life in a new, confusing country in which they experience suspicion from anyone different in color or accent. In the courses on the history of the Christian traditions, as well as in comparative world religious traditions, we have as a learning community looked hard at the ways in which religion fought for freedom but also took it away from people. Students from Central and South America and from the Caribbean often experienced and thus gave voice to deep ambivalence about religion. The best schools were those supported by the church. Grandparents and parents were devoted to prayer and worship, whether Hindu or Buddhist or Christian. Faith and tradition sustained families, back home and here in America. At the same time, faith and tradition erected barriers to those outside their boundaries. Several students from ultra-Orthodox Jewish groups talked of the deception and concealment necessary to have college friends, even to date outside their communities or have a boy- or girlfriend at all. LGBT students spoke fairly consistently of having to part ways with the religious communities of their childhood because of a lack of tolerance or acceptance of who they were.

On rare occasions, a student would come to me, usually after class or in office hours, with a particular spiritual question or existential personal crisis. The fact that all of us, faculty as well as students, commuted to school, that it was not a residential campus, made relationships more segmented, functional, temporary. To be sure, students would write back, requesting letters of recommendation for graduate study and for employment. Some students would take more courses with me after the first, and these were ones I got to know best, especially those who did an ad hoc major in religion and culture. This necessitated regular meetings as they moved toward completion of the major and graduation. But while interaction in class is often moving and intense, the hectic scheduling of classes by students alongside jobs and family obligations make sustained interaction less frequent. Yet some memorable students and their situations give expression to the kinds of prayer that reading, reflecting, writing, and classroom conversation create.

An Encounter and Journey of Faith

One very gifted student came to Baruch as a transfer and had decided, before starting, that she wanted to pursue a major in religion and culture, a rather unusual choice even in the large Baruch Weissmann School of Liberal Arts and Sciences. In almost four decades I think I have only worked with a half-dozen such majors, though I have worked with a number who minored. After taking several of the regular courses I offer, such as the overview historical approach to Christianity and the courses on the New Testament and World Religious Traditions, she also did as many independent study courses with me as possible. These are designed to enable students to pursue topics not covered in regularly scheduled courses as well as issues and areas of special interest.

Having been raised in a rather traditional evangelical church background, this student wanted to immerse herself in the more progressive Christian thinkers in the United States in the last century. With bibliographic suggestions and other advice from me, she was most creative. She structured for herself three independent study courses that took her through some of the major figures and writers in liberal Christianity, from Niebuhr and Bonhoeffer to Rob Bell and Brian MacLaren, among others. Her essays were intriguing. They revealed profound rethinking on her part but not abandonment of the kind of faith in which she had grown up. She and her husband, in their later twenties and both well-educated professionals, remained regular members of a congregation in the city. They had looked around for some time when they moved to New York, trying out parishes of various denominations. From many conversations about what she had read in the authors mentioned, and what she'd heard in other courses, particularly the overview of the history of Christianity, it was clear that she was working hard to move out of the comfortable, certain faith of her past. I sensed that the essentials of Christianity were not in question, but a great deal more was. The engagement of religion in the "culture wars," the all-too-easy alienation of any who disagreed, the absolute, nonnegotiable positions on LGBT people, war, the role of government, the place of women in our society, to mention a few, were too simplistic, too dogmatic, particularly where there was room for honest debate. She had heard that Rob Bell's book, *Love Wins*, was controversial for many Christians. She had simply not, in the midst of moving, working in a small business, and then trying to finish her undergraduate degree, taken the time to read it. So, Rob Bell was put at the top of a reading list for her first independent study course. The idea for focusing this course on progressive Christianity was hers, for she found a number of perspectives no longer real in living her adult life. And the thought of reading not quite "forbidden" but controversial literature was enticing.

We had many opportunities to discuss the questions that progressive religious thinkers raised and how she was integrating these into her own perspectives. These included, besides Bell and MacLaren, Donald Miller, Shane Claiborne, and Miroslav Volf. We also read and discussed a number of other writers in another course—Thomas Merton, Maria Skobtsova, Barbara Brown Taylor, Dorothy Day, Sara Miles—all voices we are listening to in this book, voices unknown to her previously. It was not that this student was now being exposed to merely a more liberal and tolerant version of Christianity. None of these authors would accurately be described as mere shills for a religion of joy, peace, and love. Taylor's *Learning to Walk in the Dark* as well as her other books dispel that very quickly and powerfully, as does Sara Miles's writings.

For me, it was a privilege to listen to this student and read the essays she crafted, occasionally to bring in the ideas of still more writers not included in her reading lists. I also shared what I was working on, namely the chapter in *Saints As They Really Are* that dealt with my own spiritual journey earlier in life, when I was in the Carmelite order and then left it. I also told her about some of the figures profiled in *Hidden Holiness*, these being books she also read in the course on contemporary Christian thinkers. From the start it was important to this student that I was not only an academic or professional specialist in religion but myself a believer and, moreover, a pastor. I was humbled by the honesty with which she listened to very different perspectives in Christian discourse from those with which she was most familiar. This was by no means a "conversion" experience, a once-conservative Christian seeing the light, becoming progressive, liberal, tolerant. There clearly was a continual challenge to what she believed, and as far as I could see, there were no important changes when it came to basics. Yet, as part of a much broader and deeper expansion of horizons she was experiencing, coming from the Midwest to the East Coast, her religious perspectives likewise were becoming more generous. She was interacting, in class, with fellow students of a far more diverse range of ethnic, class, and religious backgrounds than she had earlier in her undergraduate career and at church. And this experience of greater diversity pushed her earlier boundaries and really did enable her to listen to new experiences.

Because she was not only graduating but preparing for the birth of her first child, I have had only sporadic communication in recent years. Yet just this one student's journey to graduation and through a religion major was for me an example of how prayer includes more than the usual formal contexts of services, scriptures, and churchly locations. "Faith seeks understanding," wrote Anselm of Canterbury, and Augustine, "I believe so that I may understand." Not pitting reason versus revelation here, but rather the long tradition of room for rational inquiry, questioning, criticism, even doubt in the realm of religious faith. There were, as noted, students in several of my courses who admitted, quite without embarrassment, jettisoning all the church-going, prayer, and belief of their childhood when faced with intolerance, rigidity, and condemnation of active intellectual reflection and examination of faith.

If for church fathers and so many other writers, faith involved intellectual activity, clearly for this religion major the project of reexamining her tradition was prayerful. And so was it, I would argue, for those who, in reading Dorothy Day, Thomas Merton, and others, found that even those who remained in the church and spent their lives in writing and outreach also were capable of criticism of how the institutional church and its leaders behaved—sometimes very badly. While it was no longer the Great Depression or the era of the civil rights movements or the Vietnam war, students would connect the Christian radicalism of King and Day, Skobtsova and Bonhoeffer, with the struggle for women's rights, for the rights of LGBT people, against racism and inequality, both resurgent in the second decade of the twenty-first century.

Reading and Trust: Sharing Struggle

We read in my courses several of Sara Miles's moving books—*Take this Bread, Jesus Freak, City of God*—about the food pantry at St. Gregory of Nyssa church in San Francisco's Mission district, about Sara's own conversion experience, her struggle, and her ministering to the families of incarcerated young people, to those experiencing the effects of substance abuse and poverty in an affluent city. Likewise, we read of the setting up of houses of hospitality in the early 1930s, simultaneously in New York and Paris, by Dorothy Day and Mother Maria Skobtsova. This was not reading Butler's *Lives of the Saints*, a very traditional, even stereotypical exercise in hagiography. Rather, following the accounts of these women, as well as the experiences of Mother Teresa, Barbara Brown Taylor, and the searing memoirs of Mary Karr and Mira Bartok, students amazed each other and me with their willingness to share equally striking situations in which they were living.

One student began her reflection to the class by apologizing that she had really not been raised with much religion. There were some incense sticks burned at a local Buddhist temple on special days, and a tiny shrine in her family's living room. In the course we had encountered Mary Karr's and Mira Bartok's accounts of unbelievable childhoods with emotionally ill, severely dysfunctional parents in *Lit* and *The Memory Palace*. Karr remarked in an interview that when she gives readings, the first question asked usually is, "How come you're still alive today?" I should add here that not all the texts we read and discussed were so emotionally wrenching, and Mary Karr treats the difficult history of her parents' addiction and lack of personal control with both hilarity and grace, not to mention with forgiveness.

The student could have stuck to the text, always a safe and legitimate procedure. But rather than comment on it, she chose to do a mini-memoir of her own most challenging childhood, one in which, as a girl, she was never praised or encouraged, these saved for her brothers. As a young woman she was expected, no matter her schoolwork and job, to help her mother with housework, cleaning, cooking, and care of her grandmother, tasks that the males in the family were not expected to do. She did very well in middle school, so well that she was admitted to one of the city's most prestigious high schools, Stuyvesant, where she continued to excel academically. Home, however, was rough, and, with the decline of her grandmother's health, it became a nightmare. Asian culture demanded that an elder be cared for at home, by the family, with only minimal, necessary assistance from a visiting nurse. My student described how her grandmother would wail and scream all through the night as a result of dementia. Only the women in the family tried to calm her down, no matter the time. Care of this elderly, afflicted soul was women's work. It became normal that the student and her mother never got a full night's sleep, and sleep deprivation is devastating to both physical and mental health. Eventually the student's mother needed treatment herself, but no allowance was ever made for the student's school and work obligations.

The atmosphere of trust created by the community of students that took shape in the class meetings enabled this student to reveal so much with which she struggled. She acknowledged her long-term depression, due in part to lack of parental support for her achievement in school as well as the immense burden of helping to care for elderly relatives suffering with dementia, all this in addition to school and other responsibilities. She was on the verge of crying, but suppressed this. Immediately it was as if the rest of the class surrounded her with empathy. I heard a great deal of concern expressed, encouragement given, after her presentation. I saw, after class ended, several fellow students gathered around the student described above, providing reassurance in gestures and expressions. I was not close enough to hear what was said, but there were more tears, intense conversation. I suspect other students could speak from similar experiences.

This reflection, based on authentic *lectio divina* or spiritual reading, team presentations, discussion in class, and further reflection in essays—is such a project not prayer? If prayer is the growth of spiritual presence, if it is learning about not just God but oneself and about one's neighbors, how could this deep learning not be prayer?

Sharing One's Journey and Wisdom

I want to share the story of another class participant, someone who enrolled in several of my courses over a couple years. She was a "mature" student: she had returned to complete an undergraduate degree after years of work and parenting, and was greatly encouraged by the honesty and sharing of classmates younger than her children, maybe just a little older than her grandchildren. She was also a most encouraging, nurturing presence for them as well. The rapport with classmates unleashed in her both the need and the venue for talking about a powerful settling up with her religious tradition. She had an ultra-Orthodox Jewish upbringing, one from which she broke in young adulthood to marry. In several essays in a couple of different courses, she wrote a mini-memoir of her own religious journey, of the enormous familial pressure exerted on her from adolescence onward, which drove her out of her community into the wider Jewish as well as secular worlds bordering the neighborhood in which she once was virtually captive. There was no striking out in rage at the *frum* or observant way of life of her early years. Rather, immense gratitude is what she expressed, that, having experienced this, she now had been able to read, listen, and converse with so many friends and neighbors and learn so much not only of other faith traditions but her own, Judaism. One of her most satisfying projects was an essay based on hours of interviews with an almost legendary Roman Catholic urban priest, one known for his commitment to his community, not just that of his parish but of all the neighborhoods around it. This student, almost my exact contemporary in experience and age — we are both in our sixties and very much products of the 1960s — was for me a "living icon" of how faith can liberate, deepen, and beautify life and personality. While a grandparent several times over, she always struck me as youthful, livelier and more engaged than fellow students forty years younger than herself. This showed itself not only in religion courses but also in advanced courses on social theory in which we addressed almost every controversial political and social issue of today, from LGBT rights to income inequality and latent racism that does not use the language of hate but is hateful nonetheless. Talk about "tradition," or the literal "passing down," the "handing over" of truth from one generation to another. Her presence as a student was also the presence of a master teacher who taught not only by words but even more so by compassion, insight, patience, and understanding. I almost felt like I was in church or a monastic community, places where all my life I have learned and prayed. That's what it was like having her, this wise, experienced, discerning grandmother in my courses.

Encounters: Identity and Racism

In another course, one on social theory, a remarkable, probably unrepeatable convergence of students took place one fall semester. Not long after we began the class, superstorm Sandy blasted the greater New York City area, and our school, in lower Manhattan, was closed for a week because flooding had damaged local substations. There was no power, yet several larger ground floor spaces at the school became shelters for those driven out of their homes. Several students in the course from the boroughs most affected by storm damage—especially flooding and wind damage to homes—had to evacuate and spent weeks living with relatives. As demonstrated in the weeks after 9/11, New Yorkers are tough. They bounce back, want life and work to return to normal.

However, it was not Sandy, its destruction, or the aftermath that was notable with this particular class. Rather, it was an unusual mix of ethnic backgrounds and ages in the course that made it remarkable. There were several older students, that is, individuals in their late twenties or early thirties, a couple even in their forties. This was an advanced course that all sociology majors were required to take, and it counted as an advanced elective in a couple of other majors, such as political science and psychology. The mix of more mature, serious students with those of more typical undergraduate college age made for a greater focus and intensity in class discussion quite unlike my usual experience of the course. Given the collection of readings we go through, the range of issues from the women's movement to social justice issues and social protest, class conflict and economic inequality and the situation of LGBT people in our society, there are a lot of intense topics presented by working teams and then discussed in the group. The size of the course, about twenty, enabled rather lively discussion to take place.

Now, given all the issues that the writers we sampled served up, there were numerous moments of dynamic exchange. One of the most intense and memorable had to do with racism, identity, and racist behavior. I believe this was enhanced by the fact that in this group of twenty, there were at least a dozen "persons of color." How complex this designation and identity has become was evidenced by the actual identities and origins. One student, with a Latino last name, was African American, Puerto Rican, and Egyptian. He was married to a Dominican. "You see what my name is and how I look," he remarked in the discussion. "But who am I, really? With what group do I side?

Tell me, you guys. I know I am not sure." The question under discussion, growing out of essays we had read from W. E. B. DuBois, Dr. Martin Luther King Jr., Henry Louis Gates, and Cornel West, was: Does racism still exist in American society? Conservative political and social commentators were claiming it did not. A recent Supreme Court decision had struck down provisions of the Voting Rights Act. Numerous states with Republican majorities in their legislatures were enacting more qualifications for voting including picture IDs, while at the same time cutting the number of days on which voting could take place before election day. There had been a nasty incident in which Tea Party protestors spit on a number of African American members of Congress, including civil rights veteran John Lewis. Harvard professor Henry Louis Gates was arrested for trying to enter his own home in Cambridge, Massachusetts. In addition to Gates, notable African Americans such as actor Danny Glover, Professor Cornel West, and businessman Earl G. Graves Jr. have been stopped, frisked, interrogated, and taken into custody simply because they were black and in the wrong location, by police standards. Obviously, in the class, the face and identity of President Barack Obama also came up in the discussion of America being post-racial.

The team presentation unleased a flurry of first-person narratives from the class. This was very much in the genre of personal testimony. No one present was attacked. Nevertheless, the feelings ran strong. It was a profound and often humbling act of sharing what it was like, in everyday life, to be perceived as "other," as different, threatening, and suspicious. But also, there was the sense of being unwanted, of not really being part of the neighborhood, community, or society. There were accounts, mostly by young male students, of being stopped and frisked themselves. But I was astonished when an older student, in her early forties and from a mixed Caribbean background, spoke movingly of looks and stares in trains, at bus stops, and even on the platform in Grand Central Station. She also described others crossing the street to walk on the other side rather than next to her. She was married, the parent of two teenagers, and a human resources employee of the City of New York. A college-age Dominican woman student spoke of how often her father was stopped by police and questioned on his way to and from work. Others echoed these accounts, noting that they had experienced similar treatment as outcasts. The mother of the teenagers summed up what she and the rest were saying: "I have been treated as though I was different, to be feared, as not fitting in all of my life. All of my family has experienced the same even though we were born here, sound like everyone else, and are citizens. When I hear that we are 'over racism,' or that there is no racism any longer, I want to ask, 'For whom?' I will experience racism for the rest of my life. This is what it is like to be a person of color."

In all the years I have taught at this urban, public university, I have seen diversity of students, not so much of staff and faculty. In the early days of my teaching, the early 1980s, the diversity was not as broad, and there was more visible, obvious clustering of Latino, African American, and Asian students in public locations such as the cafeteria. There have always been ethnic as well as religious, social, and political clubs or groups at the school. There is a Muslim Students' Association, which has been infiltrated by plainclothes NYPD officers. One of our sociology majors, a young Egyptian woman whose family migrated here, was forced out of the army, where she was training as an Arabic language specialist and translator. Apparently, in a background check, her name appeared as attending social gatherings of the Baruch Muslim Students' Association. She did not go to prayers, since she was not a practicing Muslim. Faculty and student groups tried to investigate this surveillance, practiced widely on mosques and Islamic cultural centers and organizations, and defended by the then-administration of Mayor Michael Bloomberg and Police Commissioner Ray Kelly as necessary for public security.

Occasionally, there would be articles in the student newspaper and calls from a few faculty members for more diversity in hiring of staff and faculty. In recent years, probably the most significant growth has been in the admission of international students. These pay a much higher tuition that New York City residents and have impressive test scores and academic records. The diversity at Baruch has grown so that for several years the school was identified as the most diverse undergraduate institution in the country. Baruch information sites boasted of nearly 120 languages spoken by students, faculty, and staff.

But, for all the diversity, the globalization programs in various of the schools of the college, and the obviously global character of many

of the corporations, banks, and investment houses that look for interns and new employees from our graduates, when I ask a class about
racism, the majority of students say it is alive and at work, though
often not using the epithets and language of the past. Racism also now
encounters a far more complex, mixed, diverse population. A student
of color could be African American, West African, Haitian, Caribbean, or Southeast Asian. And, of course, each of these adjectives is
an umbrella, covering many particular countries and backgrounds.

How is what I have described prayer, especially, these raw, bru-
tally honest revelations of racist behavior, discrimination, shunning?
Well, here the experience of the African American church historically
is helpful. The suffering not only under slavery but also under official,
legally established segregation and discrimination was connected with
the stories of the Israelite people in the scriptures. The struggles for
emancipation and, afterwards, for civil rights were cast in the light of
the Exodus experience and the yearning of the Israelites to be free to
be able to worship and live. This connection was to be found not only
in well-known hymns and gospel music but in preaching particularly.
A most public example came in Dr. King's famous "I Have a Dream"
speech during the civil rights era. More recently President Barack
Obama's eulogy at the funeral of the pastor killed with others in
Charleston is another. In all these, prayer breaks out of the confines
of church services and even the scriptures to connect with the experiences of the people, both those of misery as well as triumph.

If one can move from the association of prayer solely to houses
of worship, sacred texts, and rituals, I would point to the testimony,
confession, and sharing that went on in this theory class, over a number of meetings, and not just on the issue of whether there still was
racism. In the courses I have described, students, supposedly not interested in politics or social issues, begin to connect, as C. Wright
Mills put it, in "sociological imagination," their lives and history, their
biographies, and the society around them. They also, without using
explicitly religious language, probed the ethical aspects of racism, of
politically produced economic inequality, of social injustice, of discrimination on the basis of gender, sexual identity, and ethnicity. No
direct equivalent of the prayer of the scriptures or the services of
church, temple, or masjid intended.

But if we are encouraged "to pray all the time," and if we are, in Paul Evdokimov's words, "to become what we pray," then is not learning a kind of everyday, uncommon prayer? Surely, as I listened to students responding to Dorothy Day's fiercely radical columns in the *Catholic Worker* newspaper and to Thomas Merton's questions about how to find sacred reality in the midst of work, home, school, and in one's own feelings and thinking, I heard many things. I heard indignation that there is so little public commitment by leaders, religious or political, to peace making and to the plight of so many who do not share in the growing wealth of less than 1 percent of our society. But I have also detected real grappling with the challenges of the poetry of Mary Oliver to quiet the frenzy in oneself, to look past the buzz of business and work to appreciate the mystery of the natural world, a mystery to be found in each of us. I have seen knowing nods as Mary Karr's or Mira Bartok's struggles with addiction and parental abuse were discussed in class by presentation teams. Young women and men constantly told that the world is their oyster are shocked when they are pressed up against the dregs of failure, as in Barbara Brown Taylor's account of her breakdown, not as a corporate executive, physician, or lawyer, but as a priest!

Prayer in the World: Does Anything Change as a Result?

By now, I hope it has become clear that so much of my experience as an educator has been in the realm of prayer and the acts of loving-kindness. In telling the many stories that make up my prayer list, you learned that alongside my years as a professor at the City University of New York, I have served in several parishes as an ordained priest. At Baruch College, I don't wear a clerical collar or anything else to distinguish that part of my profession. It is a public, secular institution of higher learning. But in full disclosure, I always tell my students what else I do, namely, that I am a priest. There is a collection of photos they can access online of the parish where I serve. But prayer isn't about some special status in a religious community. In every major faith tradition in the world, prayer is universal, for all. And like the Barbara Brown Taylor of *Leaving Church*, I have for a very long time realized one does not need to be wearing a clerical collar, vestments, or cross, does not need to be known or addressed as "Reverend" or "Pastor" or be ordained to do ministry.

Mostly I have reflected on ways in which life in the classroom, as a teacher, look to me to be moments of prayer. I could only share a few stories, but they have numerous others behind them that I remember, and even more I don't. In chapter 5, when riffing off my prayer list and all the networks of relationships summarized there, I reflected as "a man of the cloth," an ordained pastor. There is nothing that the status of professor or priest adds to prayer. It is still surprising to me that there has been and continues to be so much of a prayerful nature in teaching, but then I recall how close this profession is to the other, where preaching, leading worship, and listening to people are the stuff of ministry.

All through this book, I have emphasized the very ordinary, everyday, rather worldly character of prayer. I hope this is coming through not just in my experiences shared here but also from many of the writers to whom we are listening. James Carroll, Gary Wills, and Barbara Brown Taylor, in more popular commentaries, note that most of the four Gospels in the New Testament do not take place in the Jerusalem Temple or other equivalents of church and services, formal, "common prayer."[5] Amy-Jill Levine is perhaps the most consistent in stressing that Jesus, as a Jew in the first century of the common era, had the usual, ordinary relationship to Temple and synagogue for anyone of that time. Living the Torah, faithful and normal practice, did not mean obsession with time in sacred space and houses of learning and prayer. It is clear he frequented local synagogues, praying and teaching in them. But the real point is that the teaching and healing Jesus did was rooted in and oriented toward everyday life. The parables draw on experiences in the lives of farmers, fishermen, parents, those maintaining a home and family, doing business. In his interactions with those of the religious establishment, as Levine stresses, it is a misunderstanding to see Jesus opposing Judaism. Rather he speaks and acts within it, as a rabbi, a member of the house of Israel.[6] Thus, there is a powerfully pragmatic character to even the back and forth "learning" and debate with scribes, lawyers, and other students of the Torah. Parables seek to find concrete applications of teaching—the merciful father and prodigal son, the good Samaritan, the woman who lost her treasured keepsake coins, the farmer sowing, the shrewd property manager, the rich man and the poor man, Dives and Lazarus, and so on.

When it comes to higher education today, the headlines are not encouraging. There is the question of whether many schools are attentive to sexual abuse, especially date rape suffered by women students. The cost of an undergraduate education continues to climb, despite a great deal of structural shrinkage such as utilizing more part-time or adjunct faculty, cutting programs or departments like classics and languages no longer deemed market-attractive. The number of administrators grows as faculty find their salaries frozen or reduced. And periodically, despite a wealth of literature and data to the contrary, the very value of an undergraduate education continues to be questioned.

Nevertheless, year after year students enroll and pursue degrees and, in the course of this, find their experience of home, their values, and very identities challenged. Over the decades, our department and the religion and culture program at Baruch have taken seriously the ideal of the humanities and social sciences to encourage students to dig beneath obvious political and social perspectives to face the confrontations their learning imposes on them. But all of this is to deepen their humanity, make them uneasy about social injustice and inequality, to sharpen their ethical sensitivity. In classes of honors students, often rather ostentatious about their very privileged status in the school, reading texts that challenge that status, their professional fixations, and career planning is a prophetic endeavor. In my introduction to social science, these honor students read—and it is surprising that it is, for most, the first time—Chris Hedges's devastating narrative *War Is a Force That Gives Us Meaning*, Michael Pollan's provocative look at where our food comes from, *Omnivore's Dilemma,* Paul Krugman's *The Return of Depression Economics*, Darcey Steinke's powerful memoir *Easter Everywhere*, Jared Diamond's *Guns, Germs, and Steel* on which cultures rule, Kathryn Schulz's riveting reflection of fallibility, *Being Wrong*, Atul Gawande's meditation on mortality, and other texts.[7] Not a theological volume among these, but what an excavation of the human condition, of our most destructive tendencies as well as most thrilling works of mercy. They complain a bit at first, but I have yet to see an honors class reject this basic approach, a humanistic one, as my teacher Peter Berger called it, to understanding who we are as persons, moral agents, and societies and why we behave the ways we do. One colleague employs a daily examination of the *New York Times* to the same end.

Has this kind of humanizing learning anything to do with prayer? Yes, decisively. As Richard Rohr argues throughout his writing and lecturing, such learning precisely attacks our dualistic thinking: us versus them, we good folk versus the axis of evil over there. Also assaulted are the dualisms of human versus natural world, of the injustices in society and my alleged lack of both responsibility for and incapacity of responding to these. Over against repressive political systems, students are asked to remember what remains liberating and hopeful in this country. While the Occupy Movement was thought politically ineffective, I know that in class after class I taught, the 99 percent and the 1 percent were persistent as talking points. Whether looking back at earlier historical periods in our own country or vastly different cultures, students were given the opportunity to compare, to wonder where we might be if there were less gender discrimination, less racism, a more just immigration policy, a thorough rethinking of defense spending and tax breaks and subsidies over against the promise of better education, health care, and environmentally sound policies.

In the examples of students I have used in this chapter, my work and relationships with them were rooted in the classroom. Of course learning takes place beyond a room with little more than chairs, a board for inkless markers, and a "smart podium" with internet access. That said, a great deal of interaction takes place in the classroom, such as the description of students' reaction to the claim of a post-racial era or the end of racism.

In my religion and culture courses, the name and concept of God appears often, not so much in the courses on social theory. Yet given how we are urged to think by the Hebrew and Christian scriptures, to speak only of these two traditions, is God ever absent when dealing with human behavior and the world, even if not invoked or named? If God is present to the human being, to the person, there is prayer.

Does prayer change anything? Is prayer the engine of change, or is it the sign that change is taking place? Prayer, as another chapter in this book argues, is about remembering. Prayer has to do with who we are, how we spend our time, with the sense we make of our work and relationships. It was reading those powerful accounts of spiritual seeking, listening to the presentation teams of students tell all the rest of us in the class what the writer said to them—and, with enormous force, how the experiences of these writers connected with their own lives, their own crises, failures, disappointments, but also hopes and triumphs. The prayer was to find so much right there, in the neighborhood, the block, the job, and the school. Once again as New Testament scholar Amy-Jill Levine says of Jesus's parables about the seed and the yeast, I am sure we can also say of prayer:

> [B]oth images are of domestic concerns: the seed parable is set in a garden or local field; the yeast parable is set at a village oven. The kingdom of heaven is found in what today we might call "our own backyard" in the generosity of nature and in the daily working of men and women. . . . The challenge of the parable can be much homier: don't ask "when" the kingdom comes or "where" it is. The when is in its own good time—as long as it takes for seed to sprout and dough to rise. The where is that it is already present, inchoate, in the world. The kingdom is present when humanity and nature work together, and we do what we were put here to do—to go out on a limb to provide for others, and ourselves as well.[8]

CHAPTER TEN

The Prayer of One's Life

Paul Evdokimov and Seraphim of Sarov

"How I pray is breathe," as Merton put it. Prayer is as basic, as integral as that, contrary to what so many of us have learned or think.[1] All through this book we have come to see that prayer is not an arcane, mysterious, or merely ritual practice. Rather, prayer is natural and intimate. Our prayer is to eventually become so much a part of us that our very breathing, our very living, becomes prayer. There is no opposition between the "uncommon" prayer of everyday life and liturgical, communal, formal or "common" prayer any more than there is opposition between prayer and service, contemplation and action.

We have listened to a collection of diverse voices thus far, a few theologians and clerics, some poets and writers, some of my own experiences. Coming from the Eastern Church, I would also like to listen to a couple of voices that might not be widely known or heard. I want to look at the lives and listen to the words of some who made incarnate the integration of prayer in daily living. They are "living icons" who bridge the world of the nineteenth century with our own time: Seraphim of Sarov (1759–1831) and Paul Evdokimov (1900–1969).[2] The label "living icons" comes from Maria Skobtsova, as noted earlier, and is applicable to all seeking God.[3] These two have in common that they were in the Eastern Church, so they prayed at the same liturgy on Sunday, celebrated Easter in the ebullient, extreme manner typical of the Eastern Church. Evdokimov wrote a number of essays on Seraphim and gave a great deal of reflection to what Seraphim said and did in his life—much of what I say here is indebted to him. But there were many differences. Seraphim was a priest and monk. Evdokimov was married, the parent of two children and a professor and lecturer. They both lived in the modern era, but in very different centuries, Seraphim never leaving Russia and Evdokimov migrating to Paris early in his life and staying there for the rest of it.

These two do not dwell on the techniques of prayer but integrated prayer into their lives, along with liturgical worship and intense service to their neighbors. Seraphim is certainly the most popular Russian saint. A monk and priest at Sarov, he was also a hermit, for a time a recluse, and in the last years of his life an extraordinary elder or counselor. Able to read people's hearts, his luminous face showed how the Spirit dwells in us. He was a gifted healer, an "icon" of the spiritual life, as Paul Evdokimov called him. Rooted in traditional Christian life he was constantly moving beyond traditional statuses, activities, and confines.

Paul Evdokimov was part of the Russian emigration to France, a gifted student who received a scholarship to study at the Sorbonne. He was in the first graduating class of the St. Sergius Institute, a student of Father Sergius Bulgakov. Just as Maria Skobtsova fed, clothed, and sheltered those in need during the Depression years of the 1930s and the Nazi occupation of France, Evdokimov also worked with the French resistance to hide people pursued by the Gestapo. After the war, for almost a decade, he directed hostels run by an ecumenical agency, CIMADE (Comité inter-mouvements auprès des évacués) for the care of the poor, refugees, and other distressed people.

As a theologian with experience in pastoral and service work, he eventually taught at St. Sergius Theological Institute, L'Institut Catholique, and the Ecumenical Center in Bossey. He was an ecumenical observer at Vatican II and became an important voice for the Eastern Church in the West. He was one of the founders of the international Orthodox youth movement, *Syndesmos*. His studies were wide ranging: the historical contributions of Russian theologians; the Eastern Church's understanding of the Mother of God and of the Holy Spirit; the theology of the icons, prayer, and the liturgical services; the significance of the church and desert mothers and fathers for modern society; and, most especially, of the vocation of all the baptized and the ways in which holiness found distinctive patterns and shape in modern life—these are but some of his gifts as a teacher to the church and our time. The visions of his teachers Berdyaev, Kartashev, and Bulgakov are present in his writing along with his own singular sense of being a person of prayer, a "liturgical being," a witness to Christ both in the world and the church.

Seraphim of Sarov: A Life of Prayer

> The true aim of our Christian life is the acquisition of the Holy Spirit. As for fasts, and vigils, and prayer, and almsgiving, and every good deed done because of Christ, they are only means of acquiring the Holy Spirit. . . . Of course, every good deed done because of Christ gives us the grace of the Holy Spirit, but prayer gives it to us most of all, for it is always at hand, so to speak, as an instrument for acquiring the grace of the Spirit. For instance, you would like to go to church, but there is no church or the service is over; you would like to give alms to a beggar, but there isn't one, or you have nothing to give . . . you would like to do some other good deed in Christ's name, but either you have not the strength or the opportunity is lacking. This certainly does not apply to prayer. Prayer is always possible for everyone, rich and poor, noble and humble, strong and weak, healthy and sick, righteous and sinful.[4]

In the nineteenth century, the figure of Seraphim shines brightly, a true "seraph," a flame of fire in the dark and cold of the Russian Church of that time. The collection of his sayings was edited and censored by Metropolitan Filaret of Moscow, probably Russia's greatest preacher in the nineteenth century and a hugely influential cultural figure. Despite this editing, something of Seraphim's creative and distinctive personality still radiates, much as it does from the well-known account of his encounter in the Spirit with his friend Nicholas Motovilov.[5] The *Chronicles* of the Diveyevo Convent nuns and others, finally being translated into English, also retain something of his unusual traits, as have biographers.[6]

For Seraphim, the Spirit was warmth in a world that had grown very cold, not due to lack of faith but to the weight and decadence of an institutionalized state church. He himself experienced some of the legalism and rigidity of this institution, from of all sources members of his own monastic community. His ministry to the sisters at Dive-yevo was criticized, threatened, as was his merciful reaching out and healing of the many who came to his monastery to be prayed for and touched by him.

Looking back on him in historical context, despite the beloved popular pictures of him feeding his friend, the local black bear, of him hunchbacked and walking with an ax handle or kneeling in prayer on the rock for a thousand days and nights, Seraphim still refuses to be imprisoned by popular piety just as he refused to be captured by all the various statuses and roles he occupied in his life. He was a light in

Seraphim of Sarov

the midst of the forest, in a church in deep need of renewal, in a time of great cultural stirring, in a society of political questioning.

His official recognition as a saint was delayed, derailed by the Russian church hierarchy, and only the insistence of the Romanovs led to his canonization in 1903, despite decades of widespread, not just local, veneration. Donald Nicholl recounts how over a century after his death, and decades after the close of Sarov monastery, people would bring fir branches around his feast days into the antireligious museum that had been the Kazan cathedral.[7] They did this because they instinctively knew that his relics were there, and they wanted to bring him reminders of the forest he so loved in Sarov. And when the end of the Soviet era finally came, those relics were indeed rediscovered and brought back to Sarov, his spiritual home, along with many of his personal effects that had been hidden and kept from destruction—his cross, monastic cowl and mantle, sandals, Bible, rosary, and his favorite icon of the Virgin.

Seraphim embodied many traditional elements. Yet Evdokimov as well as other biographers observe that in his person, actions, and words he stepped out of the usual, expected forms, overturned the stereotypes and myths that have accrued to "spirituality."[8] It is no surprise that he was so beloved to many of the leading Paris Russian émigrés. Seraphim surfaces in Sergius Bulgakov's writings as an example of the humanity of God, through the Incarnation, at work in a person.[9] Seraphim also has a major place in Evdokimov's work.[10]

Seraphim stands out by his willingness to follow the Spirit through traditional monastic life in community to a hermit's vocation, then to years as a virtual recluse, and finally to an intensely active ministry of healing the distressed and organizing the Diveyevo women's communities. There was consistent criticism of his character and activities by local bishops and by his abbot and other members of the Sarov monastic community. Filaret of Moscow's editing of Seraphim's words, very likely the smoothing out of details of his life, suggests the unease with which Seraphim was regarded.[11]

Despite an overwhelming popular cult, many icons, pilgrimages to his tomb, healings, and prayers, it took the pressure of the Romanovs, Nicholas and Alexandra, to push through the decision for Seraphim's canonization in July of 1903. His early invisibility in the Sarov community gave way to notoriety for his reclusive behavior, his unusual dress, and his detailed instructions for the construction of churches, the mill, and the walkway at Diveyevo, requested by the Virgin Mary herself in a vision. This is not to mention the healings of both Michael Manturov and Nicholas Motovilov of clearly psychosomatic afflictions, and the subsequent relationship between him and these two associates. There is Seraphim's warm, fatherly, and to some, scandalous relationships with the Diveyevo nuns, his direction of their physical and spiritual existence down to details of prayer, dress, and work.

The famous encounter, recorded by Motovilov, richly illustrates both Seraphim's personality and position.[12] On a snowy winter afternoon, in a field outside his hermitage in the Sarov forest, Seraphim allowed Motovilov not only to see the luminous results of being in the presence of God, in communion with Him, he also enabled Motovilov to share in this experience himself.

The most unusual nature of this "encounter" and the even more radical content of what Seraphim had to say is often overlooked even today. Seraphim stressed the absolutely *universal* character of holiness. Everyone can acquire the Holy Spirit. Such is not the result of saying many prayers, lighting candles, keeping the fasts, or attending numerous services. All this activity had but one purpose—allowing the Spirit to make his dwelling in us. God deeply desires the holiness of *every person*. Whether one was a monastic, ordained, a lay person, rich or poor, single or married—none of this matters. Motovilov described almost blinding light, warmth despite the winter cold, beautiful fragrance, and, above all, indescribable joy and peace, exactly what the New Testament indicates the real presence of the Spirit to be.

Healed miraculously by the Mother of God in his childhood as well as in later life from a brutal attack by robbers, the recipient of numerous visits by her and other saints who constantly said, "He is one of us," the seer of visions of Christ at the liturgy, Seraphim's biography appears to be standard hagiography. To be sure, many details seem made to conform to the classical models of a monastic saint. But if one looks carefully, there are important details of difference.

Though a monk and priest, Seraphim chose to dress as the peasants of the surrounding area, in an unbleached smock, birch-bark sandals in summer, boots and coat in winter. To be sure, he would put on the monastic habit and vestments when going to communion at the liturgy in the monastery church. He lit candles for those who came for healing. He also rubbed holy oil on their arms and legs, gave out bread and wine and water to everyone, an extension of the Eucharist, even an image of the feeding of the multitudes by Christ in the wilderness. He raised his own vegetables, cut wood, and cleared brush, exactly as the local farmers and earliest monastics did. He read the daily prayer office and lived in the pages of the Bible that he read constantly. In the *Chronicles* and other sources, visitors from small children to troubled young adults are urged to read the Gospels along with him. The accounts tell of the monastic community's resentment at the hundreds of visitors lined up daily to see him, crowding the corridor outside his cell. Memoirs report that all kinds of people came: Orthodox, Catholics, Protestants, Jews, Muslims, nonbelievers. There is no record of anyone being turned away. In the end, he does not conform neatly to the category of monastic saint.

In Seraphim, the categories of priest, monk, even of *staretz*—elder or spiritual father—are never really rejected. But in moving through and beyond them and other identities, he transcends them all. He flees from even routine monastic life to his hermitage, and both there and back in his monastery cell, the door is shut to all, even his confreres. But then the door is opened to all, to the irritation of many, and never closes again. Having "fled the world," he belonged to the world, and through him, very reluctantly at first, the monastery too was opened to the world, a prefiguring of the wonderful openness of the elders of Optina monastery, of Elizabeth Feodorovna and the Mary-Martha monastery in Moscow, of Maria Skobtsova at the Rue de Lourmel and Noisy-le-Grand houses of hospitality, of Paul Evdokimov at the hostels in Bièvres, Sèvres, and Massey.

It does not take much to connect this radical embrace of all people and similarly radical orientation of acceptance, love, and service to our time. While the figures of holy people are always capable of being "used" for various political and religious points of view, it is difficult to ignore the power of their witness, and this is the case with the well-loved figure of Seraphim. Often portrayed with the bear who came to his hermitage for food, and looking more like a kindly old grandpa, there is more to him than that cuddly image.

Seraphim, mostly by his lived example, extends the possibility of life in the Spirit to every person, in every situation in society. Any prestige due to status, ordained or monastic, is obliterated. Gone too are any stereotypes of what holiness looks like, of what ascetic practices are necessary. He keeps all the monastic rules and churchly traditions. Yet his life and his words make it clear that these are but means to an end and never an end in themselves. When one has recognized the Holy Spirit, prayers cease, for the Spirit takes over, praying in one's life, making all of one's life prayer. "Acquiring the Holy Spirit," he said, "is the whole point of the Christian life," and "if one is saved," becomes holy, "thousands around will also be saved." Each person was his "joy," every person, no matter how desperate, was being illumined by the Spirit. No wonder his greeting year round was "Christ is risen." No wonder Thomas Merton thought so highly of him.[13]

Paul Evdokimov: Prayer Incarnate

It is not enough to say prayers; one must become, be prayer, prayer incarnate. It is not enough to have moments of praise. All of life, each act, every gesture, even the smile of the human face, must become a hymn of adoration, an offering, a prayer. One should offer not what one has, but what one is.[14]

Preaching at Paul Evdokimov's funeral, Fr. Lev Gillet, himself a great spiritual writer and mystic, said that Evdokimov was one who "worshiped in spirit and truth." Knowing him for close to forty years, Fr. Lev said Evdokimov was at ease in the invisible realities of the kingdom, while at the same time diligent, effective, enormously solicitous for those around him. Prayer and life were a constant unity for him.

As with Seraphim, so too for Evdokimov: prayer is hardly an arcane spiritual practice. Rather its genius is that it summarizes all that the scriptures say, the whole of life is to be "in Christ" and the Spirit. Prayer does not drive us from the world or restrict our being, but on the contrary it opens and widens our love, our service. Today, when

Paul Evdokimov, ca. 1960s.
Photo courtesy of Mrs.
Tomoko Faerber-Evdokimov.

the temptation for many is to make of the church and the liturgy an oasis apart from other believers and the world, Evdokimov argues precisely the contrary.

> Liturgy . . . teaches the true relationship between myself and others and helps me understand the words, "Love your neighbor as yourself." . . . Liturgical prayer makes the destiny of every person present to us. The liturgical litanies lead the individual beyond himself, toward the assembly, toward those who are absent, those who suffer and finally those who are in their agony. Liturgical prayer embraces the city, nations, humanity and asks for peace and unity of all. . . . [E]very soul knows by experience that one cannot stand alone before God, and that, liturgically, one saves oneself with others. The pronoun in the liturgy is never in the singular.[15]

Evdokimov put this into practice, whether bathing and feeding his young children while his wife was teaching or working on his thesis as they slept. He did so in the years of lay pastoral ministry in the hostels, leading evening prayers, listening to the joys and miseries of those residing in them. Later he would also live out his prayer as a teacher and in his writings. Olivier Clément called him a "go-between" for the church and the world.[16] In his essays one hears Sartre, de Beauvoir, Camus, Jung, as well as the Gospels. He argued that a chair of atheism be set up in every theological school, so profound were the questions that modern thinkers put to the community of faith. No modern theologian has so deftly probed the problem of human evil despite a supposedly good and just God. His image of the God who suffers along with us, who empties himself in love to become one of us, who pursues us with an absurd or foolish love, could only stem from prayer and loving service to the suffering, the pattern of his life.

His contemporary Mother Maria Skobtsova, as we earlier saw, insisted on the integration of prayer into the fabric of one's life, echoing John Chrysostom's vision of "liturgy after the liturgy." The heart of the brother/sister, the neighbor before us becomes the altar. Hence we can speak of the prayer pervading all of our life, our everyday work becoming the "sacrament of the brother or sister." Evdokimov, as well, spoke often in his writings of how the face of the person before us becomes an icon of Christ. His moving memoirs of the years he spent directing houses of hospitality capture this, as do the recollections of many who knew him.[17]

It is impossible not to see in Seraphim as well as in Paul Evdokimov and Mother Maria, for that matter, the amazing "evangelical inversion," the turning upside down of things that the gospel works in all human situations. Seraphim began life tall and strong, later shrunk due to injury and age. But this little man, huge in holiness, is very accurately depicted in the last section of Mother Maria's essay, "Types of Religious Lives."[18] The radical life of the gospel is described as giving away to others the love one receives in abundance from God. If we cannot love the neighbor whom we can see, it is impossible to love the God we cannot see. Seraphim, healed many times himself, made God's healing available to thousands of others, in his time and down to our own.

Consciously or not, Mother Maria followed a path like that of Seraphim. She was, as we learned, a child prodigy, a poet ingénue, an engaged political and social activist. Her life conformed neither to the bourgeois nor the traditional Orthodox patterns. She had several marriages, lost two of her children fairly early. While still having her son Yuri with her, it is as if she needed to add more and more people to her family—those she sheltered, clothed, and fed, and to whose miseries she listened. Her critics fault her for not living the classical pattern of monastic life. She was often absent from other daily services.

Evdokimov understood this well. It is not just how many services we attend, how many prayers are recited. The point is that we *become* our prayer, that *all our life* becomes prayer. The true measure of Maria's prayer was not how many vigils she attended, not the question of whether she should have sat consoling people in a cafe over a glass of wine, or whether she should have participated in Berdyaev's seminars and contributed essays to his journal. The real sign came when she and her co-workers were arrested by the Gestapo and hauled off to the camps. Those who knew her in Ravensbrück testified to her courage and her support of the despairing women around her. They described the Bible readings and prayers she led. In the end, she took the place of another in the truck to the gas chambers. She lived what she prayed.

The perennial opposition of Mary and Martha, of contemplation versus action, of prayer versus life, is a fiction when one looks at the lives of these three. The very idea that one could take preference over the other was abolished in Seraphim's cell, in Evdokimov's hostel, in Skobtsova's house of hospitality, and at the Ravensbrück camp. God's humanity, his taking on of all that creaturely existence entails in the Incarnation, brings together the love of God and of the neighbor as the gospel itself expressed it. Here is how Mother Maria put it.

> "It is no longer I who live, but Christ who lives in me." The image of God, the icon of Christ which truly is my real and actual essence is the only measure of things, the only way given to me. . . . Christ gave us two commandments: to love God and to love our fellow man. Everything else, even the Beatitudes, are merely elaborations of the two commandments which contain within themselves the totality of Christ's Good News. . . . It is

remarkable that their truth is found only in their indissolubility. Love for man alone leads us to the blind alley of anti-Christian humanism and the only way out of it is, at times, to reject man and love for him in the name of all mankind. But love for God without love for man is condemned. . . . These two commandments are two aspects of a single truth. Destroy either one and you destroy the whole truth.[19]

Perhaps another way of putting this is to see prayer as the celebration of the sacrament of the present moment, finding how, in the Incarnation paradise here and now, God has come to fill all things. Evdokimov is able to connect prayer with the greater sweep of looking for God, of trying to live in and with God in our time. It is a particularly intriguing vision, not so much of traditional piety lived more unobtrusively or of even just a simpler approach. It is a kind of spiritual existence so common it is uncommon. It is a hidden holiness, about which I have reflected and written earlier.[20]

It appears that a new spirituality is dawning. It aspires not to leave the world to evil, but to let the spiritual element in the creature come forth. A person who loves and is totally detached, naked to the touch of the eternal, escapes the contrived conflict between the spiritual and the material. His love of God is humanized and becomes love for all creatures in God. "Everything is grace," Bernanos wrote, because God has descended into the human and carried it away to the abyss of the Trinity. The types of traditional holiness are characterized by the heroic style of the desert, the monastery. By taking a certain distance from the world, this holiness is stretched toward heaven, vertically, like the spire of a cathedral. Nowadays, the axis of holiness has moved, drawing nearer to the world. In all its appearances, its type is less striking, its achievement is hidden from the eyes of the world, but it is the result of a struggle that is no less real. Being faithful to the call of the Lord, in the conditions of this world, makes grace penetrate to its very root, where human life is lived.[21]

CHAPTER ELEVEN

The Prayer of Contemplation and Action

Richard Rohr

In many ways prayer—certainly contemplative prayer or meditation—is planned and organized failure. If you're not prepared for failure, you'll avoid prayer, and that's what most people do. Prayer is typically *not* an experience of immediate union, satisfaction, or joy; in fact, quite the opposite. Usually you meet your own incapacity for and resistance to union. You encounter your thinking, judging, controlling, accusing, blaming, fearing mind. So why pray? Julian of Norwich, my favorite mystic, uses the word "sin" to mean a state of separateness or disunion. She writes that you become aware of your state of resistance or separateness, and then when you try to sink into the experience of *one-ing*—Julian's word for unitive consciousness—you realize you can't get there by yourself. You can't make it happen. You can't make yourself one. Julian writes in *Revelations of Divine Love* (Chapter 78), "Only in the falling apart of your own foundation can you experience God as your total foundation and your real foundation." Otherwise you keep creating your own foundation, by your own righteousness, by your own intelligent and holy thoughts. . . . What we're doing in prayer is letting our self-made foundation (or False Self) crumble so that God's foundation can be our reality. Prayer is a practice in failure that overcomes our resistance to union with Love.[1]

A Franciscan Perspective: "Alternative orthodoxy"

Barbara Brown Taylor is a writer on the spiritual to whom many have gone for her insightful, free-of-traditional-piety take on faith and living this out. Quite a few of the writers to whom we have listened are attractive for precisely the same reason. There is nothing conventional about their spirituality. Those of us who are tired of the usual box of religion are relieved and excited by their daring to step out of the pattern.

The same is true for Richard Rohr, who brings rich personal experience to bear on the spiritual life and on prayer in particular. You initially might be scared away from prayer by what he has to say. Mostly, it seems to be an experience of failure, your own and, worse, God's. And yet there is something that pulls you in, something almost seductive. Right here you encounter what makes Rohr such a sought-after teacher and best-selling author. He gets to the heart of faith without the usual sentimentality and pieties. He also connects faith and life with intelligence as well as good humor. Many of the main themes of Rohr's work are brought together in the passage quoted above. Also very explicit are the references to Julian of Norwich, his "favorite mystic," and the more implicit invocation, through the talk about the false and true selves, to Thomas Merton. Much like Barbara Brown Taylor and Christian Wiman, Rohr recognizes that even the spiritually dedicated would like to avoid the dying/falling/descending movement in favor of the rising/restorative possibilities. Yet the great tradition of prayer insists on both. New life only comes from some kind of dying or descent. It is one of the most attractive characteristics of Rohr's writing and his teaching, that he has no illusions about his own failures, his own weaknesses, or anyone else's.

Richard Rohr is a Franciscan friar and priest of the New Mexico province of the Order of Friars Minor. Born in Kansas in 1943, he has been a youth pastor, prison chaplain, educator, and parish priest since his ordination in 1970. In 1971, with the support of then-Archbishop of Cincinnati Joseph Bernardin, Rohr formed the New Jerusalem community of lay people, a community different from traditional religious orders and parishes. As with others in renewal movements within the institutional church, he had his run-ins both with his order and with the ecclesiastical establishment. In the late 1980s he began what is today the Center for Action and Contemplation in Albuquerque, New Mexico. It is a school, conference center, and base for his work of writing, teaching, and lecturing. According to some, Rohr is the most highly regarded spiritual writer at present working in Catholic circles. On February 8, 2015, he was a guest on Oprah's Super Soul Sunday program.

Over the years he has taken up a number of areas: men's spirituality, ecology and spirituality, scripture, the integration of contemplative prayer and life, the spirituality of the Twelve-Step Program. In

Richard Rohr

social justice and peace issues, he has supported the acceptance of LGBT people in the church, including some kind of recognition of same-sex marriages. He was called in by his bishop, Michael Sheehan, in 2003 to confer on his teachings and their conformity to Catholic teaching. Sheehan then wrote an open letter affirming Rohr's willingness to remain within the magisterium. He has enjoyed good standing in the Santa Fe archdiocese, his province, and order. His Sunday homilies from the local parish at which he assists are linked online at the center's website.[2]

Most recently he has done a book on the "alternative orthodoxy," as he and others call it, of the Franciscan spiritual tradition, that of Francis and Clare but also Bonaventure, Duns Scotus, and others.[3] He evokes very strong praise and criticism, the latter from traditionalists. They are alert to his consistent criticism of institutional religion, that of his own Catholic Church as well as other churches. In particular, his targets are ecclesiastical legalism, which makes paramount the obedience to rules and adherence to usually narrow statements of doctrine, as well as clericalism. His openness toward LGBT people, to sexuality as an important form of human expression, not just behavior that can occur only in limited boundaries, make him a progressive who would appear to be at odds with the resurgent conservatism of the Catholic Church up until Pope Francis. But he remains in good standing not only within his order but within his diocese.

Rohr writes with intelligence and clarity. He is intentionally ecumenical, drawing freely from the Catholic, Eastern, and Reformation traditions, as well as non-Christian sources, Sufi and Buddhist among others. In his own self-definition, he is "catholic" in that he excludes no one but also, without embarrassment, because of his Roman Catholic and Franciscan formation and experience. He draws a good deal on psychology, Jung in particular, but he uses and cites the scriptures most of all—he was a teacher of scripture in his order's formation program. After the scriptures, there is a diverse procession of writers and thinkers upon whom he leans: Julian of Norwich as well as Teresa of Avila, John of the Cross, and Augustine, and of course his own order's great founders Francis and Clare of Assisi. A major influence on Rohr's thinking is, by his own admission, Thomas Merton. This is especially evident in Rohr's commitment to the integration of contemplation and action, his concern for the retrieval of the contemplative way and prayer, and, in particular, in his interest in the life-long conversation or transformation process, the pursuit of the "true self." But other shapers include Karl Rahner, Rene Girard, Kathleen Dowling Singh, Ilia Delio, Dorothy Day, Ken Wilber, among many others. He has been interviewed or appeared with Brian MacLaren, James Martin, Thomas Keating, Cynthia Bourgeault, Joan Chittister, Laurence Freeman, James Finley, Shane Claiborne, and the Dalai Lama.

Rohr speaks with humility but also confidence. One hears in him the voice of an experienced pastor and teacher. He both remembers and draws upon his past in his writing—childhood in the 1950s, formation in the Franciscans in the 1960s, pastoral ministry and teaching afterwards, leading into a great number of lectures, retreats, conferences, and books on the spiritual life. He has become one of the spiritual voices most often listened to in the past decades.

Basic, Classic Themes

Richard Rohr's rooting in the Franciscan tradition is a principal reason for his renown. But also significant is the way he draws synthetically from many sources, both those within the history of spirituality as well as depth psychology, history, and anthropology. Rohr's critical attitude and his openness are threatening to some. He emphatically argues for the importance of experience in the life of faith, a feature of theology for much of the past century, including such as Rahner, Congar, Küng, Schillebeeckx, and certainly those *ressourcement*, or "return to the sources," figures so important for the shaping of Vatican II. There is a strong connection with what psychology and history have to say, as well as a serious ecumenical openness, one that reaches out to non-Christian traditions. Following in the path of Thomas Merton, there is a central place in Rohr's vision for the struggle to discern one's true self from competing versions. That the Pauline movement of dying and rising, falling and ascending, is central to his outlook should warrant his certification within the tradition, something he claims for himself. He calls himself a "radical traditionalist," and he identifies his Franciscan roots, as mentioned, as an "alternative orthodoxy."[4]

Not because of direct connections but because of shared sources and the larger tradition, other figures to whom we have listened in this book share many if not all these perspectives. Despite a resurgence in sectarianism, a rejection of ecumenical work, there remains, especially at the local church and pastoral levels, a great sense that the division of the churches is a tragedy and scandal, and also regard for the authentic faith of other Christians. In the last half century or more, this openness has been connected with the civil rights and women's movements and, more recently, the situation of LGBT people in both church and society. We are more and more understanding that Christ broke down the walls of enmity, fear, and distrust among us. The gospel of Christ, as preached and enacted by Jesus in the Gospels, but also in the other literature of the New Testament, does not exclude or segregate but instead actively reaches out to include those outside the community, outside social standards of propriety. As scripture scholar Amy-Jill Levine shows most strikingly, this is authentically the Jewish vision too, not some Christian correction of insularity and hyper-particularity.

No matter the writers we are listening to, it seems that the life of faith and thus of prayer is radically open and, I would further say, centripetal—moving us toward community. It is interesting that "community" is not a separate theme for Rohr, but implicit in several of them.

That scripture, and therefore also the rest of the tradition of faith, liturgy, and prayer, is validated by experience and, in turn, that the complex of tradition informs, shapes, validates our experience are affirmations of how the divine and the human, joined in the Incarnation, also function in practice for us today. This puts aside the notion that all that is not religious—science, politics, culture—is merely a profane, secular world at odds with God. Over and over, the realization is that all the dualisms so easily assumed need to be put, as the scriptures do, in a more integral or unitary relationship. This is true whether it is divine/human, mind/body, spirit/flesh, male/female, Jew/Greek, master/slave—and so for numerous other dichotomies that inhabit both our consciousness and world. God is source, and as such God constantly is self-giving and, by this outpouring of life and love, drawing all back to God.

Falling and Rising

Crucial in the themes of Rohr's writing is the recognition that we "fall upward," namely, that dying and descent is transformative. It is the paschal mystery and movement so central to St. Paul, to Francis and Clare of Assisi, to John of the Cross and Teresa of Avila, to Seraphim of Sarov and Thomas Merton, Dorothy Day, and Maria Skobtsova, to the "little way" of Thérèse of Lisieux, and much later and in a different context, to Alcoholics Anonymous.[5] The dynamic is also one that Carl Jung recognized, namely, that in the first half of life we learn to abide by rules and to perform within the boundaries and structures of the world around us, which means family, the broader society, the state, church, economy, and education.[6] Rohr describes the first half of life as the construction of a durable container, the internalization of rules that shape and direct us. But in time, we will face numerous contradictions to all the structure we have made our own. Also, not all "first half" formation is effective, hence we will see many seeking, for the rest of their lives, the second half, to make up for what they did not receive in the first half. Rohr also points out the endurance of first half rituals, rules, and order well into and throughout the second half because freedom and creativity are too frightening. The trouble, however, is that we cannot protect ourselves from failure, from falling, from defeat and disappointment. Julian of Norwich recognized that both the fall and recovery are God's mercy at work in us!

Rohr, over and over again, emphasizes that unless the grain of wheat dies, falls into the earth, nothing can grow. Put differently, there is "necessary suffering."[7] To try to run from suffering that is part of our lives is, for Jung, the source of much neurotic behavior. Rohr also speaks of this as "incarnational mysticism," the embrace rather than rejection of Christ's humanity, of Christ's suffering and death as intrinsically linked to resurrection.

For Rohr, the holding together of both movements, falling and rising, are sound psychologically and theologically. There is an integrity in maintaining the connection that avoids the over-spiritualizing, the hyper-divinization of Christ while simultaneously rejecting the reduction of Christ to merely human heroics of revolutionary or martyr. For each of us to squarely face what surely is a "tragic" sense of life, the utter inevitability of suffering and death, is, at the roots, to affirm life. Again, he cites Jung as seeing our lives as "luminous pause" between the great mysteries of birth and death that are themselves linked.[8] Rohr employs the homesickness and homecoming of Odysseus as an epic, literary model. One can only return, one can only truly "be" home, after one has left, been deprived of it. Homecoming is not so much a reward or "happy ending" as the completion of our quest, the discovery and acquiring of the true self. Or as Teresa of Avila puts it, when we find God in ourselves we also find ourselves in God.

The second half of life depends on the first but is not bound to the same rules and boundaries. These no longer should contain us. We should learn the rules well, says the Dalai Lama, so we can better break them.[9] As contradictory as this sounds, it is in fact most healthy and right, namely, that where rigor originally guided us, mercy allows us to be generous. It is, as Rohr suggests, the "generative" phase in Erik Erikson's view of life development. We possess what the Eastern Church calls a "bright sadness," a theme during Lent.[10] We know enough to be sad, but we know too much to be crushed and so can encounter ourselves and others around us with joy.[11] We do not have to correct, refashion, or reshape others any more than we need to keep doing the same to ourselves. We are not so compelled to achieve, to accumulate, to dominate, to succeed. One could also describe this as an "inner brightness," possible once we have let go of old hurts and grudges, old taboos and prejudices—when the Beatitudes guide us as much if not more than the Ten Commandments, when love is the power, as Afanasiev says, rather than the law, whether in our personal lives or in the church or the larger cultural context.[12]

Rohr describes, at some length, the battles that emerge as we try to get to the second half of life, that is, to "fall upward." The central struggle, one that runs via Merton throughout Rohr's writing, is that with the "shadow" or "false" self. This, he makes clear, cannot be evaded. And we are wrong to think the false self could or should be annihilated. After all, the false self is produced by the first half of life formation, which enables us to move beyond it, to fall upward. But to face the shadow self is humiliating. The more that we try to justify who we think we are, what we feel we should be, the harder it goes for us, the more costly it is.[13]

But the second half of life, as Rohr sketches it, is not to be thought of as nirvana. It is authentic solitude, peace, and wisdom, but also distance from the active existence of institutions and professions of the first half of life. The world may be larger, our spirit more expansive, but our circles of colleagues and friends, necessarily, will decrease.[14] This said, falling is not humiliation but finally being able to really stand upright, really speak truthfully, though at lower volume and more briefly. Dying, in terms of gospel inversion, is rising. Giving oneself to others, giving away what one has accomplished, what one has accumulated is gift in itself. We should be able to see this in the lives of people who have gone on before us. I have been privileged to do precisely this in the work of listening to not just the writers in this book but the many others from earlier volumes. Rohr meditates on a Merton poem from the late 1950s to show how the movement into the second half sounds.[15] One could do the same with Dorothy Day's columns for the *Catholic Worker* paper, in so many of Merton's journal entries, or the memoirs of Sara Miles and Barbara Brown Taylor.

The Prayer of Falling and Rising

That the movement of falling and rising is prayer should warrant no lengthy defense or explanation. In an earlier book, *Everything Belongs*, Rohr links prayer, prayer lived out and enacted, to the paschal pattern of Jesus's dying and rising. That his institute is named "The Center for Action and Contemplation" is an expression of the broader vision he has, as a Franciscan friar, that prayer is always completed, made real, in its enactment. One hears the echo of not only his spiritual father, Francis of Assisi, but also a modern teacher, Thomas Merton, in Rohr's stressing that prayer is not primarily words or rituals but a stance, an attitude, a waiting in love, a realization that life is not about me but about God and community.[16]

Merton affirms that we must seek the true self and, in so doing, we get a better sense of our real relationship to God and to others. Prayer, or better, living prayer or prayerful living, is real healing—*salus*/salvation—really what all therapy aims at.[17] Prayer enables us not just to heal the splits and divisions within ourselves, it enables us to see ourselves as we truly were created to be, in relation to God and to others.

> Prayer lives in pure moments of right here, right now. This is enough, this is fullness. If it is not right here right now, it doesn't exist. If we don't see God now, why would we know God later? If we don't see God now, would the eyes be prepared to see God later? The mystics say no. We will not recognize God later if we cannot recognize God now. It is a matter of seeing God now through the shadow and the disguise. Prayer lives in a spacious place. It is free of personal needs or meanings or even interpretations.[18]

Because it is a way of being, in prayer we see everything in a new light. In the Buddhist phrase, we clean the mirror in our prayer.[19] Merton used "contemplation" as a synonym for prayer. Following him, Rohr reminds us that in contemplative prayer we recognize God present everywhere, in all people.[20] We see things as they are, not as we want them to be, not just as they have something to do with our own interests, and there is real freedom in this seeing.[21]

As a Trappist hermit at Gethsemani abbey asked Rohr to say, over and over in his preaching, lecturing, and writing, God is never "out there," "up there," but rather in here, in me and you, here and now.[22] As Paula D'Arcy aptly puts it, "God comes to us disguised as our life."[23] Rohr also sees here the happy meeting of the vision of the Eastern Church, that of *theosis* or "divinization." The view is neither heretical nor eccentric. We are made in the image and likeness of God, as affirmed in Genesis. So, then, everything belongs to God. God is the flame, as Symeon the New Theologian and other Eastern Church writers choose to put it, from which we all take the flame of life, all of us sharing in God's life.[24]

Prayer, Integral and Integrating

God uses everybody and everything. Prayer is surely not a rare treat, an unusual activity, a periodic obligation. And as God is always with us, then, as Julian of Norwich says, a favorite writer of Rohr, even "sin shall not be a shame to humans but a glory."[25] While clergy use and prefer law and guilt, and often, even unwittingly, monopolize public prayer as celebrants, prayer is the ultimate empowerment of the people of God.[26]

> The gift of contemplative prayer is not a way of thinking. It's much more a way of not thinking. It's not a way of talking; it finally moves beyond words into silence. It moves into the mystery that is too deep for words. . . . I have never met anyone who is at peace who is in their mind, and I have never met anyone in their head who is at peace. Prayer must lead us beyond mind, words, and ideas to a more spacious place where God has a chance to get in. While the prayer of words is an attempt *to express to ourselves* our dependence on the great mystery, the prayer of silence is not so much to express, but *to experience* that dependence. We acknowledge and rejoice that we are the beloved, created out of nothing. I sit as content as a child on its mother's lap. I sit and wait until I know that truth in my body.[27]

As for Merton, so too for Rohr: the contemplative way is not, as it might seem, just about personal wholeness and spiritual growth. When we are able to be still, silent before God, to experience God not up or out there but in here, now, we will be better able to view the large picture—of the church as community, as the people of God. We will come to realize that "a Christian alone is no Christian," in Tertullian's words. We have in all Christian traditions proceeded as if Christianity was primarily an individual phenomenon, "me and Jesus," when the New Testament has no sense of this exclusively personal faith at all. Trying to create church or be the church as individuals with "souls saved" just has not worked. "We are more than our private lives."[28] But if people have come to understand themselves as taken up into the great compassion of God, then they will understand that liturgy calls us to action together to feed, to shelter, to seek social justice.

It is not possible, then, to accuse Rohr, or for that matter Merton or any other proponents of contemplative prayer, of quietism, obscurantism, or disdain for the world and its troubles. While prayer is not primarily words, we will nevertheless need to use words in our relationships and our actions, and if we are living in and from our prayer, our words will be more considered, and they will have greater weight and reality to them. With Teilhard de Chardin, we will know that nothing is profane, secular, or distant from God for those who have learned how to see.[29] Everything that is, is holy. The sacred and the secular are no longer opposites, no longer at odds with each other. Is this not the most thorough incarnational grasp of how we are to relate to ourselves, to the world? Does this not help us to resist accepting and dealing with "things as they are," what Dorothy Day called the "dirty rotten system," whether of the state or the church or the culture?

Some find Rohr, as well as Merton and Day before him, threatening, their radical sense for action a social-political distraction from salvation, their commitment to contemplation smacking of Buddhism, an ecumenical flirtation. It could not be further from the truth. It is telling that over the years Rohr has sided with those working for change, especially for LGBT rights. Along with many others, he has applauded Pope Francis's emphasis on mercy, on finding ways to welcome and reach out to those marginalized by the church.[30]

To me, it is always a bit frustrating that when going to a Dorothy Day or a Thomas Merton for spiritual insight, the sheer passage of time has an effect on their impact. If they were alive now, in the early twenty-first century, what would they say about the struggle for women's rights, for the rights and protection of LGBT people, about income inequality, about religious and racial discrimination, about the situation of those divorced and remarried and thus officially excluded from the church's sacramental life? There are many other questions, too, of the impasse in ecumenical relationships, the all too easy swing of so many religious leaders to the political right in the past decade, thereby making Christian faith equivalent to only traditional ethical perspectives, citing certain proof-texts to support as unchangeable the official church positions on same-sex relationships, same-sex marriage, and divorce. And this then translates into political positions, very much those of the "culture wars" that have been part of American culture now for several decades.

I would locate Richard Rohr solidly within the gospel as recovered by the Second Vatican Council, within the Great or Catholic Tradition, very much where Pope Francis has positioned himself. His deliberate, thoughtful positions are a faithful reflection of where past great teachers would be today. Toward the end of *Everything Belongs* Rohr makes a good point, one that is attributed to Teresa of Avila and of which Dorothy Day was fond.

> There is a certain fear of death that comes from not having lived yet. . . . Something in me says, "I haven't done 'it' yet." I haven't experienced the stream of life yet. I haven't touched the real, the good, the true and the beautiful—which is, of course, what we're created for. When we know we have experienced the stream of life, we will be able to lie on our deathbed like Francis and say, "Welcome, sister death." I'm not afraid to let go of life, because I have life. I am life. . . . It's heaven all the way to heaven. And it's hell all the way to hell. Not later, but now.[31]

He is also channeling Julian of Norwich who consistently sees God's mercy covering over so much in our lives, transforming our sin and defects so that "all will be well." But the more basic thrust of all of Rohr's thinking is that God is always present and at work and that seeking God and trying to live in God, as opposed to often conventional, constricted religiosity, is life itself. That is where so many of the writers to whom we have listened take us, though it is no judgment on the worth or importance of the prayer of church services, books, or other texts, the "common prayer" that is most often what we think of when we hear of "prayer."

Disconnected Prayer

But as heard here, in even a few passages, Rohr insists that prayer *can* be words, even words in a book or at a service, but never *only* these. Prayer, he says many times, is spacious. Prayer spreads out to all corners of our lives, our work, our thoughts. Behind this is Merton's insistence that contemplation cannot be separated from action, that prayer is wound into, around, and through our living.[32]

The attitude that prayer can be spoken of or described, that techniques for prayer can be laid out without connection to the rest of everyday existence, long ago came to bother me greatly. I was raised in a pre–Vatican II Catholic atmosphere, after my family migrated to the Roman Church from the Ukrainian Greek Catholic. In parochial school, then later, in the Carmelite order's minor seminary, novitiate, and undergraduate studies, until I got to the Catholic University of America, it was natural to separate prayer, liturgy, and faith from the "distractions" of daily life.[33] These texts were impenetrable, already dry and antiseptic almost fifty years ago when we were exposed to them. One was counseled to keep batting these away during prayer, whether the mass, the divine office, or meditation, like swatting at pesky mosquitoes when camping or sitting in the backyard in the summer.

Years later, one can still find this "I want to be alone with God" attitude in some books on prayer. It even appears in Merton's early writing, in *The Seven Storey Mountain* and in an early article included in a recent collection of his essays.[34] This autobiographical piece, "The White Pebble," was written in 1949 not long after his ordination and the publication of *The Seven Storey Mountain*. In it, Merton's expressed passion for God is powerful, his dedication to baptism, monastic life, and priesthood fierce. Yet the tone is one of detachment, disconnection. Other people, daily tasks, the realities of work, ideas — all are missing. God and the spiritual life, and, of course, prayer, seem to float alone, away from the world, from others.

This was hardly the case, however, for Merton as time went on, as both his journals and published works attest. Life and prayer, action and contemplation, faith and the world are revealed as inseparable. The edgy, almost sarcastic tone of "Day of a Stranger" is a powerful statement. Merton's "epiphany" at the corner of Fourth and Walnut in Louisville is a more lyrical account. Daniel Horan makes a strong case for Merton's several "conversions" in his life as writer and monk.[35] Contrary to the judgment of some, namely, that Merton has no connections to us in the twenty-first century, he emphatically argues that Merton (still) matters.[36] Horan also stresses the continuing relevance of Merton's connecting contemplation with radical engagement with the world. Along with this, Merton's commitment to a profound ecumenism remains most relevant for us.

The same is true for Rohr and the others to whom we have listened. With experience and thus credibility in his pastoral work over several decades, he understands the indissoluble connection of action and contemplation, of life and prayer. There is no need to struggle to build a bridge from prayer to life. It's already there. The students I teach, the parish members with whom I talk, the memories of my parents now deceased and of childhood at home, now too the memories of my own adult children growing up, the things I need to make dinner, the difficulties of a relative, the struggles with chronic illness of a friend—like all those names on my prayer list, these "distractions" are just some of the fragments of my life.

I much prefer now, later in my life, the advice not only of the ancient desert mothers and fathers but of Merton in his later reflections, of Richard Rohr and many others we have listened to here. Let all these faces, names, events, interactions pass into God as they pass through my consciousness. If the monastery kitchen pots and pans were to St. Benedict as precious as the eucharistic vessels, are not these incarnations of the experience of myself and others, where Jesus entered and remained, God's humanity, the divine incarnate?

CHAPTER TWELVE

Conclusion

The Prayer of Incarnation

Incarnation: God Embodied, Prayer Embodied

More than any other element of the Christian tradition, the Incarnation speaks most powerfully to the ways in which prayer permeates life. Throughout the Hebrew Bible there are numerous encounters between God and human beings. They are most often terrifying. Warnings are given to keep prostrate, eyes to the ground, lest the sight of God annihilate the human creature. Smoke, a cloud, a pillar of fire, an earthquake on a mountain top, a fearful warrior—these are some of the ways in which God appears, though God has a great deal to say, a word that almost is ceaseless, through the prophets and other teachers and writers and leaders. Eventually, the Christian community comes to understand that God came even closer and in nowhere as fearful a manner—as a baby, then a man, like everyone else except for sin. God's humanity is a shock but also the greatest joy and encouragement. Now God gets hungry and eats, gets tired and sleeps, works, ages and dies, as we do.

The émigré Russian scholar Nicholas Afanasiev—historian, exegete, canonist, and more—quipped that most Christians are actually more comfortable with a Christ who is mostly divine and only a little, if at all, human.[1] I am sure he was thinking, as more recently

MacCulloch also has, of the Christological controversies of the early centuries, set in ancient religious and cultural contexts that had lots of room for divinities, the more the merrier, but which could not really understand incarnation, the humanizing of gods. Better to keep humans human and gods godly.

Now while this division may hold in some traditions, even in them the connections between Creator and creation, between divine and human, remain intimate. The Trappist monk killed with several of his community in Algeria, Christian de Chergé, was acutely aware of the difficulty of the Incarnation in the Muslim consciousness. No matter the important position of Jesus in the Qu'ran, the thought of his divinity was seemingly impossible for the radical monotheism of Islam. And yet de Chergé found ways of talking about Jesus as the communication of God, as the one who truly submitted to the Father, also drawing on Vatican II and Teilhard de Chardin to talk of a Christ "greater" than traditionally spoken of by Christians, without regard to the rest of humanity and faith traditions.[2]

This is not just an ancient attitude nor a doctrinal debate, a theological conflict over Jesus from centuries ago. It is very much a modern one, an issue of our times as well. Now, as James Carroll argues, we have had so much of the overly divine, institutionalized versions of Christ. Carroll, a popular religious writer, is hardly alone in this stance. For the last century at least, from Bonhoeffer to Küng to Schillebeeckx, John F. Meier to Amy-Jill Levine, N. T. Wright, Rowan Williams, and Luke Timothy Johnson have been pressing questions about how we understand Jesus.

We want to see the dwelling of the divine among us, God sharing our flesh, our life. And, if this is so, if God is "everywhere, filling all things," as an Eastern Church prayer puts it, then is not our prayer also everywhere, filling all things with God, fulfilling our creation in the image and likeness of God? Prayer has to do not only with God but with ourselves. Carroll drives this home very powerfully.

> "The point of incarnation language," the Catholic theologian Roger Haight writes, "is that Jesus is one of us, that what occurred in Jesus is the destiny of human existence itself: *et homo factus est*. Jesus is a statement, God's statement, about humanity as such." Humanity is the presence of God. The presence of God,

therefore, lies in what is ordinary. Not in supernatural marvels. Not in a superman with whom we have nothing actual in common. Not in saints. Not in a once-only age of miracles long ago. Not first in doctrine, scholarship, or theology—but in life. Doctrine, scholarship, and theology are essential as modes of opening up that life and its meanings, and there is no separating the life of Jesus from interpretations of it. The interpretations must always be examined, and criticized. . . .

But the *life* is our object. The life of Jesus must always weigh more than his death. And, to repeat, the revelation is in the ordinariness of that life. His teaching—his permanent Jewishness, his preference for service over power, his ever-respectful attitude toward women and others on the social margin—is available to us because his followers passed the teaching along, which continues. His encounters with beloved friends, disciples, outcasts, antagonists, and Romans, all arranged in a story that is more invention than memory, are valued as occasions of his encounter with the Holy One—but they are *typical* encounters, not supernatural ones. Again and again he turned to God, and, as the tradition says, he turned *into* God—but that, too, occurred in the most ordinary of ways. Day by day. Act by act. Choice by choice. Word by word. Ultimately "lifted up," as John says, on the cross which *was* the Resurrection. And the cross is central to this meaning not because God willed suffering but because, in Jesus, God joined in it. "The quality of the suffering," in Eliot's phrase, is changed. And that includes the extreme suffering of war.

Leaving us with? A simple Jesus. An ordinary Christ. One whom the simplest person can imitate, the most ordinary person bringing Christ once more to life—day by day, word by word, bread by bread, cup by cup. In all of that we see divinity, which, paradoxically, is what makes Jesus one of us. Whatever sort of God Jesus is understood to be, it must be the God who is like humans, not different. If that seems impossible, then what we think of God—*and of humans*—must change. This is essential to the New Testament and "the very logic of Christian faith."[3]

Some theologians would balk at the interpretation of Incarnation as Jesus becoming divine in his continuing life with the Father, through some kind of "adoptionist" process, a decidedly "low" Christology. But Carroll is clear that one cannot purge divinity from Jesus. More importantly, he is only echoing centuries of Christological struggle in highlighting the ways in which Jesus is an image of what all believers can become—children of God who have more fully come to mirror the God whose image and likeness they bear.

If what Carroll says sounds familiar, if you think you have heard it elsewhere, from someone else, this is accurate. You have heard it. It has been a powerful and controversial theme for Pope Francis. He has returned to it, over and over again—to the presence of God everywhere, not just within the boundaries of the institutional church and organized religion. He has repeatedly emphasized the compassion of God and need for our compassion and acceptance of others. In his own way, Francis keeps attacking the dualism by which religion and religious people separate themselves from others, seemingly putting the ethical line between evil and good "out there" instead of through the heart of each of us, thereby setting "us" off from "them."

But he also rejects the dualism that separates the divine from the human, the spiritual from the material, the religious from the secular. Sticking with the core insight of the Incarnation, he sees the presence of the divine everywhere. We know about Jesus because of what his people, his followers said, prayed, and wrote about him, what they experienced, how they felt and what his friends then did on the basis of these words—how they lived.

Jesus was born as one of us. He lived among us and lives among us still. He talked about the way of teaching or Torah in fresh, lively words. He put those words into practice, made them human, by healing, by speaking the truth about the poor and marginalized, about the state and society—how we live. All of this was and is prayer. After all, we stand in church when the Gospel is read, don't we? We treasure the other readings both from the prophets and historical and wisdom books as well as from all those letters written to the first churches and their people, in Rome, Corinth, Thessalonika, Ephesus, and other places. All of these texts tell us that Jesus died and rose, and it is in his people that he remains present, in their breaking of the bread, in their prayers, and in their love and care for others. There is no time of day, no activity, no place that cannot be prayer.

This is, I hope, what we have learned in this book. The experience of connection, of communion with God and each other is what we have been listening to throughout. God is not up or out there but here, in and with us. Our prayer is more than words: it is our lives. We incarnate God over and over again. We become what we pray.

NOTES

ONE Introduction

1. Stephen Prothero, *God Is Not One* (New York: Harper, 2010).

2. Julian of Norwich, *Showing of Love*, chap. 5, in *The Complete Julian of Norwich*, ed. John Julian (Brewster, MA: Paraclete Press, 2009).

3. Julian of Norwich, *Showing*, chap. 49.

4. Thomas Merton, *The Sign of Jonas* (New York: Harcourt, Brace, 1953), 362. Also see my essay, "'Mercy within Mercy within Mercy': Thomas Merton's Merciful God," *The Merton Seasonal* 39, no. 1 (Spring 2014): 3–6.

5. Pope Francis, *The Church of Mercy: A Vision for the Church* (Chicago: Loyola Press, 2014); Walter Kasper, *Mercy* (Mahwah, NJ: Paulist Press, 2014).

6. T. M. Luhrmann, *When God Talks Back* (New York: Knopf, 2012).

7. Nancy T. Ammerman, ed., *Sacred Stories, Spiritual Tribes: Finding Religion in Everyday Life, Everyday Religion* (New York: Oxford University Press, 2013), and *Congregation and Community* (New Brunswick, NJ: Rutgers University Press, 2001). Also see Diana Butler Bass, *Christianity for the Rest of Us* (New York: HarperOne, 2006).

8. Michael Plekon, *Living Icons, Hidden Holiness,* and *Saints As They Really Are* (Notre Dame, IN: University of Notre Dame Press, 2002, 2009, 2012).

9. F. Procter and W. H. Frere, *A New History of the Book of Common Prayer* (St. Martin's Press, 1965); Diarmaid MacCulloch, *Thomas Cranmer* (New Haven, CT: Yale University Press, 1995).

10. Friedrich Heiler, *Prayer*, trans. Samuel McComber (Oxford: Oxford University Press, 1932).

11. Philip Zaleski and Carol Zaleski, *Prayer: A History* (Boston: Houghton Mifflin, 2005). There are libraries of books on technique by important spiritual writers like Basil Pennington, Cynthia Bourgeault, Thomas Keating, and Richard Rohr, to mention only a few. Tim Keller, the very successful pastor of Redeemer Church in New York City, has produced a volume: *Prayer: Experiencing Awe and Intimacy with God* (New York: Dutton, 2014). Carmelite

nun Ruth Burrows's contribution is another respected one, *Essence of Prayer* (Mahwah, NJ: Paulist Press, 2006), as is Ronald Rolheiser, *Prayer: Our Deepest Longing* (Cincinnati, OH: Franciscan Media, 2013). Thomas Merton himself published a number of essays on contemplative prayer, beginning with *Seeds of Contemplation* (Norfolk, CT: New Directions, 1949), which was revised as *New Seeds of Contemplation* (New York: New Directions, 1961), with several other anthologies posthumously issued.

12. A summary of the results from the survey can be found at http://www .lifewayresearch.com/2014/10/01/americansprayforfriendsandfamily-2.

13. See, for example, http://www.pewforum.org/2012/10/09/nones-on -the-rise.

14. For numerous studies of membership, affiliation, identification, and attendance, see the Association of Religion Data Archives, http://www.thearda .com/Archive. Other resources include the Public Religion Research Institute, http://publicreligion.org; the Insights into Religion website, http://religion insights.org; and the Hartford Institute for Religion Research, http://hirr .hartsem.edu.

15. Linda McCullogh Moore has focused on the integration of prayer into ordinary living in *The Book of Not So Common Prayer: A New Way to Pray, A New Way to Live* (Nashville: Abingdon Press, 2014).

16. Burrows, *Essence of Prayer*, 1, 3.

17. Barbara Brown Taylor, *Learning to Walk in the Dark* (New York: HarperOne, 2014).

18. See Douglas Christie, *The Blue Sapphire of the Mind: Notes for a Contemplative Ecology* (Oxford: Oxford University Press, 2013).

19. Mary Oliver, *A Thousand Mornings* (Boston: Beacon Press, 2013), 34.

20. For more information, see an interview conducted with Christian Wiman at https://www.commonwealmagazine.org/being-prepared-joy.

21. Christian Wiman, *My Bright Abyss* (New York: Farrar, Straus, Giroux, 2013).

22. *Mother Maria Skobtsova: Essential Writings* (Maryknoll, NY: Orbis, 2003), 185.

23. Amy-Jill Levine, *Short Stories by Jesus: The Enigmatic Parables of a Controversial Rabbi* (New York: HarperOne, 2014), 125.

TWO The Prayer of Theologians and Others

1. Diarmaid MacCulloch, *Silence: A Christian History* (New York: Viking Adult, 2013), 191.

2. MacCulloch, *Silence*, 191–216, and *A History of Christianity* (New York: Viking, 2009), 222–67. Also see Maggie Ross, *Silence: A User's Guide* (Eugene, OR: Wipf and Stock, 2014).

3. Rowan Williams, *Faith in the Public Square* and *The Edge of Words: God and the Habits of Language* (New York: Bloomsbury Academic, 2012 and 2014).

4. See Rowan Williams, *Sergii Bulgakov: Towards a Russian Political Theology* (Edinburgh: T&T Clark, 1999); James Pain and Nicolas Zernov, eds., *A Bulgakov Reader* (Philadephia: Westminster Press, 1976); Paul Valliere, *Modern Russian Theology: Bukharev, Soloviev, Bulgakov* (Grand Rapids, MI: Eerdmans, 2000). Boris Jakim and Thomas Allen Smith have been indefatigable translators of Bulgakov, so now his major works are available: *The Lamb of God, The Comforter, The Bride of the Lamb, Unfading Light, Jacob's Ladder, The Burning Bush, The Friend of the Bridegroom* (Grand Rapids, MI: Eerdmans, 2008, 2004, 2002, 2012, 2010, 2009, and 2003), among other titles. Also see Aidan Nicholas, O.P., *Wisdom from Above* (Herefordshire: Gracewing, 2005).

5. Among many publications see Pope Francis, *The Church of Mercy: A Vision for the Church* (Chicago: Loyola Press, 2014), and Walter Kasper, *Mercy: The Essence of the Gospel and the Key to Christian Life*, trans. William Madges (Mahwah, NJ: Paulist Press, 2014).

6. Sarah Coakley, "Prayer as Crucible: How My Mind Has Changed," *The Christian Century* 128, no. 6 (March 2011): 32–40.

7. Thomas Keating, *Open Mind, Open Heart* (New York: Bloomsbury Academic, 2006), and *Intimacy with God* and *The Heart of the World* (New York: Crossroad, 2009 and 2008); Basil Pennington, *Centering Prayer* (New York: Image, 1982); John Main, *John Main: Essential Writings* (Maryknoll, NY: Orbis, 2002); and Laurence Freeman, *First Sight: The Experience of Faith* (New York: Bloomsbury, 2011) and *Jesus, The Teacher Within* (New York: Continuum, 2001).

8. Thomas Merton, *The Hidden Ground of Love: The Letters of Thomas Merton on Religious Experience and Social Concerns,* ed. William H. Shannon (New York: Farrar, Straus and Giroux, 1985), 63–64.

9. Coakley, "Prayer as Crucible," 33.

10. Sarah Coakley, *Powers and Submissions: Spirituality, Philosophy and Gender* (Wiley-Blackwell, 2002).

11. Coakley, "Prayer as Crucible," 36–37.

12. See Sarah Coakley, *God, Sexuality, and the Self: An Essay "On the Trinity"* (Cambridge: Cambridge University Press, 2013).

13. Coakley, "Prayer as Crucible," 39–40.

14. Sarah Coakley, with Paul Gavrilyuk, eds., *The Spiritual Senses: Perceiving God in Western Christianity* (Cambridge: Cambridge University Press, 2012), and Sarah Coakley, *The New Asceticism: Sexuality, Gender and the Quest for God* (New York: Bloomsbury Academic, 2015).

15. Sarah Coakley, "Meditation Is Subversive," *The Christian Century* 121, no. 13 (June 29, 2004): 18–21.

16. Sarah Coakley, with Sam Wells, eds., *Praying for England: Priestly Presence in Contemporary Culture* (New York: Bloomsbury Academic, 2008).

17. See also Coakley, *The New Asceticism*.

18. Rowan Williams, *Being Christian: Baptism, Bible, Eucharist, Prayer* (Grand Rapids, MI: Eerdmans, 2014), 61.

19. Williams, *Being Christian*, 69–70.

20. See, for example, http://www.rabbitblog.com, http://www.salon.com/writer/heather_havrilesky, and http://nymag.com/author/Heather%20Havrilesky.

21. Heather Havrilesky, "Our 'Mommy' Problem," *New York Times*, Nov. 8, 2014, available at http://www.nytimes.com/2014/11/09/opinion/sunday/our-mommy-problem.html.

22. For her own narrative see, Heather Havrilesky, *Disaster Preparedness: A Memoir* (New York: Riverhead, 2010).

23. Patricia Hampl, *The Florist's Daughter* (New York: Harcourt, 2007).

24. I was most gratified to read of her sitting down, with her father, to a plateful of pirogi at her grandparents in Johnstown, Pennsylvania. Pirogi, as you will see in chapter 8, are dear to me.

25. The full column is available at http://nymag.com/thecut/2014/09/ask-polly-life-is-a-struggle-why-keep-going.html. Also see http://aeon.co/magazine/psychology/how-did-i-end-up-growing-old.

26. Alexander Schmemann, *For the Life of the World* (Crestwood, NY: St. Vladimir's Seminary Press, 1973), 11–16, 34–35, 42–43.

27. Havrilesky, *Disaster Preparedness*, 238–39.

28. Sara Miles, *City of God: Faith in the Streets* (New York: Jericho Books, 2014), 196–97.

29. Sara Miles, *Take this Bread* (New York: Ballantine, 2007).

30. More information about the frescoes can be found at http://www.saintgregorys.org/events/detail/dancing-saints-online.

31. Sara Miles, *Jesus Freak: Feeding, Healing, Raising the Dead* (New York: Jossey-Bass, 2010).

32. Miles, *City of God*, 38–39.

33. Miles, *City of God*, 59.

34. Miles, *City of God*, 103.

35. Miles, *City of God*, 136–37.

36. Miles, *City of God*, 181–84.

37. Miles, *City of God*, 195–96.

THREE   The Prayer of a Hermit

1. Thomas Merton, "Learning to Live," in *Thomas Merton: Spiritual Master, The Essential Writings*, ed. Lawrence S. Cunningham (Mahwah, NJ: Paulist Press, 1992), 358. Cunningham notes in an early draft it was titled, "Learning to Learn." Another version of this chapter was presented as the paper "Merton and

the Inner Journey" (with Fiona Gardner), at Merton 100: Living the Legacy, the Fourteenth Annual International Thomas Merton Society Meeting, Bellarmine University, Louisville, KY, June 4, 2015.

2. Merton, "Learning to Live," 366.

3. Victor A. Kramer, "'Crisis and Mystery': The Changing Quality of Thomas Merton's Later Journals," 77–97, and Jonathan Montaldo, "Loving Winter When the Plant Says Nothing: Thomas Merton's Spirituality in His Private Journals," 99–117, both in *The Vision of Thomas Merton*, ed. Patrick F. O'Connell (Notre Dame, IN: Ave Maria Press, 2003).

4. Montaldo, "Loving Winter," 99–100.

5. Michael Mott, *The Seven Mountains of Thomas Merton* (Boston: Houghton Mifflin, 1986).

6. Very much in focus with what I am saying here, see Jonathan Montaldo, "To Uncage His Voice: Thomas Merton's Inner Journey toward *Parrhesia*," *The Merton Seasonal* 39, no. 4 (2014): 9–20.

7. Gordon Oyer, *Pursuing the Spiritual Roots of Protest: Merton, Berrigan, Yoder, and Muste at the Gethsemani Abbey Peacemakers Retreat* (Eugene, OR: Cascade Books, 2014).

8. Thomas Merton and Ralph Eugene Meatyard, *Meatyard/Merton, Merton/Meatyard* (Louisville, KY: Fons Vitae, 2013).

9. Maria Skobtsova, *Mother Maria Skobtsova: Essential Writings*, ed. Helene Klepinin-Arjakovsky (Maryknoll, NY: Orbis Books, 2003), 81.

10. See throughout, Patrick Hart, ed., *Thomas Merton/Monk: A Monastic Tribute* (Kalamazoo, MI: Cistercian Publications, 1983), esp. 19–58, 93–102, 261–64; and Basil Pennington, ed., *Toward an Integrated Humanity: Thomas Merton's Journey* (Kalamazoo, MI: Cistercian Publications, 1988). Also see Victor A. Kramer, "Merton's Contribution as Teacher, Writer, and Community Member: Interview with Flavian Burns OCSO," *The Merton Seasonal* 3 (1990): 71–89, and "Looking Back to Merton: Memories and Impressions; Interview with Matthew Kelty OCSO," *The Merton Seasonal* 1 (1988): 55–76; and Paul M. Pearson, "A Dedication to Prayer and a Dedication to Humanity: Interview with James Conner OCSO," *The Merton Annual* 23 (2010): 212–39.

11. Thomas Merton, *Dancing in the Water of Life: The Journals of Thomas Merton*, ed. Robert E. Daggy, vol. 5, 1963–1965 (San Francisco: Harper San Francisco, 1997), 237.

12. Thomas Merton, "Rain and the Rhinoceros," *Holiday* 37 (May 1965): 8, 10, 12, 15–16. It is also available in *Thomas Merton: Selected Essays*, ed. Pat F. O'Connell (Maryknoll, NY: Orbis, 2014), 216–24.

13. Merton, *Dancing in the Water of Life*, 87, 89–90.

14. Merton, *Dancing in the Water of Life*, 239–42.

15. The second version of the essay was published in *The Hudson Review* 20 (1967): 211–18, and then by itself as *Day of a Stranger* (Salt Lake City, UT: Gibbs M. Smith, 1981).

16. Thomas Merton, *The Courage For Truth: Letters to Writers*, ed. Christine M. Bochen (New York: Farrar, Straus and Giroux, 1993), 225.

17. Montaldo, "To Uncage His Voice," 13–15.

18. Merton, *Day of a Stranger*, 12–19.

19. Merton, *Dancing in the Water of Life*, 240.

20. "Day of a Stranger," second draft, typescript in the Thomas Merton Studies Center, Bellarmine University, Louisville, KY, 1–2.

21. Roger Lipsey, *Make Peace Before the Sun Goes Down: The Long Encounter of Thomas Merton and His Abbot, James Fox* (Boston: Shambala, 2015).

22. Merton, "Day of a Stranger," in *Thomas Merton: Spiritual Master*, 218.

23. Merton, "Day of a Stranger," in *Thomas Merton: Spiritual Master*, 218.

24. Merton, "Day of a Stranger," in *Thomas Merton: Spiritual Master*, 217.

25. Merton, "Day of a Stranger," in *Thomas Merton: Spiritual Master*, 215.

26. See Merton, *Day of a Stranger*, 22–23.

27. Thomas Merton, *The Sign of Jonas* (Mariner Books, 2002), 362.

28. Merton, *Dancing in the Water of Life*, 177–78.

29. Merton, "Day of a Stranger," in *Thomas Merton: Spiritual Master*, 215.

30. Merton, "Day of a Stranger," in *Thomas Merton: Spiritual Master*, 217.

31. Thomas Merton, *Thoughts in Solitude* (New York: Farrar, Straus and Giroux, 1958), 92, also 99, 101, 114.

32. Thomas Merton, *New Seeds of Contemplation* (New York: New Directions, 1961), 29, 30, 31.

33. Merton, *New Seeds*, 34.

34. Merton, *New Seeds*, 35.

35. Thomas Merton, *The Hidden Ground of Love*, ed. William H. Shannon (New York: Farrar, Straus and Giroux, 1985), 63–64.

36. Merton, "Day of a Stranger," in *Thomas Merton: Spiritual Master*, 221.

37. Merton, "Day of a Stranger," in *Thomas Merton: Spiritual Master*, 219.

38. Thomas Merton, *Conjectures of a Guilty Bystander* (Garden City, NY: Image Books, 1968), 132, 158.

39. Thomas Merton, *The Asian Journal of Thomas Merton*, ed. Naomi Burton, Brother Patrick Hart, and James Laughlin (New York: New Directions, 1973), 318.

40. Merton, *The Asian Journal*, 318–19.

41. Montaldo, "Loving Winter," 117.

FOUR The Prayer of Poets

1. From an interview with Oliver at http://writersalmanac.publicradio.org/bookshelf/oliver.shtml.

2. From an interview with Oliver at http://www.oprah.com/entertainment/Maria-Shriver-Interviews-Poet-Mary-Oliver.

3. I have to thank my daughter Hannah for having introduced me to Mary Oliver's poems, only one of the many treasures that Hannah's education, experience, and wisdom have brought me. Hannah was also the instigator of my using my life and experience in writing about everyday paths to God and holiness, some of which I have used in this book. Paul, our son, likewise has encouraged me in sharing what I have seen of real spiritual worth despite so much that blunts this in the institutional church and stereotypic "religion."

4. From the interview at www.oprah.com/entertainment/Maria-Shriver-Interviews-Poet-Mary-Oliver. Also see her recent interview with Krista Tippet at http://www.onbeing.org/program/mary-oliver-listening-to-the-world/7267.

5. Mary Oliver, *New and Selected Poems* (Boston: Beacon Press, 1992), 1:94.

6. Oliver, *New and Selected Poems,* 1:110.

7. Benedicta Ward, trans., *The Desert Christian: The Sayings of the Desert Fathers* (New York: Macmillan, 1975), 110.

8. Mary Oliver, *Thirst* (Boston: Beacon Press, 2006), 16.

9. Oliver, *Thirst,* 17.

10. Oliver, *Thirst,* 23.

11. Oliver, *Thirst,* 24–25.

12. Oliver, *Thirst,* 37.

13. Oliver, *Thirst,* 31–34.

14. Oliver, *Thirst,* 40–41, 42–43, 50–51, 52–54.

15. Oliver, *Thirst,* 57.

16. Oliver, *Thirst,* 44, 45.

17. Christian Wiman, *My Bright Abyss* (New York: Farrar, Straus and Giroux, 2013), 155.

18. Christian Wiman, *The Long Home* (Story Line Press, 1997).

19. Christian Wiman, *Hard Night* (Copper Canyon Press, 2005), and *Ambition and Survival: Becoming a Poet* (Copper Canyon Press, 2007).

20. Christian Wiman, "Mortify Our Wolves," *The American Scholar,* Autumn, 2007.

21. Christian Wiman, *Every Riven Thing* (New York: Farrar, Straus and Giroux, 2010).

22. Wiman, *My Bright Abyss,* 56.

23. Wiman, *My Bright Abyss,* 57–58, 59–60.

24. Wiman, *My Bright Abyss,* 3.

25. Wiman, *My Bright Abyss,* 4.

26. Wiman, *My Bright Abyss,* 13.

27. Wiman, *My Bright Abyss,* 17.

28. Wiman, *My Bright Abyss,* 23.

29. Wiman, *My Bright Abyss,* 15, 30, 67.

30. Wiman, *My Bright Abyss,* 25.

31. Wiman, *My Bright Abyss*, 25–26, 68–69.

32. Wiman, *My Bright Abyss*, 77.

33. Wiman, *My Bright Abyss*, 66.

34. Wiman, *My Bright Abyss*, 67.

35. Wiman, *My Bright Abyss*, 47–49, 81–83, 63–67.

36. Wiman, *My Bright Abyss*, 81.

37. Wiman, *My Bright Abyss*, 87.

38. Wiman, *My Bright Abyss*, 94.

39. Paul Valliere, *Modern Russian Theology* (Grand Rapids, MI: Eerdmans, 2000), 11–15, 186–87.

40. Wiman, *My Bright Abyss*, 121.

41. Wiman, *My Bright Abyss*, 122.

42. Wiman, *My Bright Abyss*, 134.

43. Wiman, *My Bright Abyss*, 138–44.

44. Wiman, *My Bright Abyss*, 139–40.

45. Wiman, *My Bright Abyss*, 165.

46. Wiman, *My Bright Abyss*, 178.

47. Mary Karr, *The Liars' Club* (New York: Penguin, 1996), *Cherry* (New York: Penguin, 2001), and *Lit* (New York: Harper, 2009).

48. For example, see http://nymag.com/arts/books/features/jeffrey-eugenides-2011-10.

49. The full interview is at http://www.theparisreview.org/interviews/5992/the-art-of-memoir-no-1-mary-karr.

50. Mary Karr, *Sinners Welcome* (New York: Harper Perennial, 2006), 69–93.

51. Karr, *Lit*, 240–46.

52. Karr, *Lit*, 247–55.

53. Karr, *Lit*, 267–98.

54. Karr, *Lit*, 330–38.

55. Karr, *Lit*, 349–54.

56. Karr, *Sinners Welcome*, 54–55.

57. Karr, *Sinners Welcome*, 9, 31, 38, 52, 61.

58. Karr, *Sinners Welcome*, 61.

FIVE The Prayer of Forgetting and Remembering

1. Esther de Waal, *Seeking God: The Way of St. Benedict* (Collegeville, MN: Liturgical Press, 2001); Kathleen Norris, *The Cloister Walk* (New York: Riverhead, 1997).

2. Jim Forest, *Loving Our Enemies: Reflections on the Hardest Commandment* (Maryknoll, NY: Orbis Books, 2014).

3. I wrote about this at length in Michael Plekon, *Saints As They Really Are* (Notre Dame, IN: University of Notre Dame Press, 2012), 105–50.

4. Amy-Jill Levine notes such words of Jesus do not fit into the vision or vocabulary of first-century Judaism as do most else he said. See her *Short Stories by Jesus: The Enigmatic Parables of a Controversial Rabbi* (New York: Harper-One, 2014), 83–87.

SIX   The Prayer of Darkness

1. Barbara Brown Taylor, *Leaving Church: A Memoir of Faith* (San Francisco: HarperSanFrancisco, 2006).

2. Barbara Brown Taylor, *An Altar in the World: A Geography of Faith* (New York: HarperOne, 2009). For another account of ways of encountering God in everyday life, see Lauren F. Winner, *Wearing God: Clothing, Laughter, Fire, and Other Overlooked Ways of Meeting God* (New York: HarperOne), 2015.

3. Barbara Brown Taylor, *Learning to Walk in the Dark* (New York: HarperOne, 2014).

4. Taylor, *Learning to Walk*, 4–5.

5. Taylor, *Learning to Walk*, 6.

6. Taylor, *Learning to Walk*, 7.

7. Taylor, *Learning to Walk*, 12.

8. Taylor, *Learning to Walk*, 86.

9. Taylor, *Learning to Walk*, 54.

10. Taylor, *Learning to Walk*, 87.

11. Taylor, *Learning to Walk*, 165–70.

12. Taylor, *Learning to Walk*, 149–63.

13. Taylor, *Learning to Walk*, 91–109.

14. Taylor, *Learning to Walk*, 110–31.

15. Diarmaid MacCulloch, *Silence: A Christian History* (New York: Viking Adult, 2013), 69–84.

16. Taylor, *Learning to Walk*, 138.

17. Donald Cozzens, *The Changing Face of the Priesthood* (Collegeville, MN: Liturgical Press, 2000), *Sex, Priestly Ministry, and the Church* (Wilmington, DE: Michael Glazier, 2003), *Sacred Silence: Denial and Crisis in the Church* (Collegeville, MN: Liturgical Press, 2004), *Freeing Celibacy* (Collegeville, MN: Liturgical Press, 2006), and *Notes from the Underground: The Spiritual Journal of a Secular Priest* (Maryknoll, NY: Orbis, 2012).

18. Taylor, *Learning to Walk*, 148.

19. Taylor, *Learning to Walk*, 165–82. Another sacred object at Chartres Cathedral is *le Sainte Chemise*, the shawl supposedly worn by the Virgin Mary during the birth of Jesus.

20. Thomas Merton, *Thoughts in Solitude* (New York: Farrar, Straus and Giroux, 1958), 79.

21. Taylor, *Learning to Walk*, 185.

22. Taylor, *Learning to Walk*, 181; Merton, *Thoughts in Solitude*, 79.

SEVEN   The Prayer of Care for Those in Need

1. The extensive literature by and about Dorothy Day and the Catholic Worker movement is gathered in the most extensive and best biography of her: Jim Forest, *All Is Grace* (Maryknoll, NY: Orbis, 2011), 338–40. Robert Ellsberg has edited both a selection of her letters and diaries: *All the Way to Heaven* and *The Duty of Delight* (Milwaukee: Marquette University Press, 2010, 2009), as well as an anthology of her writings, Dorothy Day, *Dorothy Day: Selected Writings* (Maryknoll, NY: Orbis, 2005). See also Rosalie Riegle, *Dorothy Day: Portraits by Those Who Knew Her* (Maryknoll, NY: Orbis, 2003), and *Voices from the Catholic Worker* (Philadelphia: Temple University Press, 1993).

2. In addition to the Russian and French language editions of her work, see Maria Skobtsova, *Mother Maria Skobtsova: Essential Writings*, ed. Helene Klepinin-Arjakovsky (Maryknoll, NY: Orbis, 2003). The best biography in English is Sergei Hackel, *Pearl of Great Price: The Life of Mother Maria Skobtsova, 1891–1945* (Crestwood, NY: St. Vladimir's Seminary Press, 1981). More recently in addition to a collection of Mother Maria's writings edited by Helene Klepinin-Arjakovsky, *Le sacrament du frère* (Paris: Cerf, 2001), a new and large collection has appeared, some in print for the first time: Sainte Marie de Paris (Mere Marie Skobtsov, 1891–1945), *Le jour du Saint-Esprit* (Paris: Cerf, 2011).

3. From one of the thousands of Radio Liberty talks Schmemann wrote and delivered, translation by Alexis Vinogradov, unpublished.

4. Dominique Desanti, *La Sainte et l'incroyante: Rencontres avec mère Marie* (Paris: Bayard, 2007).

5. The YMCA helped support a publishing house, bookstore, Berdyaev's journal, the theological school, and Mother Maria's houses of hospitality. See Matthew Lee Miller, *The American YMCA and Russian Culture* (Lanham, MD: Lexington Books, 2013); and Paul B. Anderson, *No East or West* (Paris: YMCA Press, 1985).

6. Antoine Arjakovsky, *The Way: Russian Religious Thinkers of the Emigration and Their Journal* (Notre Dame, IN: University of Notre Dame Press, 2013).

7. Skobtsova, "Types of Religious Life," *Mother Maria Skobtsova: Essential Writings*, 140–86, at 181.

8. See George Fedotov, *The Russian Religious Mind*, vols. 1 and 2 (Belmont, MA: Nordland, 1975) and *A Treasury of Russian Spirituality* (Belmont, MA: Nordland, 1975).

9. T. Stratton Smith, *Rebel Nun* (Springfield, IL: Templegate, 1965), 135.

10. In Hackel, *Pearl of Great Price*, xii.

11. Skobtsova, *Mother Maria Skobtsova: Essential Writings*, 173–74.

12. Skobtsova, *Mother Maria Skobtsova: Essential Writings*, 68–69. See Natalia Ermolaev, "The Marian Dimenson of Mother Maria Skobtsova's Orthodox Social Christianity," available at http://hdl.handle.net/10022/AC:P:11163, and "Modernism, Motherhood, and Mariology: The Poetry and Theology of Elizaveta Skobtsova (Mother Maria)" (Ph.D. dissertation, Columbia University, 2010).

13. Photos of the Ravensbrück embroidery from the Bayeux tapestry as well as an image of the Mother of God by Mother Maria, also embroidered, are in Jim Forest's collection; see https://www.flickr.com/photos/jimforest/sets/72157594152181792.

14. Skobtsova, *Mother Maria Skobtsova: Essential Writings*, 66–67.

15. Skobtsova, *Mother Maria Skobtsova: Essential Writings*, 70–71, translation slightly modified.

16. Skobtsova, *Mother Maria Skobtsova: Essential Writings*, 69.

17. Skobtsova, *Mother Maria Skobtsova: Essential Writings*, 45–60, 90–103.

18. Hyacinthe Destivelle, O.P., *The Moscow Council (1917–18): The Creation of the Conciliar Institutions of the Russian Orthodox Church*, ed. Michael Plekon and Vitaly Permiakov, trans. Jerry Ryan (Notre Dame, IN: University of Notre Dame Press, 2015).

19. Skobtsova, *Mother Maria Skobtsova: Essential Writings*, 154.

20. Skobtsova, *Mother Maria Skobtsova: Essential Writings*, 161.

21. Diarmaid MacCulloch, *Christianity, the First Three Thousand Years* (New York: Penguin, 2011), 112–54.

22. Skobtsova, *Mother Maria Skobtsova: Essential Writings*, 171.

23. Skobtsova, *Mother Maria Skobtsova: Essential Writings*, 184, translation slightly modified.

24. Skobtsova, *Mother Maria Skobtsova: Essential Writings*, 182.

25. See Jim Forest's lovely children's book on this rescue operation, *Silent as a Stone* (Crestwood, NY: St. Vladimir's Seminary Press, 2007).

26. Skobtsova, *Mother Maria Skobtsova: Essential Writings*, 182–83.

27. Dorothy Day, *The Long Loneliness* (New York: HarperOne, 2009), 285–86.

28. Ellsberg, *The Duty of Delight*, 459.

29. Ellsberg, *All the Way to Heaven*, 382–83.

30. Ellsberg, *All the Way to Heaven*.

31. Rosalie Riegle has collected some of these in *Dorothy Day: Portraits by Those Who Knew Her* and *Voices from the Catholic Worker*, as well as in *Crossing the Line* (Eugene, OR: Cascade, 2013) and *Doing Time for Peace* (Nashville: Vanderbilt University Press, 2013).

32. Ellsberg, *All the Way to Heaven* and *The Duty of Delight*, and Forest, *All Is Grace*.

33. See http://www.iww.org.

34. A forthcoming account of both her mother, Tamar, and her grandmother, Dorothy, by Kate Hennessy, will add much to our understanding of the lives and personalities of these remarkable women: *Beauty Will Save the World*.

35. Day, *Dorothy Day: Selected Writings*, 59–60.

36. Day, *Dorothy Day: Selected Writings*, 64.

37. Day, *Dorothy Day: Selected Writings*, 68.

38. Day, *Dorothy Day: Selected Writings*, 80–81.

39. Day, *Dorothy Day: Selected Writings*, 82–83.

40. Day, *Dorothy Day: Selected Writings*, 84–85.

41. See http://www.catholicworker.org/communities/directory-picker .html.

42. Frida Berrigan, "A Place Where It's Easier to Be Good," available at http://wagingnonviolence.org/feature/a-place-where-its-easier-to-be-good.

E I G H T   The Prayer of Pirogi Making and Other Food Adventures

1. See, for example, http://stlydias.org/about.

2. Maria Skobtsova, *Mother Maria Skobtsova: Essential Writings*, ed. Helene Klepinin-Arjakovsky (Maryknoll, NY: Orbis Books, 2003), 173–86.

3. Michael Plekon, Maria Gwyn McDowell, and Elizabeth Schroeder, eds., *The Church Has Left the Building* (Portland, OR: Cascade, forthcoming).

4. The Hartford Institute for Religious Research (HIRR) American Congregations study (2008) points to decline: worship attendance, poor financial health, weak spiritual life. Parishes are aging: six out of ten have from a quarter to half their members sixty-five or older. The 2008 Pew US Religious Landscape Survey, with a sample of 35,000, had quite similar findings: 28 percent have left their religion of origin for another or none at all; 44 percent have switched denominations; 16 percent are unaffiliated (atheist, agnostic, unaffiliated). This and other studies note that the number of religious "nones" is steadily rising. If immigrant numbers are controlled, Catholics have suffered the biggest losses. More recent Pew data, October 2012, indicate almost 20 percent are "nones"; see http://www.pewforum.org/2012/10/09/nones-on-the-rise.

5. Diana Butler Bass, *Christianity for the Rest of Us* (New York: HarperOne, 2007).

6. Robert Putnam and David Campbell, *American Grace* (New York: Simon & Schuster, 2010).

7. Lloyd Rediger, *Clergy Killers: Guidance for Pastors and Congregations under Attack* (Louisville, KY: Westminster John Knox Press, 1997).

8. Robert Putnam, *Bowling Alone: The Collapse and Revival of Community in America* (New York: Touchstone, 2001); Robert N. Bellah et al., *Habits of the Heart: Individualism and Commitment in American Life* (Berkeley: University of California Press, 1985); Nancy T. Ammerman, ed., *Sacred Stories, Spiritual Tribes: Finding Religion in Everyday Life, Everyday Religion* (New York: Oxford University Press, 2013), and *Congregation and Community* (New Brunswick, NJ: Rutgers University Press, 2001).

9. Barbara Brown Taylor, *Leaving Church: A Memoir of Faith* and *An Altar in the World: A Geography of Faith* (San Francisco: HarperSanFrancisco, 2007, 2008); Richard Lischer, *Open Secrets* (New York: Doubleday, 2001); Lillian Daniel and Martin Copenhaver, *This Odd and Wondrous Calling* (Grand Rapids, MI: Eerdmans, 2009). Also see the work of Sara Miles cited in chapter 2.

10. Richard Dauenhauer and Nora Marks Dauenhauer, *Haa Shaká, Our Ancestors Narratives: Tlingit Oral Narratives; Haa Tuwunáagu Yís, for Healing Our Spirit: Tlingit Oratory;* and *Haa Kusteeyí, Our Culture: Tlingit Life Stories* (Seattle: University of Washington, 1987, 1990, 1994); Ronald Spatz et al., eds., *Alaska Native Writers, Storytellers and Orators: The Expanded Edition* (Anchorage: University of Alaska Press, 1999).

11. Neither Hutcheon's doctoral dissertation, "From Lamentation to Alleluia: An Interpretation of the Theology of the Present-Day Byzantine-Rite Funeral Service" (Metropolitan Andrey Sheptytsky Institute of Eastern Christian Studies, 2003), nor Schmemann's lectures at a 1981 St. Vladimir's Seminary Summer Institute have been published. See Elena Velkovska, "Funeral Rites according to Byzantine Liturgical Sources," *Dumbarton Oaks Papers* 55 (2001): 21–51.

12. Amy-Jill Levine, *Short Stories by Jesus: The Enigmatic Parables of a Controversial Rabbi* (New York: HarperOne, 2014), 61–65, 109, 134, 252, 279–82.

NINE The Prayer of the Classroom

1. Hans Küng, *My Struggle for Freedom: Memoirs*, trans. John Bowden (Grand Rapids, MI: Eerdmans, 2003), and *Disputed Truth: Memoirs II*, trans. John Bowden (New York: Continuum, 2008). A third volume has been completed and is being translated.

2. Yves Congar, *My Journal of the Council* (Collegeville, MN: Michael Glazier, 2012).

3. Esther de Waal, *Seeking God: The Way of St. Benedict* (Collegeville, MN: Liturgical Press, 2001).

4. Benedicta Ward, ed. and trans., *The Desert Fathers: Sayings of the Early Christian Monks* (New York: Penguin Classics, 2003); and Laura Swan, ed., *The Forgotten Desert Mothers: Sayings, Lives, and Stories of Early Christian Women* (Mahwah, NJ: Paulist Press, 2001).

5. James Carroll, *Christ Actually: The Son of God for the Secular Age* (New York: Viking, 2014); Gary Wills, *What Jesus Meant* and *What the Gospels Meant* (New York: Penguin, 2007, 2009); and Barbara Brown Taylor, *An Altar in the World: A Geography of Faith* (New York: HarperOne, 2009).

6. See Amy-Jill Levine, *Short Stories by Jesus: The Enigmatic Parables of a Controversial Rabbi* (New York: HarperOne, 2014), throughout, and also Amy-Jill Levine, *The Misunderstood Jew: The Church and the Scandal of the Jewish Jesus* (New York: HarperOne, 2007).

7. Chris Hedges, *War Is a Force That Gives Us Meaning* (New York: Public Affairs, 2002); Michael Pollan, *The Omnivore's Dilemma* (New York: Penguin, 2007); Paul Krugman, *End This Depression Now* (New York: Norton, 2013); Darcey Steinke, *Easter Everywhere: A Memoir* (New York: Bloomsbury, 2008); Jared Diamond, *Guns, Germs, and Steel* (New York: Norton, 1999); Kathryn Schultz, *Being Wrong: Adventures in the Margin of Error* (New York: Ecco, 2011); Atul Gawande, *Being Mortal* (New York: Hamish Hamilton, 2014); and Robert D. Putnam, *Our Kids* (New York: Simon & Schuster, 2015).

8. Levine, *Short Stories by Jesus*, 167.

TEN The Prayer of One's Life

1. An earlier version of this chapter was presented as "The Jesus Prayer in Nineteenth-Century Russian Spirituality," at the Twelfth Ecumenical Conference at the Monastery of Bose, September 16–18, 2004. Published in *The Ecumenical Review* 57, no. 4 (2005): 395–405, as well as in French, Spanish, Italian, and Russian versions.

2. In Michael Plekon, *Living Icons* (Notre Dame, IN: University of Notre Dame Press, 2002), I profiled these and several other persons of faith in our time. Essays from many of these persons of faith can be found in Michael Plekon, ed., *Tradition Alive: On the Church and the Christian Life in Our Time/ Readings from the Eastern Church* (Lanham, MD: Sheed & Ward/Rowman & Littlefield, 2003). Seraphim was canonized a saint by the Russian church in 1903, as was Maria Skobtsova and her co-workers in 2004 by the Ecumenical Patriarchate.

3. Maria Skobtsova, *Mother Maria Skobtsova: Essential Writings*, ed. Helene Klepinin-Arjakovsky (Maryknoll, NY: Orbis, 2003), 81.

4. Valentine Zander, *St. Seraphim of Sarov* (Crestwood, NY: St. Vladimir's Seminary Press, 1975), 85–86.

5. Though widely published, an accessible location of this encounter is in Zander, *St. Seraphim of Sarov*, 83–94.

6. Irina Gorianoff, *Séraphim de Sarov* (Paris: Desclée de Brouwer, 1979).

7. Donald Nicholl, *Triumphs of the Spirit in Russia* (London: Darton, Longman & Todd, 1997).

8. Paul Evdokimov, "Holiness in the Tradition of the Orthodox Church," in *In the World, of the Church: A Paul Evdokimov Reader*, trans. and ed. Michael Plekon and Alexis Vinogradov, 129–39 (Crestwood, NY: St. Vladimir's Seminary Press, 2001).

9. Sergius Bulgakov, *The Bride of the Lamb*, trans. Boris Jakim (Grand Rapids, MI: Eerdmans, 2002), 292, 308, 400, 410.

10. Paul Evdokimov, *Ages of the Spiritual Life*, trans. and ed. Michael Plekon and Alexis Vinogradov (Crestwood, NY: St. Vladimir's Seminary Press, 1998), 138, 158, 189, 196, 205–9, 218, 249.

11. While the Diveyevo *Chronicles* may be the least edited source of accounts of Seraphim's personality, words, and actions, for his "spiritual instructions," most likely rewritten by Filaret of Moscow, see *Little Russian Philokalia, vol. 1, St. Seraphim* (Platina, CA: St. Herman Press, 1991). A translation of *Chronicles* is forthcoming.

12. Ann Shukman, "The Conversation between St. Seraphim and Motovilov: The Authors, the Texts and the Publishers," *Sobornost* 27, no. 1 (2005): 47–57; Michael Hagemeister, "Il Problemo della Genesi del 'Colloquio con Motovilov,'" in *San Serafim da Sarov a Diveevo*, ed. Nina Kauchtschischwili et al., 157–74 (Bose: Edizioni Qiqajon, 1998).

13. Michael Plekon, "Two Monks: Thomas of Gethsemani and Seraphim of Sarov," *The Merton Seasonal* 40, no. 2 (2015): 17–24.

14. Paul Evdokimov, *The Sacrament of Love*, trans. Anthony P. Gythiel and Victoria Steadman (Crestwood, NY: St. Vladimir's Seminary Press, 1985), 61–63.

15. Evdokimov, *Ages of the Spiritual Life*, 215–16.

16. Olivier Clément, *Orient-Occident, Deux Passeurs: Vladimir Lossky, Paul Evdokimov* (Geneva: Labor et Fides, 1985).

17. See the two commemorative issues of the French Orthodox journal *Contacts*: "Paul Evdokimov: Témoin de la Beauté de Dieu," *Contacts* 73–74 (1971): "Témoinages Familiaux" and "Témoinages Particuliers," 225–36, 237–71. Also see "Paul Evdokimov (1901–1970), témoin de la beauté de Dieu," *Contacts* 235–26 (2011).

18. Skobtsova, *Mother Maria Skobtsova: Essential Writings*, 140–86.

19. Skobtsova, *Mother Maria Skobtsova: Essential Writings*, 174–76.

20. Michael Plekon, *Hidden Holiness* (Notre Dame, IN: University of Notre Dame Press, 2009).

21. Evdokimov, *The Sacrament of Love*, 92.

ELEVEN   The Prayer of Contemplation and Action

1. Richard Rohr, from an unpublished talk, September 19, 2011.

2. His homilies can be found at https://cac.org/category/homilies/.

3. Richard Rohr, *Eager to Love: The Alternative Way of Francis of Assisi* (Cincinnati, OH: Franciscan Media, 2014).

4. Rohr identifies the following as the core themes of the Center and of his work.

1. *Scripture as validated by experience*, and experience as validated by Tradition are good scales for one's spiritual world view (METH-ODOLOGY).
2. *If God is Trinity and Jesus is the face of God*, then it is a benevolent universe. God is not someone to be afraid of, but is the Ground of Being and on our side (FOUNDATION).
3. *For those who see deeply there is only One Reality.* By reason of the Incarnation, there is no truthful distinction between sacred and profane (FRAME).
4. *Everything belongs*, and no one needs to be scapegoated or excluded. Evil or Untruth cannot be directly fought or separated from as much as exposed to the Light (ECUMENICAL).
5. The *"separate self" is the major problem*, not the shadow self which only takes deeper forms of disguise (TRANSFORMATION).
6. *The path of descent is the path of transformation.* Darkness, failure, relapse, death, and woundedness are our primary teachers, rather than ideas or doctrines (PROCESS).
7. *Reality is paradoxical and complementary.* Non dual thinking is the highest level of consciousness. Divine union, not private perfection, is the goal of all religion (GOAL).

See https://cac.org/living-school/program-details/lineage-and-themes/.

5. Richard Rohr, *Falling Upward: A Spirituality for the Two Halves of Life* (New York: Jossey-Bass, 2011), xxiv.

6. Rohr, *Falling Upward*, 25–51.

7. Rohr, *Falling Upward*, 73–86.

8. Rohr, *Falling Upward*, 87–96.

9. Rohr, *Falling Upward*, xxviii.

10. Alexander Schmemann, *Great Lent: Journey to Pascha* (Crestwood, NY: St. Vladimir's Seminary Press, 1969).

11. Rohr, *Falling Upward*, 117–25.

12. Nicholas Afanasiev, *The Church of the Holy Spirit*, trans. Vitaly Permiakov, ed. Michael Plekon (Notre Dame, IN: University of Notre Dame Press, 2007), 255–75.

13. Rohr, *Falling Upward*, 127–36.

14. Rohr, *Falling Upward*, 137–51.

15. Rohr, *Falling Upward*, 161–67.

16. Richard Rohr, *Everything Belongs: The Gift of Contemplative Prayer* (New York: Crossroad, 2003), 77–81.

17. Rohr, *Everything Belongs*, 87–89.

18. Rohr, *Everything Belongs*, 90.

19. Rohr, *Everything Belongs*, 93.

20. Rohr, *Everything Belongs*, 101–2.

21. Rohr, *Everything Belongs*, 103–9.

22. Rohr, *Everything Belongs*, 117–19.

23. Paula D'Arcy, *A New Set of Eyes: Encountering the Hidden God* (New York: Crossroad, 2002), and *Waking Up to This Day: Seeing the Beauty Right before Us* (Maryknoll, NY: Orbis Books, 2009).

24. Richard Rohr, *Immortal Diamond* (New York: Jossey-Bass, 2013), 107.

25. Rohr, *Everything Belongs*, 129–30. See also Julian of Norwich, *Showing of Love*, chap. 38, showing 13, in *The Complete Julian of Norwich*, ed. John Julian (Brewster, MA: Paraclete Press, 2009).

26. Rohr, *Everything Belongs*, 147.

27. Rohr, *Everything Belongs*, 149.

28. Rohr, *Everything Belongs*, 150.

29. Rohr, *Everything Belongs*, 159.

30. See Rohr, *Eager to Love*, throughout but esp. xiv–xxii, 6–17, 26–28, 35–43, 259–68. In late summer, August 30–September 1, 2015, Rohr joined with Ilia Delio and Shane Claiborne in a conference, The Francis Factor: How Saint Francis and Pope Francis Are Changing the World; see https://cac.org/events/conferences/past-conferences/the-francis-factor/.

31. Rohr, *Everything Belongs*, 164–65.

32. See Thomas Merton, *New Seeds of Contemplation* (New York: New Directions, 1961), but also *Contemplation in a World of Action* (Notre Dame, IN: University of Notre Dame Press, 1998) and *The Springs of Contemplation* (Notre Dame, IN: Ave Maria Press, 1992). I have found the transcriptions of the final discussions at retreats Merton gave for sisters in the last year of his life to be among the most direct and forceful expressions of his thinking, even if not as polished as some of the published material.

33. This is how prayer is described and defined in texts used in Carmelite formation, in *The Carmelite Directory*, compiled by John Brenninger, trans. Leo J. Walter (Chicago: Carmelite Press, 1951), and Adolph Tanqueray, *The Spiritual Life*, 2nd rev. ed. (Charlotte, NC: TAN Books, 2013).

34. Thomas Merton, "The White Pebble," in *Thomas Merton: Selected Essays*, ed. Pat F. O'Connell (Maryknoll, NY: Orbis, 2014), 3–14. The essay was originally published in a collection of conversion stories, *Where I Found Christ*, ed. John A. O'Brien (Garden City, NY: Doubleday, 1950).

35. Daniel P. Horan, *The Franciscan Heart of Thomas Merton* (Notre Dame, IN: Ave Maria Press, 2014).

36. Daniel P. Horan, "Merton (Still) Matters," *America* 212, no. 2 (Jan. 19–26, 2015): 20–23.

Conclusion

1. Nicholas Afanasiev, "The Church's Canons, Changeable or Unchangeable?" in *Tradition Alive: On the Church and the Christian Life in Our Time,* ed. Michael Plekon, 31–45 (Lanham, MD: Rowan & Littlefield/Sheed & Ward, 2003). Also see his essay, "Canons and Canonical Consciousness," available at http://www.holy-trinity.org/ecclesiology/afanasiev-canons.html.

2. Christian Salenson, *Christian de Chergé: A Theology of Hope* (Collegeville, MN: Liturgical Press/Cistercian Publications, 2012), 77–94.

3. James Carroll, *Christ Actually* (New York: Viking, 2014), 278–79.

INDEX

MICHAEL PLEKON is professor in the Department of Sociology and Anthropology and in the Program in Religion and Culture at Baruch College of the City University of New York. He is also an ordained priest in the Orthodox Church in America and the author or editor of a number of books, including *Hidden Holiness* and *Saints As They Really Are: Voices of Holiness in Our Time*, both published by the University of Notre Dame Press.

CPSIA information can be obtained
at www.ICGtesting.com
Printed in the USA
LVOW01s2355120816
499901LV00004B/4/P

9 780268 100018